The
Tenure
Debate

Bardwell L. Smith
and
Associates

THE
TENURE
DEBATE

 Jossey-Bass Inc., Publishers
San Francisco · Washington · London · 1973

The Jossey-Bass
Series in Higher Education

Preface

M̲y primary asset in serving as editor for *The Tenure Debate* may be that I am more or less representative of several hundred faculty and administrators who have been forced to reconfront the subject. A number of factors have stimulated this reexamination during the past few years: an increased politicization of elements within academic institutions; diminished public confidence in the performance of colleges and universities, especially the quality of teaching within them; a nationwide debate about the purposes and direction of higher education; and severe financial constraints. These and other factors prompted reconsideration of tenure, as many began to argue that tenure, though created to safeguard academic freedom and promote job security, has actually contributed to featherbedding, protection from responsible critique, and financial insolvency.

Although the current debate about these issues is only a few years old, it is nevertheless striking that the literature on the subject is relatively sparse. There has not, for instance, been a thorough discussion of academic tenure in its many facets, except for scattered essays in the *Bulletin* of the American Association of University Professors (AAUP) and elsewhere, since the 1959 publication of *Tenure in Higher Education* by Clark Byse and Louis Joughin. The present collection is an attempt to deal with several relatively neglected issues, with the purpose of stimulating, not of settling, the arguments.

While an obvious need exists for comprehensive, balanced studies of tenure, there is also virtue in dealing, as this book does, with a limited number of issues from diverse perspectives, with the primary intent of fostering further inquiry rather than advocating particular recommendations. With the knowledge that a study on tenure had been commissioned jointly by the AAUP and the Association of American Colleges (AAC) and was due to appear at approximately the same time, it seemed only appropriate to approach the topic in a different fashion. It may be that these two volumes will supplement each other. It was decided, for instance, that no chapter dealing extensively with the history of tenure or any bibliography on tenure and related subjects need appear here since the AAUP/AAC study (directed by William Rea Keast) includes both. (The Keast study, tentatively titled *Academic Tenure,* will be published by Jossey-Bass in 1973.)

Although several topics and points of view are absent from *The Tenure Debate* (comparison of tenure situations longitudinally in different institutions; the economics of tenure, especially as this is now changing; attitudes toward tenure on the part of various constituencies within higher education; and suggested alternatives to tenure), the book does cover many aspects of the subject and represents a variety of viewpoints. Originally, there was to have been a chapter by a faculty member from the counterculture, but the first three persons approached had recently been converted to the relative merits of tenure. (While a small sample, it may be significant at a time when those with unorthodox views have reason to feel insecure.) With these caveats registered, Chapter One makes clear what *The Tenure Debate* does attempt.

From the start it was hoped that the debate over academic tenure might be seen more as an important opportunity to discuss a host of issues to which tenure is inevitably related than simply as a clash between its supporters and its opponents. While these factions exist, there is less clarity about the crucial matters of academic freedom and the relationship of tenure to it than has existed in recent decades. Furthermore, more people from different intellectual and value persuasions have entered the lists than ever before. Among them are national and state legislators, collective bargaining agents, and nonteaching professionals within higher education. With the lessened isolation of the academic profession from regular and complex ties with the community, it becomes increasingly necessary to promote intelligent debate about education itself and in this wider context the debate about tenure.

In conclusion, I would like to acknowledge the assistance of two persons who provided initial and continuing help. The original idea for the book was that of Ann Orlov. Her conception of the need for a book on tenure which might reach not only an academic audience but also several publics concerned with higher education helped to shape the collection at various stages. I acknowledge also the contribution made by Harold Hodgkinson, whose wide acquaintance with the field of higher education helped in the selection of contributors.

Northfield, Minnesota   BARDWELL L. SMITH
September 1972

Contents

xiii

Contributors

THOMAS J. COTTLE, *member of the Education Reseach Center and Medical Department, Massachusetts Institute of Technology*

KENNETH E. EBLE, *professor of English, University of Utah; director, AAUP Project to Improve College Teaching*

HAROLD L. HODGKINSON, *project director, Center for Research and Development in Higher Education, University of California, Berkeley*

JOHN C. LIVINGSTON, *professor of government and political science, and acting dean, Sacramento State College*

WILLIAM F. MCHUGH, *professor of law, American University Law School*

JOEL G. MAGID, *director of freshman English,
Newark College of Arts and Sciences, Rutgers
University*

ROBERT M. O'NEIL, *provost and academic vice-
president, University of Cincinnati*

JOHN R. SILBER, *president, Boston University*

BARDWELL L. SMITH, *dean (1967 to 1972) and John
W. Nason Professor of Asian Studies,
Carleton College; also on the Yale University
Council and chairman of its Committee on
Yale College*

MARTIN TROW, *professor of sociology, Graduate
School of Public Affairs, University of
California, Berkeley*

ARVO VAN ALSTYNE, *professor of law, University of
Utah; chairman of the Commission to Study
Tenure at the University of Utah*

The
Tenure
Debate

Chapter *1*

What Price
Tenure?

Bardwell L. Smith

Since 1970 concern with the issue of tenure has arisen again within the academic profession. Faced with what appeared to be sudden financial exigency, a scarcity of available positions, and the prospect of considerably lessened mobility, the academy is now presented with new, dilemmas. In various senses the question of what price tenure has become an important one. Is a rapidly rising proportion of tenured faculty injurious to the liveliness and diversity of a campus? How will colleges and universities bear the obviously increased economic costs which accompany this trend? Should quota systems be established to offset the "negative" features of a fully or largely tenured faculty? Is tenure the effective guardian of academic freedom it has been heralded as? What threats to academic freedom exist for which tenure offers little, if any, protection? What previously neglected problems come to light as one reexamines this important subject?

A short time ago I would have described my position on

1

tenure as neutral. Developments on my own campus as well as else-where plus a fairly comprehensive reading of the literature have moved me from neutrality to ambivalence. At present, I am strongly appreciative of the merits academic tenure can have, yet strongly suspicious that tenure is neither the cause of nor the solution to the principal problems facing higher education today. Such a reaction may be typical of many who have done their homework on this sub-ject.[1] In fact, from its formation in 1915, the American Association of University Professors (AAUP) has never argued that academic tenure was a sufficient protection of academic freedom, only that it was a necessary one. While the debate over its necessity will con-tinue, I am persuaded that the principal value of the current con-troversy is that it has promoted inquiry into issues which previously have not been thoroughly discussed. If the controversy over tenure is not the sole stimulus to these discussions, it has certainly added a realistic and vital ingredient.

Of the issues facing higher education none is more important than the following: the evaluation and improvement of teaching; the balance between teaching and research, and which kinds of research are appropriate to a university; the ingredients and process of shared governance; the complex relationship between the acad-emy and society; and the dimensions and vehicles of learning avail-able. The confluence of several forces since the early 1950s poses problems and opportunities which were nonexistent when tenure first became an established practice. Among these, none exceeds the vastly increased access to higher education and the virtually infinite sources of learning which are now permanent factors within society at large.

Being unrepentantly dialectical by inclination, I suspect two or more sides exist to any dogma. Certainly, each dogma tends to

[1] Besides the *Bulletin* of the AAUP since 1915 a few of the key works include R. Hofstadter and W. P. Metzger, *The Development of American Freedom in the United States* (New York: Columbia Uni-versity Press, 1955); R. M. MacIver, *Academic Freedom in Our Time* (New York: Columbia University Press, 1955); C. Byse and L. Joughin, *Tenure in Higher Education* (Ithaca: Cornell University Press, 1959); and L. Joughin (Ed.), *Academic Freedom and Tenure: A Handbook of the American Association of University Professors* (Madison: University of Wisconsin Press, 1969).

create an equal and opposite dogma, forcing one to cope with the values and liabilities of both. The advocates of meritocracy, for instance, scorn the "lowering of standards" they envision as characteristic of changed admissions patterns or tenure for all. Egalitarians, in turn, counter by viewing older standards as but a ruse for perpetuating elites for their own sake. Both are right, yet each misses the other's strengths. The same game of attack and counterattack, the game of credentials, may be played between senior and junior faculty, between faculty and nonteaching professionals, between the students and "adults" of any academic community. The debate over tenure is often bandied about as a "pure" issue, involving primarily attacks upon academic freedom from the Yahoos outside. In fact, decisions on tenure often are sullied by the power struggles which are as evident in the academy as elsewhere.

Of the eleven authors of this volume, several were able to meet for a brief conference to discuss the purpose, scope, and content of this volume. Subsequently several of the chapters were circulated for comments. From the start it was clear that the book would necessarily cover a limited range of subjects and that its primary value would be catalytic, moving discussions of tenure into areas relatively neglected by others.

Within these limitations the volume falls into three parts: the first examines the dilemmas of tenure from decidedly different perspectives, each chapter taking a critical position regarding the current practice of tenure without necessarily arguing for its abolishment; the second focuses essentially on the areas of faculty responsibility, career development, and the improvement of teaching prior to and after the tenure decision; and the third explores the conflicting intramural and external pressures which necessitate a wider examination of tenure.

The chapter by Thomas Cottle is a unique treatment of the subject, providing insight into the pathos and anxiety of the faculty member who sweats out his years on the probationary treadmill. This familiar syndrome, heightened by the prestige of an institution, is portrayed with its self-seeking on the one hand and its taste of self-corruption on the other. With wit and irony Cottle creates a fantasy of tenure neurosis which rings true to anyone who recognizes the seduction of "standards of worth" measured in instrumental terms. The image is as valid for the measurement of student as of faculty ability and emerges as a devastating commentary on the competitive system and anyone who allows himself to be captured by it. The villain is not tenure but those who misuse it.

John Silber's chapter argues against the assertion that tenure is effective in protecting academic freedom. All rhetoric to the contrary, that is, that tenure for some protects freedom for all, Silber identifies ideological and personal constraints which all too often exercise tenure decisions as a means of fostering subtle conformity. Furthermore, he regards the timetable for making these decisions as largely responsible for reinforcing an emphasis upon routine rather than creative research and prefers an extended period during which one could provide "stimulus and encouragement" as well as periodic reviews to all faculty.

John Livingston goes beyond both Silber and Cottle in scoring the fundamental purpose of tenure—not in theory but in practice—the deselection of incompetents. Arguing that ours is a tenured society in which the mores of social Darwinianism still prevail and in which the achievement ethic is nowhere more active than in the educational arena, he suggests tenure for everyone. As he sees it, the task is not to eliminate but to strengthen the weak. In contrast to the competitive struggle of the marketplace, Livingston advocates a model akin to the family, essentially a model of collegiality.

The tone of Part Two shifts from explicit critique to an emphasis upon how the academy can assist its members both to evaluate their performance and to improve their capacities for learning, teaching, and scholarship. The value of Arvo Van Alstyne's chapter stems in part from its report of a case study executed by an institution which reexamined with care its own tenure policy and practices. This was the same institution (the University of Utah) which the AAUP investigated as its first "case" in 1915. The present Utah statement essentially reaffirms the institution of tenure on traditional grounds. Van Alstyne's chapter is a rehearsal of the basic premises and provides a summary of the arguments for and against tenure.

The next two chapters, by Kenneth Eble and Harold Hodgkinson, pursue this problem further. As director of the AAUP Project to Improve College Teaching, Eble appropriately makes a contribution in this area. While finding no particular correlations between effective teaching and tenure, Eble cautions against both the under-valuing of tenure for this reason and complacency about the effectiveness of teaching. His two-year study of what institutions do to help faculty evaluate and improve their performances presents a discouraging picture. Eble also argues strongly for a climate of freedom in which the instructor can affirm unorthodox positions without fear of censure or job loss. While not claiming this freedom is guaranteed by tenure, he contends its abolishment would only undermine the situation further. The real task, nevertheless, is to focus on the need for competent and imaginative teaching.

Hodgkinson's chapter is concerned with how faculty become motivated toward effective performance as teachers and how the tenure system might explicitly encourage their self-assessment. Underscoring the necessity for adequate feedback from colleagues and students, he outlines a number of suggestions which encourage open observation and candid discussion, a contrast to the customary "closed classroom." Also, he recommends a growth contract approach to learning and teaching, pertinent to students and professors alike, which can help individuals evaluate performance and design the areas they would like to emphasize next. The import for tenure is that judgments about strength and weakness can then be made on the basis of agreed upon and specific indices, not vaguely phrased abstractions. As with Eble, the focus here is how to improve the quality of what tenure is designed to protect and encourage.

In the final chapter in this section Joel Magid makes a series of recommendations which define "ways of recognizing the importance of teaching and service for promotion." Because of the differences within and between institutions, one can expect that proposals which appear sound for one context may be inappropriate or inadequate elsewhere. The value of Magid's contribution, however, is less in the specific proposals than in their reminder that each institution and its components must go through the difficult and necessary task of working out acceptable approaches to the recognition and rewarding of significant teaching and service. Magid's particular recommendations have received careful consideration in one state university; they would seem to have value in a variety of settings.

Part Three extends the consideration of tenure into areas of governance, conflict resolution, and academic freedom within higher education and its interplay with societal forces. Each of the chapters in this part focuses upon threats to the self-determination of the academy, whether from internal unrest and pressures or from external developments. The analysis of faculty unionism and tenure by William McHugh raises a host of issues on a complex subject. Outlining first the emergent causes of faculty unionism, he proceeds to examine workings of the collective bargaining process with regard to tenure, job security, due process, and academic freedom. His fundamental claim is that faculty unionism can facilitate a reliable grievance system, displacing systems which frequently are both unclear and ineffective. This particular chapter will be to many readers the most controversial, as it strongly affirms the merits of a process which remains suspect, if not anathema, despite its affirmation by the AAUP. The central questions are whether collective bargaining can coexist with significant institutional autonomy, whether adversarial relationships are inevitable, whether student demands can sustain their impact, and whether the process not only permits but encourages diversity. The task ahead is to shape whatever emerges in ways which edify the process and the structures of higher learning.

Robert O'Neil extends the picture by showing how certain developments are essentially an attack on the academic profession itself, not the tenure system. He focuses on attacks from state legislatures; high-level study commissions within education, foundations, and the federal government; criminal courts and grand juries; and the collective bargaining movement. Group efforts outside the academy to determine faculty work load conditions and sabbatical practices are seen as part of an emerging public attempt at curtailing the autonomy of higher education. If "tenure was meant to afford its holders an exemption from political pressures, fiscal fortunes, and assaults upon the academy," the implications of these developments for academic freedom are crucial. Not only do they suggest that age-old assaults are more insidious and on a larger scale, but they indicate that tenure alone will prove less effective than before.

The final chapter in this part broadens the perspective still further by examining the educational scene at various points during recent decades. In it I maintain that the case for or against tenure must be viewed not only historically but within the rapidly shifting context of the self-determination of the profession. If the role of tenure in protecting academic freedom since 1915 has been noteworthy, the threatened autonomy of higher education now calls for safeguards beyond tenure. Since 1945 especially, the complexity of developments within higher education and its relationship to society require major attention. The issue of accountability and the tension between "the imperative of university neutrality and the imperative of university morality" (as labeled by Kingman Brewster) are seen as central to the problems facing both the academy and the nation.

The chapter by Martin Trow stems from research sponsored by the Carnegie Commission on Higher Education. It is an analysis of the largest data base available on the distribution of academic tenure in higher education. Trow examines the scene by size and quality of institutions, by academic fields, by age and rank of faculty, by highest degree held, among other categories. The data were gathered in 1969, and it will be important during the next few years to keep track of any significant changes, as some at present are predicting that the incidence of tenure will climb to 75 to 80 per cent in the near future. Others, arguing for rigorous evaluation procedures, predict the reverse, a decline rather than further increases. To ask "what price tenure?" is to rattle old skeletons in new closets. On the one hand, the question relates to the price tag which accompanies an increasingly tenured faculty. On the other hand, it asks about the psychic costs to individuals not granted tenure, whether for professional or market reasons. The classic dilemma always returns: Do the advantages of tenure offset the disadvantage of having to live with one's mistaken decisions? The specter of deadwood locked into an institution for thirty years remains the primary argument against tenure, but it may be a false issue.

In a profession which predicates its existence on the necessity for an open approach to learning, there surely is no excuse for not expecting its members—students, faculty, administration, and nonteaching professionals—to evaluate their own performances regularly and rigorously. Indeed, the academic climate of any institution cannot remain free or healthy unless the process of evaluation is both candid and effective and unless opportunities for self-development are extensive. As a trustee of my acquaintance put it, "What makes any person settle back into a state of 'innocuous desuetude'?" The deadwood problem says as much about the institution as about the individual.

While the current tenure debate is still in its infancy, the most promising initial consequences are that for the first time in higher learning serious attention is being given to the problems of both evaluation and improvement of teaching. On campuses throughout the country one can observe the beginnings of responsible faculty evaluation, not only at the point of tenure but also during the second, third, or fourth year of teaching. Until now, the primary frustration of any academic dean has been the absence of a climate favoring adequate and responsible means of evaluating faculty. In my estimation, nothing is more irresponsible in the academic profession than withholding accurate and significant feedback. I do not mean to imply that this evaluation is simple, but it is necessary. To inform a nontenured faculty member that his contract is not being renewed without providing reasons and evidence has now become unacceptable. More important, however, is the necessity of providing feedback long before the tenure decision is made, the kind of professional feedback which can assist faculty in assessing both weaknesses and strengths. And this process must continue beyond the granting of tenure, at regular intervals throughout one's career.

The forms which this feedback will take and the variety of its sources will have to be worked out locally, but there will probably be general agreement that students must be party to the evaluations of teaching in ways which are effective and acceptable to the faculty. Procedures must be agreed upon and made public, and due process must prevail. One would wager that if the academy sustains its seriousness about teaching evaluation and improvement, tenure will not remain a false issue. Threats to academic freedom are constant; the main justification for tenure lies in the protection of this freedom.

Chapter *2*

Pains of
Permanence

Thomas J. Cottle

How well I recall my earliest hours in that black leatherette swivel chair in front of the handsome brown desk. A job! A real job with money, an office, and a phone—the accoutrements of fame, surely—and the smell of Harvard literally oozing out of the empty bookshelves, desk drawers, and file cabinets. And what a job! What a gorgeous step into heaven itself, and right before the eyes of absolutely everyone. No slinking around this time; no hiding from professors and teaching assistants who waited breathlessly for a six month overdue term paper; no dodging of classmates to whom low grades and remissions of all sorts would have to be confessed. No longer any of that. Swivel about now and catch the rays of the sun that penetrated the tall white stone building and glowed, for certain, on just one single man, one solitary inheritor now on his way. Work be damned; the momentum of a faithful, prestigious, and glorious name would carry one right to the sun, and then, beyond. Way beyond.

Do you know what they think in Utah, Colorado, Rhode Island, Arkansas, and rural Illinois when a beaming hostess one night proudly announces, "Ladies and gentlemen, may I introduce to you Professor Greatman from HARVARD?" Can anyone know what Americans out there, on the other side of the academic wall feel when they see Harvard standing before them? I mean, does anyone know? Well, let me tell you. They die; they swoon; they lose all sense of conscious purpose and throw ethics and protocol to the winds. They are veritably overcome by competitive urges and choked, actually left gasping, by the noxious fumes they themselves generate from the motors of sheer envy. Oh God, this must be it! This must be the utter meaning of life; the first moments of fortune, of power. I can feel myself becoming handsome and taller. Oh, Beauty, beauty of Education, had I known this would come, I swear I would have loved my schools and my teachers. I would have worked. You know how I would have worked. Anything; I would have done anything to achieve this leatherette chair and everything under the sun into which it might now swivel me. If I had only known. But can I make it last? Can I keep it all with me, forever? The corner office with two views, the name on the door? The women in the adjoining room who await my impulses, my demands, my orders, my buzz? Can I keep it? Please, please let me keep it! I'll take care of it as no one else can. Please don't ask me to give it back.

My first few days as a junior faculty member, but a few years ago, remain with me, vivid, alive, fat with prideful ecstasy, and free of the anxieties and sense of being engulfed that would so quickly strike, almost as retribution, but a few weeks later. There was, in those brilliant hours of luxurious freedom, such a mood of accomplishment, of arrival, that I hardly dared to breathe the word *professor* (though I was but a lecturer) or the name of the school to anyone for fear that my unequivocal achievements would cause my listeners to whimper and crawl away. That I was at the bottom of the hierarchy lightly tethered to a three-year contract and that my chances of maintaining this status, any status, were rather slight didn't phase me at all then. Well, maybe a little. I just sat there in my office, writing letters on that gorgeous letterhead, hour after hour. What a humble, lovely gesture to write to me, my friends must have thought, having received a gushing, newsy missive out of the blue. That's a modest man, considerate and kind, they must have uttered to their contemporaries. Little did they know my motives, my own personal Maileresque advertisements for *myself*.

Yet despite the aggrandizement and my search for fame, which would, ideally, leave me filthy with prestige and enviable recognition, I was aware of a sound, a movement in the stillness that was my sterile, sanitized office. "Never mind what it might be," I told my new furniture, my new friends. "You will see, just as soon as my Japanese prints go up on the walls and my books fill these yawning shelves, you will see, I shall be ensconced. I shall have moved in. There *will* be a presence in this room, a presence that others will feel even as they pop their heads in the door asking me to lunch with them, a presence that, like the stink of gymnasiums, will refurbish me somehow and revitalize my image of importance and pure worth."

But there was that sound, that movement in my office. No omen, no prevision; nothing like that. Perhaps a missed heartbeat now and again; a bleep in an electronic recording of my measured destiny; a fright that it could all fall through. It is not even the fear of retribution that overcomes some of us reared in a particular tradition at a time when the ways of the world unravel so easily, and jobs and women (if one is a man) seem to be less complicated or overwhelming than they once did. More accurately, it is a perfectly sanguine assessment of the situation and a recognition of what rises to the surface as the truth. It would not last, not because it was too good or premature in coming, but because soon enough the world would turn and the sun would no longer penetrate the corner office where I and my meager possessions lolled together.

No, but this couldn't be, I reasoned early in the first autumn. Things change; the odds, a thousand to one, are against us, to be sure; but every once in a while, as I had already learned, one of the junior people "makes it." He gets tapped, pronounced permanent senior faculty, and is bedecked in the cloaks of foreverness. I better not say anything, of course, I thought one day riding the elevators, but I could be that one in a thousand. Others, obviously, had ridden the same elevators and had juggled the identical thoughts, but I, after all, was different. They knew it too. Or did they all entertain this last thought as well?

What it meant, in these earliest days, as the myths and histories and vignettes of tenure were communicated to me by the experienced junior guys—there were no women—about to take their next career steps, was that I didn't have even a week of luxuriating in my untold freedom before the issue of academic tenure was already in my mind. Indeed, in the center of my mind. Often I would feel as though I had just been traded to a pennant contender or, better, moved up from the (graduate school) farm system to the big club. Getting to know colleagues, making believe I could present myself in any way I wanted since no one had known me previously, pretending that I could invent a new and ideal personality, I felt a sort of happiness, a consummate gratification. I could help this club even though none of its members spoke too much of the pennant or, even worse, of being traded down to a spot even lower than that from which they had commenced their ascent. I feared none of this, for I had just arrived. I was not about to depart like these other poor devils. And anyway, they had had their days, their bout with the sun and the furniture and offices absolutely identical to mine. Now it was my turn, and perhaps my turn would just be different from theirs.

But the senior men and women did have something. No doubt, they did possess a certain, well, elegance, confidence, a sense of belonging that shone through their lovely ways. One could see it in their offices. Special rugs lay on the vinyl floors, tons of books lined the shelves, and the framed prints, photographs, etchings, and paintings that covered their walls had permanence, enduring life written all over them. There was something else as well: the reprints. Everyone had reprints of their articles laid out modestly but nonetheless visibly on certain appropriate shelves. Millions of them were everywhere—piled on top of one another, labeled and pasted in green and brown covers, falling out of cabinets. It was utterly frightening. Then too, there were the baskets of correspondence, the piles of free books, and the look of someone having worked for long years and now being smack in the middle of something, while I was only beginning. There were no reprints in my office. Even by laying my books lengthwise on the shelves I still could not fill out the space allotted to me. My office was empty, nothing was in process, nothing was completed. It was lifeless and empty, and the sun, which shone still, seemed now to gleam a hazy light on my special, impermanent corner.

If anyone doubts the sociological notion of secondary socialization they're crazy. Never have I learned how to act, how to be, what criteria to employ in examining this or that as obligingly as I did in that first year as a university faculty member. That experience of being on the other side of the fence, of being in the locker room with major league stars, was being etched in my head. I could hardly believe those first few departmental meetings, sitting next to the authors of my textbooks. Do you call them by their first names? You can't. You're so new, so young, so undeserving of all this. Damn right you call them by their first names! That way no one confuses you with the graduate students. But how do you acquire what they possess? How do you become what they have become, even those who, ironically, you assess at close hand in terms of baseball hitting averages? This one's a four hundred hitter, we used to say, can hit three sewers easy. That one's about a two-sixty hitter. How *he* got tenure remains a mystery. It was strange to think that some of my contemporaries actually would disagree with our batting average computations. He thought X was a four hundred hitter? Just because he has written one crummy little study that everyone knows but would just as soon forget? So, part of the socialization began with having idols, heroes, and gods. To be given an inscribed copy of one of their books or articles, as is customary, was at first utterly stunning. "To Tom from Constantine." Constantine. Constantine. And the book would move, magically, in my hand.

Do you suppose Freud's wife really called him Ziggie? Might I ever attain such fame that the students would joke about learning that my wife calls me Tommy? Identification, socialization, emulation, adaptation, obedience, behavior, achievement, they were all there, marching arm and arm, willing to teach me, grabbing me to join the parade, and I loved it! I wanted it, all of it. I wanted tenure. I wanted the chance to say, "Well, let me think about your gracious offer." I wanted to still that growing movement, that ubiquitous noise that followed me about, even at home, in the evenings every so often.

There was no doubt at the time that the whole world was becoming divisible: the senior men and the junior men. That's all there was to it. Those early department meetings caused me anxiety, particularly when I realized how young several of the senior men were. That seemed outrageous. Men but a few years older than I had already inherited the objects of permanence that I had seen accumulating in the offices of the great ones. People I had not even heard of, and they could never be fired. Never. Well, they could be, it was told to me eight million times, if they got caught in bed with a Radcliffe undergraduate. "How about a graduate student?" someone laughingly asked. "How about playing it safe," I thought to myself, "and trying B.U. or Wellesley?" Never mind all that, the competitions, the suppressed tensions, and restlessness had already begun. Always, it seems, the commencements, the births inevitably arouse news or anticipations or wonderings of the end, of termination and demise. Three weeks in my black swivel chair with the high back and I was already jotting down on a yellow pad the names of schools that might someday award me tenure.

I have to laugh as I read what I have so far written. There is a quality to my recollections that makes them uncoil like a short story, only because the pains of several years ago cannot be retrieved, and, thankfully, as so many have discovered, the human animal, the naked ape, the junior faculty member is able to look back and see the absurdity. But not while the pains are alive. Never once. They are *the* hidden curriculum, *the* noise that accompanied me during the days in which I began to write articles for professional journals, in the days when I sat in my office crystalizing philosophical statements on the nature of professional achievement and existential glory. Like, if I just do my work, I will be discovered. They will come to my door asking me to perform this duty or honor them by writing this book. And then someday they will say, he did his work, he did it well, he published, and so we now reward him. The senior members of the department in conjunction with the members of the Harvard Corporation are pleased to announce the elevation of Thomas J. Cottle to the esteemed rank attained by one in a thousand.

Now, again, others must have dreamed as I did. They were tremendously intelligent, interesting, and productive others, too, publishing something everywhere I turned. I recall on several occasions scanning the journals in the departmental library. I imagined that the few present must have felt uplifted at the sight of a young professional seeking to keep up with the vast literature of his field. How wrong they would have been, for I was checking to see who was publishing and, even more, where and how much. I didn't even check to read article titles, merely the names. The anxiety. I felt as my eyes reluctantly canvassed the glossy front pages of the journals was staggering. Please God, don't let them publish something in this issue. It was all right for the others out in the boondocks like Kansas and Utah and Illinois, but please, not here. Then the next day I would encounter one of the young productive ones: "Hey, Jack, saw your piece in the AJS. Great! When do you have time to do all that work?" Jack would be pleased, as well he might, and respond modestly, "That was the last thing I've done in about six months. I can't seem to get to my work anymore." (Work, of course, always implying out-of-class research, writing, and pro-fessional duties. Never teaching.) About two months later, Jack's book would be published and I would start to tally up the points. Lots of points for books, a little less for articles, except of course articles published in the more prestigious journals. Anthologies were more difficult to assess; one would have to inspect the book to learn just how much original work the person had done. Surely they couldn't be considered "real" books, so one needn't worry too much. Still, when the advertisements began to carry news of the forth-coming anthology and a few months later the book appeared, one's role as expert was slowly coming into focus, and one's chance of tenure, like a marker on a monopoly board, moved several squares forward to the property that skyrockets in value. "Who'd you say was publishing your dissertation, Harry?"

I watched my colleagues closely, knowing full well that from time to time I was actually immobilized by my competitive drives. Talk about comparative analysis. This, of course, is not universal, but genuinely universal are the periodic checkups that somehow disclose one's chances or yield a glimpse of one's destiny. He'll get it. I'm sure of it. He'll be the one. The least deserving and they'll pick him. You'll see. The whole damn system is so unconscionably unfair. There was an element of truth in these laments, too. As the first year passed, we naturally began to witness, from an extraordinary distance at first but later on a bit closer, the tenure considerations of one of our older colleagues. Little competition was involved here because this man's destiny affected our own not at all. Then too, we heard the tales of this or that case for whom not getting tenure proved to be utterly traumatic and pitifully demoralizing. That's stupid and unnecessary, I would always say. One's family and one's work supersede these ridiculous, politically charged, irrational tenure decisions. Stupid people get this thing about their college and its town, this disease, this tropism that prevents them from leaving. It's stupid. I said these things always thinking to myself, please, someone, it just shouldn't happen to me. So if I never say a word about wanting tenure when I don't get it no one will know my hurt and despair, and no one will be able to gloat with jealousy from the thought that he is still alive, holding on to any chances that might still exist.

During these first involvements with others' tenure deliberations, two paths of action invariably passed through my mind. First, sue the senior faculty and the university corporation. Get a legal case. File for nonsupport or bad sportsmanship if need be, but get them. Second, seek another career. This route I contemplated over and over again. Run away to law school, work in a shoe store, open a bowling alley, purchase a franchise for a drive-in chicken restaurant, become a farmer. Do anything, I told myself, but avoid intellectuals; instead, make a lot of money and convince yourself that what you presently are experiencing through this other person's career is not for you. Strangely, when later on the considerations were being made about me, the law suits and alternative careers never regained their initially enticing thrill.

When the older ones exited I clung as mightily as I could to the hope that the sun might shine again on me in all the brilliance of my first few days. Never did I invest interest in anything as much as I did in the mail. I cathected mail. It would deliver to me the one letter that would reform my life and redesign my future status. I rose feet off the ground and pounded a fist into an invisible face when an article got accepted. I was a football coach witnessing his

team move slowly but ineluctably down field, converting each third
and eight into a magnificent first down. I was catching up. Maybe
those other guys now might see *my* stuff when *they* scanned the
journals. That is, if they scanned journals. But rejections from
editors were horrendous. They destroyed me. I was a failure, unpro-
ductive, unworthy. Tenure? I'd be lucky to get my contract renewed
and be given the same office next term. I mean, every once in a
while you have to add something to your curriculum vita. A book
review, a paper delivered at a professional meeting, a birth of a
child, something had to enlarge that document by a few lines now
and again. Maybe one could list the articles he had submitted for
publication. That was legitimate, but it looked cheap.

No one representing opportunity, of course, ever knocked
on my office door. Students came by, naturally, but American
opportunity failed to appear, despite the fact that I always set a
place for him (or her). It seemed to be going elsewhere, or so it
felt. Yet all of this prompted a new dimension and with it a new
anxiety, namely, that the other guys knew better than I how to play
"the politics of the system." They were political animals, not naked
apes at all. They were flesh peddlers, grabbers, weasels consistently
buttonholing the right person, meeting the important agent, connecting with the most instrumental wheeler-dealer they could find.
They were dashing off to every meeting, conference, and weekend
retreat. Twenty-eight years old and they were sidling up to this guy
or that guy, cajoling this editor or that program chairman. The
whole thing was immoral, I decided. Let 'em all get tenure. I'd just
as soon not have any part of it if those are the compromises and
obsequious gestures one must make, the inequities one must endure.
It's a dirty, pretentious, illegitimate racket, this tenure thing. It's
no different from getting elected president. Let 'em have it; I'm
liquidating my shares. The writing isn't worth it. To think that I
even once had tried to dictate articles in hopes of increasing my
productivity. Teaching is what matters. That's the only valuable
activity going on in colleges. That no one gets rewarded for it with
a trillion billion brownie points is proof of its greatness and proof
of the ludicrous and psychotic nature of tenure. I am a teacher first
and foremost, not a tenure-grubbing, professional whizbang on the
make. The kids matter. The blue books and term papers will get

my attention, not tenure, that fakery. So I'll end up in the boon-docks. Tough darts, at least I'll know I acted nobly for those four years in the sun. They'll know it too. The world sorts out the grub-bers from the honest laborers.

And that's exactly what I went to tell a wonderful man only a few years older than I when it became clear he would not be given tenure. The negative decision was tearing his insides out, eating him up alive, and I was thinking Supreme Court decisions, shoe stores, and medical school. Seeing him in his office during his last week in Cambridge made me reminisce on the few funerals that I had attended, with the courageous mourners sitting in the front chairs of the funeral parlor working desperately to keep back the tears. You may cry now, I always want to say to them. You may cry like a child, for nothing hurts more than bereavement and bitter, bitter loss. You may cry, and feel angry too, for it *is* unfair. Cry, my friend, so I need not feel such uneasiness and dread stand-ing before you here amidst the cartons of books mailed in last week from California from a man with an unfinished dissertation of obviously mediocre quality who can't wait for you to leave so that he may occupy your office, your swivel chair, your cabinets and bookcases, your very life space. You know, my esteemed friend, that in my heart it will always be your office, regardless of what happens, just as my office will always be my office. Isn't that also right, my dear, departing friend?

The passing on of these good people whom we all rallied around had the first truly antitenure effects on me. In the first year, when I took a long summer vacation and even slept on a secret beach somewhere and read mystery stories free of any work anxiety, the coming and going of departmental people mattered little. It was as though I belonged to an army platoon sending some of its men back to the front or home. But my name then was not about to be called. Tenure still sizzled as an ideal, a universal ideal, one presumably honored by everyone and surely earned by the most deserving and prominent. In my second year, when I spent much of my vacation time working, but traveling a bit as well, the gleam of tenure remained intense, although the colors of its borders seemed to have undergone certain modification. An unknown had received tenure; a well-known person had been dismissed. It was not making sense, but that year must have been anomalous.

During my third year I took no vacation, never saw the ocean, read not one mystery, worked almost all the time, and made one trip: to the national professional meetings to deliver a paper, no less. I had waited long enough in my office for opportunity. When it never came I altered my philosophical resolutions and military strategies: slightly less dreamy hopes for tenure, slightly more political grubbing around. It all had come upon me slowly and indistinctly. A friend, brilliant in social-psychological observation, asked me one day whether I had noticed that at lunch in the departmental cafeteria I spent most of my time speaking to the highest-ranking faculty personage present? My posture, he claimed, told the same story. I was literally leaning toward the famous and the tenured. Had I not noticed this, I who was usually so perceptive? But there I was in San Francisco reading my paper, drinking in the lounges with the big shots, and thinking every other minute, if this doesn't make it for me nothing will. I've got to have a book, then a reader perhaps, then two, maybe three more meetings; and that's as much as anyone can ask of a junior man. I'll *cause* opportunity to happen. I'll arrange it so that every day the mail brings something—a smell of tenure, a glimpse of controversy, an indication of calculable progress. I'll go to the meetings and retreats, get myself on some universitywide committees, lunch with at least one editor from every publishing company, get to know a few department chairmen around the country, undertake some internationally oriented research so that I can start to expand my reputation on a few new fronts, maybe hobnob with the granting agencies and anyone from the society pages, buy a sports car. I'll of course be as subtle about it as I can.

"Look, it's not selling out," I found myself telling two young students one day early in my third year. "It may not actually be publish or perish anymore, but let's just say it's close enough that I think we'd better do a little writing." The two young men were easily convinced. They believed everything I said, and sadly I noted that they too craved publications, believing them to be essential for their own admission to graduate school. They wanted coauthorship and a chance, perhaps, to deliver a paper at the regional meetings the following April. The disease was spreading. As I had been infected so was I now infecting those younger and more vulnerable, those whose systems could not possibly have generated the appropriate antibodies in a million years. Typhoid Annie, I smiled to myself walking home, meet Tenure Tommy.

Two strange, indeed bizarre events occurred during that, my third year. First, two men with tenure quit the department. They did not have to leave, mind you; no one caught them with a Radcliffe or a B.U. or a Wellesley girl or any girl. They left because better situations arose for them. Better situations? What could be better? Sure, something on the side with Jeanne Moreau or Sophia Loren, but I mean in academics, where would they go? What could they covet? Was there actually something that transcended that was more regal than tenure? But they left, and, contrary to my impudent predictions, they never returned, not even to visit, as far as I could discern.

The second event had to do with living through the tenure ordeals of a special friend—the man, in fact, who had pointed out my obsequious cafeteria ways (ways, incidentally I had abruptly terminated by fixing my schedule so that I could lunch at home). At any rate, lasting several months, this one ordeal was more than even we, the rooting audience, could tolerate. He was getting it, he wasn't getting it. He was in New York, California hunting other jobs. Then he was being given tenure here and having to tell the other places he probably would not be accepting their offers, fantastic as they were. Then he wasn't getting tenure again and the negotiations elsewhere had to be reopened. Throughout this time a whole host of things were being said about him, many of which seemed to be doing little more than documenting what people had believed about him prior to studying his record and credentials. For the first time I was witnessing the machinations of a tenure consideration and being let in on the private information of the transactions. Secondhand, thirdhand, fourthhand stories, vignettes, vituperations, scandals—unreal, but they hurt this man, and they made me sick and frightened inside.

Out of this real misery emerged a genuinely potent argument against tenure. If this was what it entailed, I didn't want it.

The academic freedom clause seemed irrelevant. At least I had not known of violations. But this sort of unparalleled negotiation was excessive. I wanted nothing to do with tenure. Well, maybe a little I wanted it. But not this way. For weeks I commiserated with my friend, and after arduous self-searching, I decided in my heart of hearts that I wanted him to earn tenure because he wanted it so intensely. His case, moreover, caused me to conceive of still another parameter of the permanency struggles and existential dilemma I saw playing itself out in various forms on the different floors of the building. I was making close friends, then losing them. This one whom I loved had left town, this one had moved to another school in the same city, two more now resided over fifteen hundred miles away. Were still alive? Could they even breathe in Texas and Oregon and Hawaii? My cohort—a word I had come to use more and more in graduate school—was disintegrating; they were vacating their apartments and rented houses to younger people, selling homes where we had visited with them, and leaving me! A new team was gradually forming in my mind, a team composed of all the people who had come up for tenure and been defeated. It was a good team: sound, young, a lot of punch, a winning attitude, incredible talent and energy. It was the visiting team, the away team, the road company; in a matter of time I would be joining them for sure.

Maybe I wouldn't, though. Maybe that one chance would arrive, maybe that one turn of the world would strike my head just right and suddenly I would become the newest arrival, the seasoned rookie on the senior men's squad, the squad of confidence and international glamour. It could happen, I thought, even at the end of my third year. It could happen. It won't. But it could happen. You never know. It won't.

In the first days of my fourth year I felt a hurt, not a deep hurt, more a pain of recognition: Not only did the undergraduates that one autumn appear so young I believed them to be tourists from a local high school, but the new junior faculty members looked scarcely any older. By now I had been perfectly socialized. A few publications, a clipping from a newspaper now and again, a few profoundly insignificant appearances on panel discussions, and a status disconnected from both the younger faculty and the senior

people. More disarming, the younger faculty were now coming to
me for information and tips about the department. At first I
thought that presumptuous of them, but had I not done the same
thing three years before without realizing that that was what I had
been doing? So I told them all I could. Work hard. Honor your
students, be prepared to spend the entire first year doing little
beyond getting adjusted, think of the work of the day and the years
will take care of themselves.

The words, actually, didn't sound too bad, a bit like William
Osler, perhaps, admonishing medical students. But it wasn't at all
what they wanted to hear. Not in the slightest. They inquired instead about the tenure deliberations of this person or that, my close
friends. "Hey, what was the real story there?" Did these guys, these
legends, that is, care that they didn't get tenure? they asked. As
graduate students completing their dissertations, they had heard the
stories, even in Ann Arbor, Evanston, Madison, and Santa Cruz.
Their details, ironically enough, coincided quite remarkably with
the truth as I had fashioned it. So our discussions would turn that
inevitable corner and once again we would trot out the batting
average of the present senior faculty crop; the cycle was completed.

It bothered me that the reports of my friends—who, I
advised these younger people, had left pleasantly enough, weighted
down as they were with bountiful offers—were disseminated in such
a way that noble human beings were being transformed into symbolic figures and legendary creatures. It bothered me, too, that while
we never discussed it these new heads were obviously sizing up my
chances for tenure just as I had sized up others' chances several
years before. "You have, what, Tom, three, four years left on your
contract?" they would ask deferentially, but I knew they were assay-
ing the property just as I had. The same old monopoly game was
still in session, only the players varied, and history grew. Everyone
rolled the dice about in his hands, inspected the board, and com-
puted the probabilities. Who owns the utilities and the railroads?
they were asking, knowing damn well who owned the peak-roofed
hotels on the blue, green, and yellow properties, the big properties,
the permanent properties. As *I* was now competition for them, it
would soon be time for me to go through the wretched labors not
of childbirth exactly but of adult birth, shall we say. And while I

cannot ever know the real experience of childbirth, I was, perhaps, not unlike a young woman carrying about the seed of something in my body that was nowhere near ready to emerge, and I was a bit frightened by it, the prospect as well as the process.

In our own particular department a letter was sent to all junior faculty members who definitely were not getting tenure. Kindly, the senior people wished to afford as much time as possible for their younger colleagues to seek employment elsewhere. It was a tastefully written letter, but to receive it, indeed merely to know of its presence anywhere in the building, to be aware even of the electric typewriter where it was taking form, terrified me. Every letter I received from my chairman during that fourth year caused me to perspire. Here it comes. This is it. But they've been known to change their minds. No, this letter is going to say, halleluja, you are the new chairman of the department! Not only do we give you tenure, we have arranged that from this day forward you will be immortal and eternally lovely. You will be twenty-nine or thirty-two forever, and you will never lose your hair or gain weight, and no one will ever again reject anything you write or say, for that matter, and the students will flock to your elite and oversubscribed seminars even when you are boring and totally unprepared, which of course you no longer will be.

The letter never came. Something else happened instead. The university faculty voted to institute a new rank of associate professorship without tenure. Prior to this, it had been my understanding that the rank of associate professor automatically carried tenure. So this was a new turn of events, indeed a glimpse at the future, for if one were elevated to this new position, could stardom and bright sunlight lie far beyond? Not on your life, I reasoned. Here was the acid test. Now at last we would know where we stood. If ever a rank order of favorites, of reasonable bets for tenure, of sheer love existed, here it was. I remember thinking at this time, however, that an associate professorship without tenure was not the real thing, not the genuine item. It was a bit like pastrami without mustard. Edible, still kosher, but not the real goods. Still, opportunity in a new form was extant somewhere in the building, hunting surely for my modest fourth-floor office.

I was never elevated to associate professor without tenure.

But no matter, for no sooner had I comprehended the terms of this new proposition than I erected rationales for why it would be injudicious for me to receive it. I wanted no early clues. No fluid sample to determine the sex of the unborn child for me. When it was ready, full term, it would appear, and I would either stand before the world with tenure—legitimate tenure, that is, defined in the ways it traditionally had been—or, as the old joke goes, I would return to my home quietly, sip a cool drink, eat dinner, take a hot bath, and slit my wrists.

I should not pass too quickly over this point of honoring traditional modes of advancement and rewards. Perhaps the central theme of my discussions with friends about tenure was that teaching ability and professorial reputation played too insignificant a role in the decision. I recall speaking to undergraduate students on several occasions about why one of their favorite teachers was no longer at the school. For the while, our sentiments and reveries were identical. He was such a wonderful man, a decent man who took interest in the young, we agreed. He was a bit of a godhead even, selflessly defending the eternal inequities manifested by the young. Yes, yes, we lamented, his leaving was regretable. In fact, it represented something of a betrayal and outright rejection. Yes, I agreed, it did all that. Then suddenly, I realized our perspectives were not at all consistent, for whereas I had been blaming the senior faculty for not awarding tenure to the man in question, the students were hurting from the belief that the man had quit voluntarily, sold out for more money if a bit less prestige. The recognition of the reality shocked them, for collective adoration, they believed in their hearts, should have been sufficient to bestow tenure on their heroes. Once again the establishment had committed a criminal error and contributed to the dehumanization of universities and hence civilization.

The students' sense of angered bewilderment was not unshared by some occupying my own cohort. Why shouldn't the teaching count for more? we would ask again and again and again. Intrinsic rewards are nice and all that, but as sociologists we know more than most about mobility channels and the social structures that determine them. You can't eat rewards or live under the roofs of student idolatry. Intrinsic rewards don't buy one of the gorgeous old Victorian houses off of Brattle Street or on the top of Gallows

Hill. We're knocking our brains out, bathing in the miniscule but still cherished waters of mini-fame, in the ripples, that is, of so-called local reputations, while the big shots are already scanning the globe to find someone to replace us. Coals to Newcastle, someone muttered once. I might have muttered the phrase myself, but my mind was already at work attempting to figure out just exactly how one does establish that gargantuan reputation and list of superb publications that entice the Newcastle people to become interested in *your* coal.

That was exactly the point: Despite the rising number of what we label educational alternatives, despite the obviously unjust weighings made during tenure considerations, and despite the recognition, which, I think, all of us in this one institution shared—that caring for a student was sweet and kindly but hardly a criterion of manly, mature achievement—the fact was that I had reached a point where I craved tenure on the oldest, strictest, and most traditional criteria extant. I wanted the university to scan the world of scholars, living, dead, unborn, anywhere, and proclaim me to be the best candidate. Ideally they should also say in their proclamation letter that my marvelous teaching and devotion to young people were important features for them, but fundamentally it had been my scholarship, imagination, creativity, and productivity that simply obliged them to rank me alongside Freud, Marx, Durkheim, and Weber. Yet, fantasy aside, how could I even live with tenure when those who would be my new colleagues occupied such colossal status outside the university? How could I even use the same bathrooms with them or attend the same meetings with them, and, worse, decide the fate of younger faculty folks with them? Was it true, I asked my friend one day, that a study had demonstrated that those recently appointed tenure experience the highest anxiety of any faculty status group? He said that a study had revealed exactly this. I shook my head from side to side and looked soberly at him, all the while urging my face to appear that of a sociologist gorging data and ruminating on the implications of occupational mobility and status anxiety. Inside, however, I longed for that reported anxiety tenure was supposed to fetch. Try me, I told my secret guardian. Give it to me and you'll see how quickly I can transform that rippling anxiety into temerity, aggressiveness, and conquering strength. Give it to me, I dare you, and I'll show you a quivering boy transformed into a man of earnest dedication to his work and to his school.

The department was crazy, I continued to believe, the system of tenure preposterously constructed. Why recruit an unknown kid—how I was aging—finishing some run-of-the mill dissertation, and throw me out? It didn't make sense. But forget me. Let's just speak sociologically. The students, don't you see, are being hurt by all this; it's part of a systematic oppression of them. The two undergraduates listening to me concurred. The senior men are busy with all that they do, I resumed, and here we are, the junior slobs, willing to take the small salaries and the pressure and that complicated status routine one plays out at professional meetings where one constantly feels that the status he derives from his institution comes to be embarrassingly higher than the status he earns by token of his being and his work, just to teach people like you. But no, I went on without taking a breath, they go bring in punk, hotshot graduate students with no real teaching experience, which, if they did have it, no one would care about anyway, to replace us. It makes no sense. The whole thing is destructive to the system.

The students concurred again and looked serious, even worried. They nodded their heads just slightly in thoughtful obeisance. Then one said: "But many of the senior people are great teachers and many of the junior ones stink. And you can't forget that many of the junior guys who were good teachers when they first came, when we were freshmen, say, have become totally disinterested in students and less and less prepared for their courses, which they repeat without alterations year after year as they battle to attain the brownie points needed for tenure." (The kid knew all about brownie points.) Then the other student, who all the while had appeared wholly uninvolved in the matter, the matter being, of course, my fate, quietly uttered his only words of the afternoon: "If they didn't choose unknown, punk, hotshot graduate students with crummy dissertations and no teaching experience, like you say, then *you* would never be here."

The one bit of evidence and piece of finalized resolution that sustained me during my fourth year was that I had convinced myself that tenure decisions were politically biased, ruthlessly determined, and injudiciously transacted. Senior men pushed for their former students or against the students of their competitor colleagues, or for scholars who shared their perspectives and approaches. A candidate's reputed politics could overrule his talents, the weight of a person's articles and books could prove to be, alas, either embarrassingly slim or indecently heavy, and an undefinable but frightfully omnipresent element called life-style was being invoked at every turn. He just isn't our kind of person, I imagined one senior man would say to another. I just can't articulate it any better than that. And the other would nod and, in the manner and tone of the old Mike Nichols and Elaine May routine, enunciate: I know *exactly* what you mean. I know *exactly* what you mean. Well, then it's settled. No tenure for *him*. Anyway, we always have another go around should we want a second shot at him.

These were my fantasies and projections, naturally predicated on the shreds and morsels of "hard data" regarding tenure decisions that I could assemble from people here and there. Naturally, too, my images reflected the fantasies and projections of other junior people and their wives, who, sadly enough, were always sucked into these heart-rending issues. The whole thing by now was a family affair. Dinner or cocktail parties had become important events for the acquisition of tenure. Perhaps guest lists should be altered so that a little political figgly miggly might be served up with the hors d'oeuvres. Maybe more or fewer students should be invited. Maybe unmarried people or couples without children looked bad somehow to an unseen tenure committee. After all, listing family information on curriculum vitae was formal practice, and certainly this information meant something. From time to time I wished I had been born someplace more exotic than Chicago. I wondered about the style of our furnishings and how well received were the pieces of art that hung on our walls.

The projections and fantasies emanating from tenure considerations were inevitable as there was never an empirical method for knowing just what constituted these practices. What *were* they looking for? The worst source of information was the victim, the man from the department up for tenure, for his information was so painted over by hopes and anguish that almost nothing of any validity could be discerned.

Precisely such thinking and wondering persuaded me that at last I was assessing the tenure prospect in proper and rightful contexts. My very vantage point and perspicuity would save me. Tenure, alas, was not worth it. The team without it was incalculably superior, while the machinations for its bestowal were ugly, ignominious, and castrating. I would play out my years and silently depart. The students would weep, maybe tear down a few buildings in righteous furor, but I would go the way of my departed friends. Quite possibly, a new fantasy went, we would all be together again somewhere, even in the boondocks. Better still, we would start a college of our own and bring to it exactly whom *we* wanted. Now this was a unique and positive idea. The Ford Foundation would underwrite it, viewing us as an experimental college literally exploding with the unspeakable talent that had so threatened and intimidated the old guard. We would retrieve all our friends. Our families would play together in the mountains and in the oceans, and, just short of a beauteous commune, this emancipated colony college would flourish, restoring creativity where before moribund scholarship had reigned.

But wait, was it possible that this was exactly what the senior faculty had done? Was it not they, after all, who had fetched their school chums and former junior faculty colleagues and reassembled them right under our noses in the elegant houses of Cambridge, Belmont, Brookline, Winchester, and Lexington? Was it not in fact *their* families who now combed the mountains of Vermont and New Hampshire or trudged upon the dunes and beaches of "the Cape" and Martha's Vineyard in search of winter and summer pleasures? The department, the university, it suddenly dawned upon me, was *their* colony, their brainy house of communion, aggrandizement, and bliss. They had been there before us, and, like the most settled of totemic pilgrims, they stood unwilling to move over and make room for anyone but their rightful inheritors.

Well, no matter, I thought. The Ford Foundation could keep its money. I was by now bitterly disillusioned by the whole process. When I fail to advance and claim a foul, the insiders and losers will know precisely how unstable, unpredictable, and frightful is the bumpy jaunt to permanence.

And so I rested content for the while, contending that my

earlier public hunches had been accurate and erudite. Tenure was a tainted status, and if I never attained it that would be just fine. I would say this to myself and then wait. But there would be no response. No longer did I detect that movement in my newer but smaller fourth year office, and no longer did I sense that mysterious noise. If I don't make tenure it's just fine. I'll do my work and honor my students. So. Then I would wait. No response. Nothing but the stillness. At last the tension was over, the tenure anxiety permanently quieted. Liberation veritably engulfed me, arriving as opportunity never had in a rather unique form, given this age of multimedia liberation packages. I alone had passed beyond the formidable ladder of success that all the world, surely, dared each of us to ascend. No longer would I have to suffer the pains of permanence.

A few more thoughts and my recollections of the tenure ordeal have all been duly accounted for. It took a fellowship year at a university located right in the center of what I had always called the boondocks to make me realize that my new found transcendence and absence of pain were the concluding movement of the tenure socialization process. They not only were utterly predictable reactions but were perfectly functional and indeed required for the success of the academic system. My imagined liberation was in fact the neutralization of emotion and denigration of purpose, expectation, and reward that I was meant to experience as the prospect of tenure loomed nearer.

What was not intended, however, and what would be the most frightening reflection of the junior faculty years began to form out of the discussions with my new boondock colleagues, themselves luxuriating in a year of freedom, bedded in space far removed from the normal vicissitudes and trials in universities one knew surprisingly little about. The fright was that in those early faculty years I had become totally preoccupied with tenure, and in a laryngeal sense of identity I had lost my voice. I had my work, my faithful list of projects and intentions, but I needed a foreign place and a group of men and women who did not share my discipline and with whom I could not talk shop to make these sickening points clear. With them, with whom I felt no competition and for whom I prayed for great success, conversation vacillated between elegant intellectual issues and the most earthy, pornographic, filthy, mundane slop one could ever hear. And I loved it all, the ideas and the junk, for both helped me to become a bit more honest with myself and to disengage from the inevitable topics and dilemmas of academic mobility and projected career. Between the highest and the lowest common and wondrously uncommon denominators of these conversations, I came to value my talents, capacities, and drives, however meager, gross, or farfetched they might turn out to be. Naturally a new bunch of prejudices, insecurities, anxieties, pitfalls, and invidious comparisons associated with this new perspective was born. Now batting averages had to be assigned to new players, but this time I felt, somehow, that the game was better suited to me. I could feel that my insides were being tapped, plumbed even, and as they were, the pretensions I had refined crept quietly away. I felt light again, maybe even a touch pure.

Most interesting, I came to depend on a sense of marginality, a boondock orientation, an opportunity to invoke and then rely on one's sense of having been excluded. It was not exactly dangerous in the center, in the hub of universities. It was more the feeling that I had never felt I belonged to this center, where surely life started and where the sun disappeared beyond one's vision. Moreover, while the rewards were erected, defined, and bequeathed in the center, it was for me at the margin that the flames of creativity, innovation, and personal daring and courage shot high. The center, I mused, was an overprotective mother doing her best to bestow love but choking her child, cabining his spirit in the most unintentional way. And the poor child knew not at all of the source of his congestion and crushing anguish. He assumed it to be normal, proper, and physiologically sound. The margin, not total escape, was leaving home; staying in touch, of course, but making it in the world as best as one could on his own ingenuity, talents, backlog of resources, guile, and, at times, criminal acumen and psychopathology.

But there was one more important thing. When I invoke a sense of marginality or choose some bit of myself, some feature or element of background to lean on in order to reestablish personal uniqueness and a lost pride, I know that I have not been totally included by the ideology, by the procedures, by the people of the center, and I am frightened and angered by this sense of exclusion and lack of belonging. Furthermore, the aspect of myself I invoke for gaining marginality usually suggests something about the nature of the center that I have been repulsed or disfigured by.

I now came to believe that tenure was not evil or wrong; it was, for me, simply anachronistic. It just came too soon. I was being asked to evolve too rapidly from polite boy to responsible man without any opportunity to meet the me's that would invariably emerge upon the birth of a secondary, career-based adolescence. Not only that, I was being compelled to assess this evolution every moment of my life. Parties, gatherings, accidental meetings with colleagues on the street seemed always to bring forth discussion of salary problems and tenure. I could not extricate myself from these discussions even when I was alone.

How I wanted to be free and utterly detached from all universities, all academic obligations and tenure arrangements, all accomplished adults, and still be embraced and honored by these very institutions and people. I found and still find that I needed the sense of marginality because it provides the energy for my private thinking, writing, and personal discovery. Social, emotional, and intellectual marginality formed the breath my voice never felt. Everyone, I imagine, invokes some sense of disenfranchisement, rejection, or oppression when creating or seeking new forms of expression or style. Everyone at some age believes that his parents hate him, that his teachers have quit on him, that his friends loathe him, and that his country would adore his emigration. One needs this feeling, for at some level there is a quality of insanity, just as Freud suggested, that feeds into the mill of creativity, growth, and the search for personal identity and existential fortitude. As ironic or incomprehensible as it may seem, the few elite, prestigious, high-powered but still fabulously exceptional universities I had known, along with the web of tenure that wove about my soul the instant, perhaps, I announced where I would settle after graduate school, had throttled this insanity and had substituted for it the preoccupation with professional expectations of success and tenure. Moreover, these universities had guided insanity away from the realms where I might take potentially healthy control of it. *Where* I was in institutions, in the academic hierarchy, was all that had mattered to me.

Thus, the best I could muster was to permit the arrowheads of insanity to hit the wrong targets at the most inopportune times.

I never knew this, of course, but in those first days of the swivel chair and the empty shelves, when I truly believed that I could be born anew, I had squelched the one single element of my being that I would eventually require in order to know the profound gratifications as well as the profound anguish and pain that ultimately constitute any work, any life for that matter—the inexorables associated with and determined by impermanence.

I value the academic though still untenured position I hold now in another university. A bit of courage, a bit of fear conjoined with the counsel of honored tenured colleagues reinforced my decision to leave the university of my junior faculty years before the fatal letter arrived. Pride and all sorts of sentiments conspired to prevent me from waiting around to see just what team would choose me. The consternation of tenure has been only slightly lessened, however, in the years following my departure. I still rely on marginality and am nourished by the flames of the periphery. But I hunger, too, for the secure bosom of the concentric center, the traditional and the well-established and, of course, the guaranteed destiny. More than financial considerations prompt me to reflect on the treasures and beauties, however tarnished, of tenure. So, like a man who in all honesty feels compelled to announce his age as five, seventeen, thirty-two, and fifty-eight, and who craves to be with all his families, the people of his childhood as well as his adulthood, and at all stages of psychosocial development at the same time, a man who needs attachments as well as separateness, fullness as well as emptiness, undying love as well as periodic animosities and outright interpersonal war, I retreat to work literally wearied by the tenure considerations of others that explode about me, some yielding happiness, thankfully, others anger, hurt, and defeat. But I continue to wonder just when I might finally settle upon one enduring resolution that will unravel my persistent ambivalence toward tenure.

But then, I reason, it may be just this ambivalence that simultaneously leads each of us in new, sometimes ill-conceived, sometimes marvelous personal and career directions. It may be just this ambivalence that allows us to control these new impulses, to adapt to them as well as to the situations that in part are formed by their emergence, such that wherever we might land, in the center or at the edges, we will at least be tolerated and feel, if even for a moment, the tastes of personal worth as well as the warmth of the sun.

Chapter **3**

Tenure in Context

John R. Silber

A Pervasive Expectation

Discussions of tenure have been flawed by the absence of any contextual framework, by the failure to examine the similarities and differences in the functioning of tenure as it is operative in various human institutions. Because this defect of context has characterized discussions of tenure for more than a generation, fundamental confusions have, by frequent reiteration, become traditional. None is more glaring than the confusion of the role and function of tenure with that of academic freedom or the confused belief that in academic circles tenure functions in a manner radically different from that in business or professional life.

My purpose here is to make a modest first effort toward correcting this central defect, which, as a philosopher, I would characterize as the absence of any adequate phenomenological examination of tenure or its relation to academic freedom. Full discussion would require a book; but even a phenomenological sketch will, I believe, measurably advance our understanding of tenure.

When the average businessman, carpenter, taxicab driver, lawyer, or surgeon discusses some "wild-mouthed professor" or some careful academic exponent of a system of thought that outrages folk wisdom or a professor who is negligent or unresponsive in his duties because of psychological depression, alcoholism, premature senility, or some other cause, these professional, business- and tradesmen say, almost in unison, "If that man were in my field, he'd be fired."

The cab driver, surgeon, carpenter, lawyer, and businessman are firmly convinced that survival in their occupations depends upon continued productivity at high quantitative and qualitative levels, that they are caught up in competitive or professional forces that insure high-level competence and efficiency, and that professional and financial disaster awaits those who, for whatever reasons, fail to meet rigorous expectations. But they believe that professors or teachers in public schools, colleges, and universities, and almost everyone in civil service, at the municipal, state, or federal level, has tenure in a sense which is denied them. They believe, moreover, that tenure has destroyed responsibility and high-level performance and that the vitality, efficiency, and high competence in their fields are largely traceable to its absence.

Every college and university president knows that these are the prevailing dogmas. Every university administrator with at least two months' experience has been told, again and again, that "Professor X should be fired" and, what is more, that "he would be fired if universities and colleges operated on the same principles as the rest of American society." This charge is usually made for at least two reasons: because of the prevalent business cliché and because university administrators usually respond inadequately or confusedly.

Because the administrator has failed to think through what tenure is and how it operates in social and industrial life, he typically claims that the incompetent or the irresponsible professor cannot be fired "because he has tenure." He discusses tenure as if it were a sinecure or a magic property like the protective waters in which Achilles was dipped or the charm with which Brünhilde shielded the body of Siegfried. Administrators have spoken of tenure as if it were an absolute bar to the severance, reassignment, or curtailment of professorial activities. In order to excuse either the administrator's evasion of responsibility or his inability to give substantive answers to the questions asked by trustees, the administrator has himself encouraged the mistaken belief that academic tenure functions as a sinecure, that is, as something radically different from the disguised or unnamed forms of tenure which flourish in professions, business, unions, and so on.

If we examine these other contexts, however, we immediately see the absurdity of the distinction. I recently attended a lecture in which a leading surgeon discussed the administration of surgical services in a teaching hospital. He pointed out that in these institutions practicing surgeons include not merely teaching faculty members, resident surgeons, and students of surgery, but also surgeons in private practice who are affiliated with the hospital. In this context, he pointed out that quality is in part insured by an exercise known as Deaths and Complications, a weekly review of all hospital cases in which unexpected developments or death occur. In a typical session a case is presented, and then questions concerning procedures are asked of students and the surgeon involved by students and members of the surgical staff.

Suppose, for example, an infection develops after a Caesarean birth. What caused the infection? Investigation indicates that it resulted from the removal of a normal appendix in conjunction with the Caesarean section. Is it wise or foolish to complicate a straightforward Caesarean with an appendectomy? Was the pedicle of the appendix cut too short? Should the combining of operations be recommended in any case? And so on. The purpose of the discussion is to educate students and sharpen practicing surgeons by expanding their experience through examination of the experience of others, and to censure constructively, so as to improve professional performance, those who have made mistakes. It is a humane but stringent examination of human judgment aimed at its refinement. Deaths and Complications provides a review group in which persons can severely criticize each other without running the risk of ostracism or more severe penalties.

A member of the audience asked the lecturer, "What happens if a specific surgeon provides far more cases for discussion than any other surgeon? How do the teaching faculty and the residents and affiliated surgeons of the hospital remove a colleague who makes too many mistakes?" At this point, the distinguished lecturer said that only two courses of action were open since surgeons rarely made mistakes so flagrant that they could be charged with negligence or manslaughter. A deficient surgeon could be removed, but he would then move to a less demanding hospital or a less sophisticated medical community where he could practice without supervision. In order to avoid this, the lecturer recommended retaining the deficient surgeon on the hospital staff but protecting his patients by arranging for assistance by abler members of the surgical staff.

A candid man, the lecturer did not pretend that a doctor who graduated from a medical school, completed his residency requirements, and entered practice could be denied tenure. He pointed out that in a few cases a doctor could be persuaded to change his field from surgery to general practice, internal medicine, or some specialty less likely to endanger the lives of his patients. Basically, however, he admitted that surgeons have tenure in the sense that they have a right to continue the practice of surgery indefinitely—a right virtually impossible to rescind, barring criminal acts. We also know that the medical profession has rarely been willing to apply severe sanctions to doctors who are alcoholics or addicted to drugs.

So much, then, for the notion that in medicine "a man like Professor X would be fired."

The situation in legal practice is similar. Imagine, for instance, the senior partners of a law firm meeting to discuss a junior partner. The discussion goes as follows: "Bill's alcoholism has gotten steadily worse for the last five years. It's been three years now since he's tried a case. It's been almost five years since he has been able to meet a client effectively for more than two hours at a time. Everybody knows that he drinks too much. It's time we asked him to withdraw from the firm." And the typical reply is: "But how can we just get rid of Bill? Admittedly, he's an embarrassment to the firm. But he's brought in at least 15 to 20 per cent of our clients over the last twenty years. We still have two or three clients who swear by him, and all the clients he brought in would resent our tossing him out at age fifty-five after thirty years' service and twenty as a partner." The partnership might insist on reducing Bill's share of its income. It is extremely unlikely, however, that they would leave him severely embarrassed, either socially or financially. And we are all aware of the difficulties, regional and local, involved in removing a judge whose performance is publicly acknowledged by the legal profession to be defective.

So much, then, for the myth that in law "a man like Professor X would be fired."

We also know that in every business minor and major failings are tolerated at all levels, from executives to janitors. Except in times of severe financial strain, corporations and family businesses retain their employees by managing to overlook or resign themselves to their various shortcomings. Examples are legion and notorious, and we all know of them. When a man is fired, we can assume either that he had been with the firm for a short time or that his firing was viewed as irresponsible or unjust. Arthur Miller's *Death of a Salesman* is, in part, an indictment of the callow inheritor of a family business who met none of the obligations his father owed the older employees. An executive of one of the largest insurance companies remarked that, of its several hundred salesmen, no more than 30 to 40 per cent could be expected to produce at a reasonably high level. This level of performance, he observed, was standard for the industry and had remained unchanged over several decades.

So much for the myth that in business "a man like Professor X would be fired."

In carpentry, plumbing, and taxi-driving, the situation varies, depending upon whether the individual is a self-employed entrepreneur or the employee of a firm. If the latter, his case is covered by the preceding discussion. If the former, his case falls outside the discussion of tenure in institutional contexts but is covered by the discussion of tenure in individual or personal contexts. He has placed himself in a context of extreme individualism in which tenure obligations that arise will be obligations to himself and to members of his family. (Only those interested in the completion of the phenomenological survey of tenure are likely to be interested in the extension of tenure to individual contexts. It is, nevertheless, a relevant aspect of tenure or an alternative expression of the basic human need or propensity for order and certainty.)

My phenomenological sketch, though far from complete, leads persuasively, in my opinion, to the conclusion that tenure is an expression of the human concern for continuity and stability in personal, social, professional, and business life. Tenure, whether formal or informal, is an expectation of continued employment, of relative permanence, that grows with each year of service in the minds of employers and employees, supervisors and those supervised. It is the expectation, rising with the passage of time, that severance or alteration of service will not occur. It is also the moral conviction that employment must not be altered or terminated capriciously, that these things will occur only if changed circumstances justify their occurrence. Tenure may be seen in part as a contextual variant of the principle of nonparasitism variously formulated: "one who serves must be served"; "for unto whomsoever much is given, of him shall be much required." Both maxims express the basic human need for coherence.

Typically, the day a person takes a job he is impressed with the uncertainty of his continuance. He is on trial: probation is his mode of employment. A secretary's probationary appointment begins with her first day at work. But for an airline stewardess, probationary appointment begins with the first day in stewardess school. For a surgeon, probation begins probably with entrance to medical school, certainly with the commencement of residence. By the time a surgeon is licensed to practice independent of supervision, his practice is no longer probationary but is tenured. A surgeon has tenure in his license and also, perhaps, in his institutional position. He will continue to practice surgery for as long as he lives unless someone can prove—and proof is extremely difficult—that he is incompetent or guilty of malpractice. The lawyer's probationary appointment begins either with law school or when he joins a firm. Gradually his probationary mode metamorphoses into a permanent relationship expressed by membership in the firm or by joining the partnership. A similar relationship characterizes participation in consulting firms. The large group of associates are on probation like assistant professors, while the partners function in many ways as tenured faculty.

Tenure functions in all institutions of which I am aware as a rising expectation of continuity or permanence; the burden of proof for continuance is gradually shifted from the employee to the employer. The new employee must demonstrate his value to his institution; the firm must demonstrate to an old employee that it is justified in insisting on a reassignment, a reduction of duties, or severance. Tenure functions on a continuum, and a person's tenure claim is partly a function of his power within his profession. At the height of his powers, he reaches a zenith of tenure expectation. As his powers decline, he recognizes the growing reasonableness in a call for his removal. Removal after long service must reasonably involve either reassignment or adequate retirement or disability benefits if the employer is to be free of the charge of exploitation or of parasitism in relation to the employee.

The number of years required to establish a tenure claim must surely vary according to the nature of the institution and the demands of the job. A janitor might establish a weak tenure claim within a few weeks or months on the basis of competence and a very strong claim within five to ten years on the basis of service. A surgeon, by contrast, would need eight or nine years to sustain his claim on the basis of competence, and by that time he would already have given substantial service.

Grounds for alteration or termination of employment must likewise vary according to the nature of the institution and the responsibilities of the employee. In some fields and professions tenure once acquired through years of increasing competence and service is not likely ever to be lost by a conscientious and healthy participant (law, architecture, retail sales, interior house painting, cabinet-making are examples). In other professions, however, the claims of tenure decrease as surely as they increase through natural rise and decline in the effective performance of participants. And in some professions skills are so specialized that reassignments are almost impossible to arrange. Professional baseball and opera are two obvious examples.

One cannot even generalize concerning the claims of tenure within a single profession. The musician's profession, for instance, is incredibly varied. The concertmaster may look forward to long tenure, whereas a coloratura must resign herself to a much shorter career. A well-managed opera company must acknowledge tenure claims by members of its orchestra that are substantially more enduring than those of its singing staff. But the economics of opera production are such that no company, unless subsidized, can afford to give proper reward for service alone.

Tenure within institutions is not totally dissimilar to the claims made on one another by members of a family. In this context, we may see a kind of tenure imposed on the self-employed individual who insists on continuing to work for himself (granting tenure to himself as his own employee) as a condition for meeting the obligations he owes to other members of his family. He cannot rid himself of these obligations (except, perhaps, in a merely legal sense or in an empty physical sense through suicide) simply by deciding to disown his offspring and divorce his wife, for they have claims markedly similar to tenure (once again as expectations of continuity) in relation to him. Even in our friendships, there is a slowly rising claim analogous to tenure; responsible persons do not make or terminate friendships suddenly or capriciously. Severance of these associations requires justification.

The concept of tenure in its most humane and systematic manifestation may be found in Japan, where the entire industrial system is viewed as similar to an extended family. The imperfections in most of the tenure relationships in our society stem from the absence of this extended family concept. What we find wanting is a general system of retirement and insurance that provides dignified options for those who, through natural processes of physical, mental, and motivational decline, are no longer capable of maintaining their effectiveness in highly competitive or professionally demanding contexts. In societies such as Japan, simple firing is comparatively rare. This drastic extreme is usually avoided by means of reassignment, retirement, or hospitalization. And, ideally, reassignments and retirements are arranged within a context that successfully preserves the dignity and self-esteem of the individual.

In light of this cursory phenomenological examination, we must conclude that tenure exists as a claim of continuance and as a demand of immunity from arbitrary termination of most human relationships, whether private or institutional. Tenure is grounded ultimately in a human expectation that there be continuity in life, that there be a *quid pro quo,* that associations among individuals and between individuals and between individuals and institutions be orderly rather than chaotic, responsible rather than capricious.

Tenure exists in universities and colleges not because of the AAUP but because of human nature. When the businessman says, "In business, we would fire a man like Professor X," he talks tough, but he misstates the facts. All of us come to terms with relative degrees of competence and responsibility in all professions, institutions, and personal associations. Incompetence and irresponsibility no less than their opposites are a part of the human condition.

Tenure, Sinecure, and Academic Freedom

But if my analysis of tenure is sound, why the widespread belief that tenure functions differently in academic communities? The responsibility lies, I believe, both with academic administrators and the AAUP. I have already mentioned the confusion that has led academic administrators to explain that "Professor X cannot be fired because he has tenure." But nothing in the concept of tenure precludes firing; tenure precludes only capricious or arbitrary firing. If a tenured professor fails to meet the demands and responsibilities of his position, he may be fired or reassigned for cause. Whenever tenure is interpreted as an absolute bar to dismissal or reassignment, it loses its distinctive meaning and becomes simply sinecure. College and university administrators have, nevertheless, used tenure with the meaning and force of sinecure.

The AAUP—a highly responsible professional organization —influenced administrators in this direction through laudable but sometimes misguided efforts to protect academic freedom. And neither the AAUP nor the academic administrators have unraveled the confusions that led them astray or sought perspicuous and effective means of pursuing their common goals. Just as we failed to develop a phenomenology of tenure that would reveal its essential character in all human contexts, we never correctly discerned the relation of tenure to academic freedom. We never asked whether the principles and procedures that protect the one are compatible with the protection, or even the existence, of the other.

The transformation of tenure into sinecure was never intended by the AAUP but was rather the inadvertent result of its concern to defend and protect academic freedom. The history of the transformation of academic tenure into sinecure is a topic worthy of our best historians; but, for the purposes of this chapter, a thematic sketch must suffice. At a time when the public was hostile to and intolerant of evolutionists, secularists, economists, psychoanalysts, sociologists, or indeed of any professor whose views differed from local public opinion, the AAUP perhaps decided that the successful defense of all members of the academic community from capricious dismissal was impossible. Unable to defend all, in 1915 the AAUP suggested that the positions above the rank of instructor be tenured after ten years of service, subject to removal for cause. By so doing, the AAUP unquestionably increased the effectiveness of its protection of academic freedom for tenured faculty. It also stimulated public recognition of the need for academic freedom, even though it did little to clarify the latter concept among either professors or the general public.

In 1940 the AAUP decision to lower from ten to seven years the period of service at which tenure claims are made may have derived from numerological instincts. Or perhaps the guiding pattern among the AAUP leaders was Jacob's seven years in service to Laban. Or it may have been the pragmatic belief that by 1940 a larger subset of professors could be defended against arbitrary dismissal. Whether guided by numerology, biblical precedent, or political tactics, the AAUP could reasonably argue that a professor who has worked seven years for a university has a *bona fide* claim to tenure—that is, a reasonable expectation of continuance and immunity from capricious removal—on the basis of service. Such a professor might reasonably assume, moreover, that if he had not shown some promise of meeting minimal expectations of competence, he would have been separated from the institution at an earlier date. Although the seven-year rule distorts the essential character of tenure by disregarding its continuum features—that is, by overlooking the gradual rise in the expectation of continuance —the AAUP tenure rule, as formulated in 1915 and modified in 1940, did not absolutize tenure as an unqualified right to continuance: that is, it clearly provided that faculty members could be dismissed for cause.

As formulations of bare principles, there is little contest in the AAUP statements on academic freedom and tenure. The academic community was fighting for its life—for the freedoms to teach and to learn according to sound principles of intellectual inquiry. The AAUP tenure rule offered a significant defensive weapon (but not necessarily the best weapon; the trial procedure alone might have been more effective) against the arbitrary firing of faculty—against, that is, the destruction of teaching and research capabilities through enforced conformity to the dominant views of local communities, no matter how ignorant or prejudiced. The 1915 Declaration of Principles and the 1940 Statement of Principles on Academic Freedom and Tenure were undeniably helpful.

As formulated, however, AAUP principles provided scant protection of academic freedom for nontenured faculty or students. (Universities now occasionally use AAUP procedures to defend academic freedom of nontenured faculty. This defense has been limited, as far as I know, to cases which involve political rather than more centrally academic issues.) Moreover, scant attention was given to elaborating the concept of academic freedom or to its limits as defined by requirements of academic responsibility. Little was said about those institutional conditions or levels of faculty performance that might provide reasonable grounds for faculty dismissal or reassignment; and procedures for evaluation and assessment of competence in teaching or scholarship were not developed to guide faculties or administrations in deciding issues of continuance, separation, or reassignment. But, during those early years, when all academic communities were chastened by marauding bands of religious and racial bigots and by the austerity of their past compounded by intermittent economic depressions, these shortcomings went unnoticed, and there was no pressing need for correction.

To enforce its tenure rule, the AAUP developed a trial procedure and a common law tradition of cases interpreting the rule with force of precedent. The trial procedure guarantees every tenured faculty member subject to possible removal or reassignment the right to a hearing before a jury of faculty; the jury determines whether administrative action is justified. The professor is granted most of the traditional protections of legal due process, including right to counsel, right to confront witnesses and cross-examine them, and right to a transcript of the proceedings.

At the time the AAUP first proposed its trial procedure, it was not unreasonable to suppose that most violations of the rights of faculties would be politically motivated. Although the first AAUP Committee on Academic Freedom and Academic Tenure, formed in 1915, intended to formulate principles and procedures that would provide universal protection of intellectual freedom in universities, their concern as expressed in recommendations was more limited. Initially, the AAUP did not intend to conduct investigations of alleged violations of academic freedom, but it did so even during its first year. Perhaps because at that time most cases involved attacks from outside the university, the AAUP selected the adversary system. Although the adversary process and the jury system are crude instruments in the search for truth, they are remarkably effective in the defense of political freedom. We should not overlook, however, the serious limitations of the adversary system—agonistic both in conception and operation—in the context of a community as subtle, organic, and dependent on mutual respect and persuasion as that of a college or university.

Nor should we overlook a much more serious defect in the AAUP trial procedure that is justified by neither Anglo-American law nor the experiences of the AAUP. The AAUP jury panel, that is, does not function as an impartial body concerned primarily to determine the most reasonable and just course of action. Factional and class-oriented, it is designed to defend a member of the clan from outside interference; and all administrators, staff, trustees, and alumni are cast in the role of outsiders. Thus the unity or harmony essential to academic life is jeopardized by the AAUP reliance on an adversary process whose divisive qualities are exacerbated by the use of guild-oriented or directly partisan juries. That these disadvantages and risks are historically offset by concern for academic freedom should not blind us to the serious problems to which defects in trial procedures presently give rise.

The AAUP, I am convinced, has not used its tenure rule and its trial procedure merely to protect academic freedom. Instead it has used the trial procedure to defend the seven-year tenure rule itself. In its local chapters and nationally, the AAUP has come to the defense of anyone who has taught seven or more years. Even if no issue of academic freedom is involved and the administration has extended a professor's appointment beyond six years at his own request in the not inhumane hope that he might complete the long-awaited book, two or three articles, or demonstrate the outstanding teaching that might justify his continuance, the administration is told by the AAUP that the professor has tenure. But the meaning of tenure has changed. The AAUP asserts that he has an *absolute* claim on continued employment, that he possesses, in fact, a *sine-cure.*

The result is that the seven-year rule no longer serves as the dividing line between probationary and tenured employment. It has become, instead, the line that divides probation from sinecure. The AAUP now throws so many obstacles in the way of removal or reassignment of professors and imposes such severe penalties on most institutions that dare to recognize tenure in its true meaning that administrators have acquiesced in the transformation of tenure into sinecure and use the terms interchangeably.

Ironically, the concept of sinecure is not merely different from that of tenure, but incompatible with it. Sinecure is either present or absent: it does not function on a continuum of fluctuating expectations reflecting the growth or decay of competence or the rising claims of service. All of the complexities and subtleties characteristic of the concept of tenure are lacking in the concept of sinecure. They are likewise absent from the concept of tenure as transmuted by the policies and practices of the AAUP.

By making seven years the absolute limit of probationary employment, the AAUP imposes a uniform standard on all colleges and universities and on all departments and faculty without regard to the crucial differences that essentially alter the way in which the concept of tenure functions in these various contexts. Much can be said for the AAUP tenure principle. But we have to recognize that a principle needs to be supplemented by human intelligence, imagination, and judgment in its application, and that the mechanical application of a rule or principle destroys its value.

By specifying a uniform deadline within which the axe of severance must fall or tenure (as sinecure) be granted, the AAUP has in practice forced each academic administrator—whether senior faculty member, department chairman, dean, or president—to disregard the natural laws of development in the lives of individual professors. Through important contributions in their fields and by effective undergraduate and graduate teaching, some young men and women find themselves intellectually and emotionally by the time they are thirty years of age. Given a junior's tested character and demonstrated achievement, senior faculty and administrators can responsibly (though, admittedly, not always accurately) predict his future development. Other academics are still—even in their mid-thirties—groping about in uninteresting, unimaginative, or even psychopathological ways. These individuals likewise pose no problem for administrators; their association with the college or university is usually terminated long before the AAUP crisis year.

But no administrator has effective means for applying the AAUP rule to young teacher-scholars with six or eight years of service who, while ineffectual, confused, and indeterminate either in character or in intellectual and theoretical areas, are confused and indeterminate in ways that, far from being pathological, are exceedingly healthy, exciting, and in some cases even suggestive of genius. In the case of these individuals on whom the future of a great institution often depends, the rigid code of the AAUP poses an intolerable dilemma: the university must commit more than $600,000 in lifetime salary to a person whose character or intellectual promise is uncertain, or—though aspiring to greatness—it must fire these highly promising individuals. Neither course is defensible.

Harvard has partially avoided the rigidity of the seven-year up-or-out rule and has made tenure decisions on its own terms and at its own pace in disregard of the AAUP. Normally, tenure is not granted at Harvard to fledgling scholars; they usually serve from one to nine years without being tenured. Tenure is granted more commonly to fully established scholars on initial appointment. Although the AAUP has been reluctant to censure Harvard for disregarding its seven-year rule and has occasionally extended an indulgence even to Princeton or Yale, the AAUP has never recognized the validity or wisdom of Ivy League deviations. And it has been adamant in the enforcement of its rigid expectations in less prestigious institutions.

The natural laws of personal development by which mathematicians and lyric poets often reach peak achievements in their twenties or early thirties, while historians and philosophers, by comparison, crawl along at a snail's pace, have no place in the reckoning of the AAUP. All faculty members must develop in goosestep. Instrumental musicians and vocalists must march with composers, composers with literary critics, who in turn march with mathematicians marching with sociologists and psychologists. This uniformity, though rigid, might be tolerable if it were not so totally insulting to human intelligence and aspiration. Far greater flexibility according to the complexities of human nature is called for; and the insistence of the AAUP on rigidity and mechanism where flexibility and intelligence are required is most unfortunate. This rigidity represents a substantial violation of the academic freedom of nontenured faculty; its modification is long overdue.

Mechanical uniformity in the application of the AAUP tenure rule violates the legitimate claims—and the academic freedom—of institutions, as well as those of individuals—the right to be different, to develop programs and individuals within programs in ways that require substantially different applications of the tenure principle. A university with a vital program in the arts, for example, must employ artists—vocalists, instrumentalists, composers, dramatists, actors, painters, and sculptors—whose careers develop, flourish, and decline according to very different time frames. Such a university cannot abide by AAUP tenure rules without fundamentally distorting its proper and justifiable institutional aims. Any school of fine arts that rigidly adhered to the seven-year tenure rule would soon decay as the vigor of its faculty declined, or commit itself to a continual turnover of young nontenured artists incapable of conveying to students the power of seasoned artistic judgment. A university that ignores the performing arts and is wholly preoccupied with the purely theoretical and intellectual aspects of the arts may suffer slightly less under the uniform AAUP rule, but it cannot escape the pressures that favor intelligent differentiation.

The time required for the development of creative power and its duration are ineluctably various; why, then, should different programs and different institutions be forced into rigid conformity on this basic issue? Why should we stifle the peculiarity or genius of personal and institutional identity? Why should we ignore the motivational vitality that comes from pursuing highly individualized goals whose realization calls for flexibility and changes of pace?

The AAUP, I fear, may have become so preoccupied with the defense of tenure and so rigid in the application of the seven-year rule that its tenure rule no longer serves as a protector but rather as a destroyer of academic freedom. The seven-year rule drives young scholars in overworked fields into wanton production of the obvious, the unnecessary, or the speciously innovative. Well aware that they must make their mark within six years, young faculty rarely have the time to think, explore, speculate, and grow in silence and privacy. The young faculty member is not allowed to ripen at his own pace and thereby to produce something worthy of oral publication in the classroom and written publication in books or articles. The seven-year rule too often rewards the fast and flashy scholar rather than the scholar whose power develops at a slower pace but more profoundly. It thus encourages frantic productivity of fashionable trivia, and this in turn pollutes the marketplace of ideas and lends a specious dignity to busywork. Neither scientific nor literary invention can be commanded. While some pressure may be useful, the pressure to meet the demands for sinecure within seven years is destructive of all that is best—most sensitive, imaginative, creative, and profound—in many young academics. If the AAUP and faculty members are responsive to the realities of tenure, they will avoid absolutizing the seventh year. Rather it will be simply an important nodal point on a rising scale of tenure expectations after which severance becomes decreasingly reasonable though not impossible.

The tenure rule, through its rigidities, clearly limits the academic freedom of a college or university to develop its younger faculty and its own specialties at their own proper qualitative level. Academic institutions are also severely handicapped by such rigidity in their ability to respond to changing educational needs and to the financial reverses that most of them face. Institutions must have academic freedom to pursue their distinctive institutional goals. Hampshire College, for example, has deliberately focused on innovation and experimentation. Toward this end, it has avoided tenure appointments altogether, maintaining a probationary, transitory relationship with every faculty member. The policy is humane; it is openly declared and practiced; and its influence on the Hampshire campus is significant. This free expression of academic purpose should be protected rather than inhibited by a sound tenure rule.

Institutions that eschew all permanent ties with faculty and operate on a purely probationary basis, like Hampshire College or like Harvard with its younger faculty, must pay a price in loyalty and commitment to the institution. But they gain options for change and guarantees of quality that are lost to colleges and universities which promote their young faculty to tenured posts.

Far more serious, however, is the damage done to public and professorial understanding of academic freedom when we claim that tenure is essential to its survival. This commonly held view is ambiguous and in part mistaken. (This cliché was reiterated by President J. William Ward of Amherst College when he said, "I am not about to defend tenure. It needs no defense by me; it is necessary to the climate of freedom which sustains intellectual life in the college.") Although tenure (whether functioning properly or as sinecure) has actually protected academic freedom, it is clearly not necessary to its existence. How could tenure, held by only a *few*, be the basic weapon in the defense of a right claimed by *all* members of the academic community? Students, instructors, and assistant professors have the right to academic freedom and must exercise that right to be worthy of their responsibilities. The best nontenured faculty members assume the risks of speaking their minds to the best of their knowledge and competence quite without the protection of tenure. And academic freedom can clearly exist on a campus where there is no tenure, as shown by Hampshire College.

But even a sinecure fails to guarantee the exercise of academic freedom simply because some professors with sinecures are more concerned for salary advance or for administrative appointments than in the faithful exercise of their academic duties. Academic freedom, properly exercised, requires courage. Where courage is present, academic freedom will be exercised with or without tenure; where courage is absent, the sound and vigorous exercise of academic freedom is impossible. And when tenure becomes virtually a sinecure, as it has under AAUP interpretation, it encourages irresponsibility and, not academic freedom, but academic license.

Thus, tenure may inhibit or corrupt as well as enhance the realization of academic freedom by even tenured faculty.

Tenure has, of course, been moderately useful in protecting established scholars in their intellectual deviance from the conformists of their group. Sigmund Freud, for example, would have been a likely candidate for dismissal as he grew in intellectual power and daring had he not possessed professorial and medical tenure. Even so, his pursuit and elaboration of novel ideas required great courage and independence. Professor Nikolai Hartmann, the renowned German philosopher, remarked that, were it not for the pressure of the neo-Kantian school in Marburg (where he was employed initially as a nontenured assistant), his own philosophical development would have been substantially different. He admitted to a human weakness that pervades academic circles—the fear of deviating from established lines of disciplinary orthodoxy.

But the restriction of the vigorous defense of academic freedom to the ranks of the tenured faculty has unfortunately left the nontenured faculty exposed. Infringement by tenured professors of the rights of the nontenured faculty to develop their intellectual interests according to their own professional judgment—that is, the censuring of the nontenured faculty from the standpoint of a doctrinal orthodoxy defined by the senior men within a department—represents by far the most serious and most frequent violation of academic freedom in our colleges and universities.

Any professor can cite numerous examples of this central abridgment of academic freedom. In philosophy, for example, departments dominated by logical positivists and linguistic analysts have frequently denied appointment or promotion to young philosophers with primarily historical or metaphysical interests, no matter how able. In psychology, experimentally oriented departments have frequently refused appointment or promotion to clinical psychologists; clinically oriented departments have denied appointment to experimentalists; and departments dominated by behaviorists have sometimes gotten rid of experimentalists and clinicians who would not accept the reductionistic formulas of behaviorism.

"Doctrinal orthodoxy" may be too grand a description of the demands sometimes made by senior professors of their younger colleagues. Too often the senior men demand nothing less than conformity or deference to their own prejudices. Anything so exciting or dignified as the resistance of Newtonian physicists to the implications of the Michelson-Morley experiment is rarely involved. I refer, for instance, to the all too common decision by senior professors to remove an able young person whose outstanding teaching and scholarly promise expose their own deficiencies. Or the decision by an English department to remove a young poet because he does not write respectable academic criticism.

If we admit that the imposition of doctrinal orthodoxy by the Guildmeisters and the insistence on deference by senior professors are real—though sometimes not easily verifiable—infringements of academic freedom, then academic freedom is severely restricted for all but the most courageous or naturally conformist of the nontenured faculty. The AAUP has never defended academic freedom from coercion by academics themselves or recognized that such coercion, though of very common occurrence, is a violation of academic freedom. (Colleges, universities, and departments have, I believe, the right to a doctrinal bias; but if they exercise that right in the pursuit of their own individual educational goals, they should admit openly the restrictions they place on academic freedom and inform faculty members of these limitations at the time of their appointment.)

How are nontenured faculty—the younger faculty with minimal claims to tenure—to be protected from intellectual censorship? I acknowledge the difficulties inherent in the problem. It seems clear, nevertheless, that some review procedure insuring that assessments include responsible but nonmainstream points of view is essential in protecting younger faculty from doctrinal censorship. A vigorous dean can often prevent the dismissal of an able young scholar simply by insisting that members of his department justify their decision. By producing evidence from leading scholars and critics in praise of the young man's written efforts and by adducing student evaluations in support of his excellence in teaching, he should be able either to persuade the department to change its decision or to sustain his decision to overrule the department.

If we believe that the adversary process and common law are the only effective means in the academic community, we overlook the power of rational persuasion. My experience suggests that senior professors often change their minds when confronted by a substantial body of evidence supporting the appointment or promotion of a controversial faculty member. And I see no reason why we should defend the intellectual novelty of individuals who fail to present deviant ideas in a way that is reasonably convincing to fair-minded and competent critics.

No university can effectively pursue its educational goals, enhance the development of individual faculty members, and insure the academic freedom of all faculty and students while acting in accordance with current tenure procedures and policies. Those procedures ignore the contextual variations of human life, individual and social, and, as we have seen, they frustrate the highest ambitions and potential of individuals within the academic communities and academic institutions themselves. It is of crucial importance that administrators, faculties, and the AAUP try to accommodate policies and procedures to the essential features of tenure and academic freedom.

Chapter 4

Tenure Everyone?

John C. Livingston

Tenure protects the incompetent; it rewards and encourages mediocrity—so say its critics. In reply, its defenders assert the importance of academic freedom and the key role of tenure in protecting it. Tenure, they ordinarily add, is not in practice, and certainly need not be in principle, incompatible with weeding out incompetence. As a believer in tenure, I find myself nearly as troubled by the defense of its friends as by the attacks of its critics. I am troubled because the protection of the incompetent seems to be an inherent and necessary consequence of tenure in any academic community and because the appeal to academic freedom is unlikely either to conceal or justify that fact.

To accept most arguments for tenure is to imagine that, in the absence of a need for academic freedom, we would or should be willing to engage in evaluating, searching out, and expunging the least competent among us. I suspect that in fact we typically protect the incompetent among us not for reasons of academic freedom or even of academic due process, but for reasons which have something directly to do with our commitment to a college as a community of peers and with the fundamental character of inquiry and scholarship. If we do not discuss these latter reasons much and if we do not ordinarily admit even to ourselves that they lead us to protect the incompetent, that is probably because the arguments to which we would be led fly so directly into the teeth of what have become the givens of American culture.

Is it possible that the protection of the incompetent is a necessary condition for a community in quest of excellence? May the protection of mediocrity be the most effective way of raising the level of mediocrity? Such questions were more easily raised in other times and places. The trouble is that, in the absence of efforts to raise them, the argument for academic freedom is pressed into service to support practices which do in fact protect incompetents and which therefore run counter to the prevailing ideals of competition and merit in American life. Unless broader defenses of tenure can be developed, less dependent upon academic freedom but related even more intimately to the nature of academic life, the prospects for defending either tenure or academic freedom do not appear to be bright. I hope in this chapter to explain why this seems to be so and to consider tentatively certain matters that bear on the development of a broad defense of tenure.

Current Debate

The critics of tenure speak of the erosion of standards and the loss of excellence, of the protection of mediocrity, of the undermining of merit and achievement. It is the language of the master American myth of competitive inequality—careers open to talents, the achievement ethic, the efficacy of competition, the reconciliation of equality and liberty through the magic formula of equal opportunity. Viewed from this perspective, tenure may even appear to be un-American and undemocratic: does not its artificial protection of incompetence have the effect of destroying incentive? Does it not stand in radical opposition to the democratic rule that status is to be equated with individual merit?

In response to this challenge the defenders of tenure have

tended to advance two lines of argument. The first, on a theoretical level, holds that a competitive system of rewarding merit must be balanced against a need—peculiar to the academic world—for freedom. Academic freedom, the argument runs, can be protected only by tenure; the protection of incompetence, insofar as it occurs, is a necessary evil, a trade-off required in an imperfect world in which values conflict and must be balanced. The second and sometimes contradictory argument holds that tenure, properly administered, does not protect incompetence since it allows for dismissal for cause through proper procedures.

The trouble with this typical defense of tenure is that it accepts the basic premise of the critics. In the absence of the distinctive demand for academic freedom, it is implicitly granted, the ideal of meritocracy should apply; if it were possible to protect academic freedom otherwise, tenure would be an unnecessary evil. I do not intend to argue that academic freedom could be made secure without tenure (or, more accurately, since it is not secure even with tenure, that it could be provided similar protection), though I believe that question is more open than is ordinarily supposed. It is more open because freedom can never be had free of cost, and it may be that Jefferson was right in contending that the defense of freedom lies not in institutional safeguards but in its effective exercise, that its spirit is kept alive by a little rebellion now and then when the arrogance of power presumes to limit it. Indeed, Jefferson's view is reinforced by those who recognize that a long probationary period may have the effect of conditioning faculty to keep a low profile and play it safe. But, without seeking to resolve the question here, the relevant point for my analysis is this: The argument for tenure as an evil necessary to sustain the good of academic freedom is unlikely to be a persuasive response to the widespread clamor for bringing academic reality into line with the American ideal of competitive merit. The odds are against an argument that seeks to stake out a claim for the academic world as a unique exception to the legitimate values of American life.

The chances would be improved if the second line of defense could be made to stick—if, that is, one could argue convincingly or even seriously that tenure does not, or need not, protect incompetence. Few would care to maintain that incompetence is not protected. That cat is irretrievably out of the bag; like Alice's Cheshire friend, there is nothing left but the grin. Any faculty member would be hard pressed to recall an instance of dismissal for incompetence. However, many would argue that incompetence need not be protected by tenure.

The protection afforded by tenure, the argument runs, is simply coextensive with the existence of procedures which guarantee due process in a fair and impartial hearing, with the burden of proof on the institution. A good case can be made, however, that insofar as tenure functions in fact to protect academic freedom, it is inevitably extraordinarily difficult to fire anyone. If it is not, the way is open in dismissal proceedings for the operation of a hidden agenda in which charges of incompetence may conceal the real reasons, which involve violations of academic freedom.

At the heart of the issue here is a dilemma inherent in the application of due process to academic competence. A charge of incompetence is of necessity an overall claim that an individual has failed to measure up to some general standards of total performance. But it is a settled principle of law that it is impossible to protect against arbitrary results, even where all the other guarantees of due process are respected, when the standard or the rule under which one is judged is vague or imprecise. Thus due process requires that standards define specific behaviors, but there is no way—at least none has yet been even hinted at—to translate the specific behaviors of teachers into standards of overall competence. (For example, a code of professional behavior would doubtless include the injunction to meet one's classes and keep one's appointments; but a recent edition of the Harvard student guide to courses said of a faculty member almost universally acclaimed as a distinguished teacher that in his classes "attendance is not compulsory, either for the student or the professor.") The result is that the general charge of incompetence can rarely be brought without violating due process, but if specific charges are brought, they open the door to the arbitrary exercise of discretion in violation of academic freedom.

The claim that tenure does not necessarily protect incompetence often turns out on analysis to rest on an ambiguity surrounding the concept of competence. We may have in mind, when we use the term, at least two separate meanings. We may mean to describe some minimum threshold of critical intellect or of mastery of subject matter or technique which serves as an absolute criterion for judging eligibility for membership on the faculty. Or, alternatively, we may mean to describe a relative measure of the mastery exhibited in the performances of all those who claim or seek membership. Which of these we choose to mean makes a profound difference, and lack of clarity on the matter leads to a serious confusion. Those who defend tenure usually have the first meaning in mind, and, further, they tend to put this minimum threshold for practical purposes at or very near the bottom of the range of competence in their institutions (usually for good and honorable reasons —a matter to which I turn later).

Within the terms of their own analysis, faculty who support tenure are not engaged, then, in defending "incompetence." When the Commission to Study Tenure at the University of Utah declares that they "have identified no faculty member who advocates the perpetuation or tolerance of academic incompetence or irresponsibility," no one should be surprised by anything except the fact they found it necessary to say so. The reporting of such a finding is itself a sort of reverse McCarthyism (innocence by disassociation) which obscures the issue. Neither, very probably, are there faculty who favor lying, murder, rape, or robbery in principle, but one suspects and hopes that many oppose wire-tapping, electronic snooping, and preventive detention as measures for coping with those vices. And that is the issue. Tolerance of crime is, in one sense, the price of civic decency and liberty. Of course, faculty are willing to tolerate relative incompetence and irresponsibility; if not, tenure would not last another semester. And their tolerance, as I hope to show, is justified not alone by considerations of academic freedom but by other values as well.

But those who attack tenure ordinarily have the second meaning of competence in mind. They turn out to be invoking the ideal of meritocracy based on equal opportunity. This notion of competitive inequality means precisely "careers open to talent" in a race in which no extraneous consideration—including, and especially, incumbency—is permitted to bestow artificial favor on any of the competitors. This ideal, pushed to its root meaning, implies that in any career field the less competent should be exposed and expelled to make way for the more competent. From this perspective tenure protects incompetence. It is no answer to this argument to respond with a case that accepts in principle the demand for meritocracy and then seeks to compromise it by a countervailing claim for academic freedom or a spurious claim that tenure and meritocracy can be compatible. In such circumstances the sophisticated opponents of tenure may even be forgiven for regarding the typical academic defense of it to be disingenuous when it is only confused.

Protection of Incompetence in Society

"No strong argument is likely to come forth," writes Eble (see Chapter Six), "that keeping incompetent teachers is beneficial to teaching." My analysis leads me to the conclusion that just such an argument is necessary to any persuasive defense of the tenure system: the inept are in fact, and necessarily, protected by tenure; it is right that they should be; tenure should be accorded instantaneously at the moment of hiring; and it should continue to be approximately as difficult (that is, nearly impossible) to get rid of a tenured faculty member as it now is.

The difficulty in making a case for the protection of the incompetent and the reluctance of many who believe in it to make such a case reflect the fact that America is committed, more thoroughly perhaps than a people have ever been, to an achievement ethic. But as a national ideal it is honored in our rhetoric and systematically sabotaged in our practices. America, despite our rhetoric, is a tenured society. The unique and significant aspect of tenure in this regard is that, in contrast to the subtle and covert means by which incompetence is protected in other areas of American life, tenure does it openly. We proclaim that tenured faculty have a right to their jobs and may be dismissed only for cause proved under the conditions of due process. The result is to ensure job security for all except the venal sinner whose sins the profession, despite strenuous effort, is unable to conceal from the public. Other institutions do the same thing. Civil servants are virtually invulnerable except for reductions in force, but the structure which protects them is, through a stroke of tactical rhetorical genius, known as the merit system. Union members typically have defended job security openly, but the defense derives its "legitimacy" not through any ideological rationale but from the brute fact of self-interest backed by entrenched bargaining power.

Despite the recent faddishness of creating vacancies in college presidencies and notwithstanding the absence of formal provision for it, administrators have de facto tenure too—perhaps even more than faculty. One observer has suggested a general principle: Because the potentially most competent administrators are likely to be professors who "rank that type of job as something of a comedown," administrative incumbents are likely to be relatively less competent, with the result that there is "a greater protection of the incompetent than would otherwise occur."[1] In any case, incumbency is generally its own protection.

Even legislators, whose jobs are theoretically subject to the considered and independent choices of the electorate and who have taken of late to questioning why faculty should enjoy this unique privilege, accord tenure to themselves insofar as it is within their power to do so. Their efforts are reflected in the seniority system; the franking privilege; devices for concealing their voting records from their constituents; legislative campaign committees; a notorious reluctance to develop or enforce public standards of performance, even in matters of conflicts of interest; election laws which give flagrant advantages to incumbents; and in the political cartography of reapportionment.

The general fact, according to Goode, is that "groups do not typically expose or expel their members for lesser achievement or talent." He argues that the evidence supports this conclusion as it applies not only to unions but to informal work groups, to higher level management, and to the professions generally.

The role of tenure in American society is underwritten by both practical and ideological considerations. On the first count, some degree of protection of the inept is required for the continuity and efficiency of any social unit, irrespective of its goals. As Goode puts it, "the rigorous application of the norm of performance to the

[1] W. J. Goode, "The Protection of the Inept." *American Sociological Review,* 1967, *32*(1), 11. I have relied heavily on Goode's stimulating and perceptive essay. Where I have quoted from Goode, the references are to be found at pp. 10–15.

actions of all members of a collectivity would under most circumstances destroy both its social structure and its productivity." Practical reasons for the protection of incompetence include the fact that a minimum threshold for membership operates also as a floor, "a lowest permissible level of competence." If the most incompetent are fired, the floor is raised; those who were marginally but comfortably above it are now threatened: "To some degree, the mediocre 'need' the really inept." Moreover, in any organization which requires cooperation and trustworthy communication, no matter how committed to achievement norms, the costs of expelling or downgrading less competent members must be weighed against the costs of allowing them to remain. This is not a case of organizational efficiency versus humanistic values, but simply a measure of the extent to which efficiency in human undertakings depends upon the exercise of humanistic values. Finally, most institutions protect individual incompetence out of a compassionate concern for common human frailties and stresses (family problems, illness, marital crises, a deformed child, drinking, and, perhaps most significant, aging). Common practices include transfer to honorary or symbolic or administrative positions, assignment of simpler duties, assignment to tasks of a human relations or public relations type, or simply and most commonly lowering the expectations of performance in the job.

Beyond these practical considerations are more important ideological reasons for the general protection of the incompetent from the rigors of competition. I have referred in the preceding analysis to the prevalence of an ideology that rests fundamentally on the doctrine of equal opportunity for unequal merit—a belief ostensibly shared by both the critics and the defenders of academic tenure. The resulting view that the protection of incompetence reflected in tenure represents a gulf between norm and behavior is not confirmed by American experience. The competitive ethic has waged everlasting war, not only with a contradictory reality but with the humane and democratic values that underlie that reality.

The ideological contest here is a dispute over the meaning of equality, a dispute as old as the idea of equality itself. In America it was reflected in the Puritan dilemma between the doctrine of grace and election on the one hand and the concept of a community of believers on the other. It was reflected later in the contrast between the views of America set forward by Crevecoeur (1782) and Hezekiah Niles (1815). Crevecoeur described the "new man" he encountered in America as made different by "a spirit of independence and resourcefulness unknown to the Old World," which had its roots in "a pleasing uniformity of decent competence."[2] Niles expressed the case for competitive inequality in an arena of equal opportunity in his view that Americans were distinguished by "the almost universal ambition to get forward."[3] But, if Niles's view became dominant with the triumph of industrial capitalism, the ideological claims of a radical view of equality continued to be asserted. Even the author of *Poor Richard's Almanac,* in his "Information" for immigrants, wrote of the "general happy mediocrity" of American life. And, a century later, Lord Bryce described the two continuing and "opposite theories regarding the influence of democratic institutions on intellectual activity" as a conflict between the views of Jefferson and de Tocqueville.[4] Jeffersonian thought, he argued, holds that a radical equality stimulates the minds of people, "sharpening men's wits, . . . giving to each citizen a sense of his own powers and duties in the world, which spurs him on to exertions in ever-widening fields." The Tocquevillean view finds in equality the source of triumph of mediocrity, the resentment of excellence, and the devitalization of intellectual life. From one central perspective, this remains the basic issue in the conflict over tenure.

The case against tenure turns out to be, in one of its dimensions, a modern version of this age-old conservative analysis that standards of excellence must be protected from the clamor for the commonplace, which is the natural voice of the mediocre, that such a standard is safe only in the keeping of an elect who are the most able, and that inequality is the fence which protects it. This alleged tendency of egalitarianism to lead to the resentment of superiority

[2] J. H. St. J. de Crevecoeur, *Letters from an American Farmer* (New York: Dutton, 1957), p. 36.

[3] Quoted in L. Benson, *The Concept of Jacksonian Democracy* (New York: Atheneum, 1964), p. 12.

[4] J. Bryce, *The American Commonwealth* (New York: Putnam's, 1959), Vol. 2, p. 525.

and excellence rests, again, on a confusion of terms. One should first note that the resentment of superiority is not—at least not obviously—socially pathological, while the resentment of excellence is. For excellence simply describes the standards which define all our aspirations in the development of our talents, while superiority is a judgment of the relative worth of human beings. Equality resents superiority; it only resents excellence when men have been induced to test their own worth in a contest in which superiority rather than excellence is the objective. G. K. Chesterton provided an important insight into the implications of this distinction in his cryptic observation that "a thing that is worth doing at all is worth doing badly." To which one might add that seeing a thing done well is more likely to enable one to do it better if a glimpse of excellence rather than the status of the doer is the center of one's focus.

The clarification of this confusion is to be found in examining the meaning of standards. To be without standards (that is, institutionally sanctioned and enforced criteria for measuring the relative worth of individuals) is not to produce normless individuals (that is, individuals who lack standards of excellence for judging their own and others' work). Real achievement and excellence do not require standards of the first sort, though they obviously do require the latter. For that reason, the protection of the incompetent does not imply the protection of incompetence. The link between these two quite distinct meanings of standards is supplied in popular mythology by the Hobbesian assumptions about "natural" human motivation, assumptions which have been generally discredited by the behavioral sciences and should have been specifically repudiated in the personal experience of academic persons. Indeed, the general character of academic work, it seems to me, leads to the conclusion that standards of excellence need to be protected from inequality— from the status differences involved in the distinctions between the learned and the student, the professor and the assistant professor, the probationer and the tenured, and, above all, from that potential struggle for survival that, in the absence of tenure, pits each against all. Otherwise, our standards come to be defined by superiority, not by models (including and especially rival models) of excellence.

Much the same analysis applies to the corollary conservative proposition that equality (and the attendant job security provided by

tenure) is responsible for conformity, resistance to change and innovation, and intellectual timidity. Edward Bellamy, anticipating
reflection on mass society, provided an incisive challenge to the
alleged link between competition and individuality in his argument
that it is always inequality "which prompts the suppression of individuality by putting a premium on servile imitations of superiors."
"It is always," he added, "among equals that one finds independence."[5] Rousseau had the same point in mind when, in his *Essay
on Inequality*, he noted: "It is no easy matter to make him obey
who does not wish to command; and the most refined policy would
find it impossible to subdue those men who only desire to be independent." The result of the competitive struggle for power and
status, in this view, is that man comes to live not in himself, but
"beside himself" in a comparison with others. The result: "honor
without virtue, reason without wisdom, and pleasure without happiness." To live in oneself is not to live without standards; indeed, the
opposite is the case. As Ortega y Gasset puts it, man is "forced by
his nature to seek some higher authority." If he succeeds "of himself" in finding it in his own freely chosen standards of excellence,
"he is a superior man; if not, he is a mass man and must receive it
from his superiors."[6]

Protection of Incompetence on Campus

The reasons for protecting faculty incompetence are somewhat different from, though parallel to, those that apply to other
social situations. On a campus, there is no need or motivation for
the more able to reduce the level of their performances in order to
protect the less able. Beyond that, there is a significant difference
between the rationales for job security in the two cases. In an industrial or bureaucratic situation, as Goode argues, efficiency in
production may result from using the lesser talents of the relatively
inept in a machine-paced or bureaucratically coordinated pattern;
on a faculty, composed of self-directed professionals, job security

[5] E. Bellamy, *Equality* (New York: Appleton-Century-Crofts,
1897), pp. 391–392.
[6] J. Ortega y Gasset, *The Revolt of the Masses* (New York:
Norton, 1957), 116.

may be justified because it is a necessary corollary of the equality which must characterize their relationships.

A faculty is, almost as a necessity of its functioning, committed to the equality of its members in a way that is radically incompatible with the implementation of continuing tests of fitness for membership. At the same time, as Kerr has put it, "the great university is of necessity elitist, the elite of merit."[7] How are these conflicting claims on our loyalties to be accommodated? The second forces us to recognize that the problem of competence (that is, a minimum threshold) cannot be ignored. This claim simply dictates the greatest possible care in determining eligibility for membership in the scholarly community. The legitimate claim of elitism stops there. If there is to be a scholarly community, mistakes made in judging relative competence must be allowed to stand, protected by the inherent bias in favor of equality—a bias that must tolerate relative incompetence because it is incompatible with a continuing and universal round of efforts to discover, publicize, and eradicate it.[8] Indeed, one may suspect that, to the extent that the university arranges for the "free circulation" of its elite in a perpetual struggle to assure meritocracy, it ceases to be a university and becomes a multiversity whose members are bound together, insofar as they are, by mutual self-interest.

The radical and necessary commitment of a faculty to equality—to membership in "a community of peers"—is a condition of both its work and its governance. An academic community neither thrives on competition nor answers to the call of self-interest. It is in this respect like the family, in which there is a universal pattern of protecting the less able children from open competition. At that level we tend to recognize clearly the stakes in the competitive game. We give all our children tenure at birth and hope they will reciprocate for us. Ordinarily, we do not imagine this tenure as incompatible with the development of standards, with our ability

[7] C. Kerr, *The Uses of the University* (Cambridge: Harvard University Press, 1963), p. 121.
[8] It seems to be characteristic of white-collar employment generally, in contrast to union jobs, that relative incompetence is protected by setting higher standards for obtaining a job than for performance. See Goode, p. 8.

to instill a vision of and desire for excellence in all our children, or with the maximum development of all their powers by each of them. Indeed, almost instinctively, we recognize that tenure in the family, guaranteed by assurances of equal and continuing worth, is precisely the condition required for growth of individual competence and productive energies. The family, I suggest, is in this respect a more appropriate model for a campus than the Green Bay Packers.

If, in contrast to a family, a faculty is not bound together by love, it is nurtured by civility and trust. It is people locked in dialogue and argument—reasonable men, offering reasons to one another. Not the passion for distinction and superiority but a passion for enlightenment and compassion for one's fellow seekers make possible the trust on which such a community depends. And compassion requires a prior commitment to equality of a sort which eschews collective judgments of relative worth on which continued membership potentially and perpetually depends. What is involved here is not solely humanistic concern for others but the perspective that finds both pleasure and motivation in the company and the criticism of one's equals. Distinctions among men are probably inevitable; at least, the evaluations that lead to them are unavoidable and desirable. Evaluation will continue. The question is how, in what context, with what consequences. It may even be wholesome and productive when it is made at the same time honest, reliable, credible, and constructive by virtue of the fact we are not playing either a zero-sum or a negative-sum game.

Much more is involved in the defense of tenure than the obvious threat posed by an achievement ethic to the self-esteem of the mediocre, who, however, because they are by definition a majority, are due no small consideration. What is both crucial and confusing here can be clarified only by making a distinction between merit and worth. A judgment of merit is a specific statement about a particular professional task, a critical appraisal of the qualities of a specific performance. To be evaluated by one's peers is to have the merit of one's specific performances appraised by those who continue to constitute a company of equals and whose judgments, therefore, are to be taken seriously. Critical appraisal of one another's work, tempered always by mutual respect, is the life blood of intellectuals; but it is so not because potential rewards and threats are implicit in such appraisals, but because we assume that we can learn from one another. The purpose of evaluation is the improvement and enrichment of our ideas, our analyses, our techniques. That purpose is served only where evaluation of specific aspects of our work—our merit—is involved, and such evaluation necessarily takes the form of weighing performance against standards of excellence, not against the putative value of the work of others.

A judgment of worth, by contrast, represents a comparative ranking of the value of individuals, based on evaluation of their total professional achievements. When such judgments are collectively or authoritatively made on the totality of one's professional performance with a view to establishing formal distinctions eventuating in collective rewards or punishments, they tend to be regarded by those affected as judgments of their worth as persons. This is especially so in any activity which, like teaching and scholarship, is a "calling" in the Puritan sense of that term. No teacher or scholar worthy of the calling can be expected to imagine that an adverse judgment is a mere comment on his relative achievement in an occupational role, for his professional task is too significant a part of what he is and how he must regard himself. Thus, in any conscientious faculty, the process of peer evaluation for tenure or promotion is a traumatic, soul-shattering experience, the psychic costs of which must be weighed into any fair assessment of the practice. Peer evaluation in this sense is a contradiction in terms. Of course, peers evaluate one another's performances, continuously and unsystematically, and there is no way and no reason to impede this process. Systematic, formal, and collective evaluation in order to identify and expunge the incompetent is quite another matter. It requires a judgment that is not only different from but antagonistic to processes of evaluation which, like those proposed by Hodgkinson (see Chapter Seven), can hope to issue in improvement.

For these and other reasons, if the evaluation of the overall worth of faculty for awarding tenure (or, for that matter for promotion) is to be done at all, it is perhaps better left to administrators, whose judgments, precisely because they are not one's equals, need not be accepted as legitimate or trusted as competent. It is more important that the faculty be a community of equals than that all vice be punished or virtue rewarded. Even if it were true nowhere else in society (which, however, it is), it would be the case for the academic community that, in the Puritan minister John Wise's words, men should treat other men as equals "since no man can live a sociable life with another that does not own or respect him as a man."[9]

Wise's words bear directly on the relation between tenure and academic governance. Even Hobbes correctly understood the consequences for political legitimacy of the idea of equality when he argued: "If nature therefore have made men equal, that equality is to be acknowledged: or if nature have made men unequal; yet because men that think themselves equal will not enter into conditions of peace, but upon equal terms, such equality must be admitted."[10] In any modern secular institution, especially among a faculty, no doctrine of political legitimacy can be acceptable which does not, in the words of Macpherson, enable men to see themselves "as equal in some respect more fundamental than all the respects in which they are unequal."[11] No such assurance is remotely possible when all men are made to live in perpetual risk of public exposure and expulsion for their relative incompetence. And, under those conditions, no doctrine of obligation and no claim of legitimacy capable of supporting an academic government is possible.

Case for Instant Tenure

If, as I have argued, tenure may be persuasively defended on the basis of values other than academic freedom, it is worth considering whether it ought be awarded at the time of hiring. Instant tenure is a specter that frightens even the most partisan friends of the tenure system. A strong case can be made for the necessity of

[9] J. Wise, *A Vindication of the Government of New England Churches,* originally published in 1717. Reprinted in P. Miller and T. H. Johnson, *The Puritans* (New York: American Book, 1952), p. 262.

[10] T. Hobbes, *Leviathan,* Pt. 1, Chap. 15.

[11] C. B. Macpherson, *The Political Theory of Possessive Individualism,* as quoted in G. Lichtheim, *The Concept of Ideology and Other Essays* (New York: Random House, 1967), p. 155.

a probationary period, even one of considerable duration, as a necessary device for testing the initial appointment. But the strength of the reaction to abolishing it may also be partly attributed to the fact that it is a hostage given to the forces attacking tenure—an assurance that the professoriate does after all still share a commitment to the assumptions underlying the great American game of competitive rivalry for place and power. It permits academicians to present themselves as winning their spurs through competition; it avoids taking on frontally the master American myth of equal opportunity. Precisely for this reason, the case for instant tenure needs to be made and considered, for as a limiting model instant tenure clarifies admirably the real issues at stake. It does so because the probationary period as it now operates may be taken as a model of the situation that would prevail universally if tenure were eliminated. Thus, what we can discover of the nature of retention and tenure decisions and of the consequences and costs of those decisions may be especially useful in appraising the value of the tenure system.

The probationary period can be attacked on two grounds: on the argument that tenure decisions ordinarily and necessarily tend to expel the more competent and thus have consequences opposite to their intent; or, that even when tenure decisions weed out the less competent, the result does not justify the costs. Any analysis of the results of tenure decisions might usefully begin with Wilkinson's autobiographical comment: "I've been kicked out of two universities for my virtues and offered tenure in two others for my vices."[12] I doubt that Wilkinson's experience is unique; some years of reflection on my own academic experience confirm the impression that tenure decisions tend to reward mediocrity and conformity and to put in peril mainly those who stand up or stand out. Indeed, I am persuaded that those who have been denied tenure would compose a better faculty than those on whose brows the garland of guaranteed life-time employment has been laid. It would be a motley group, including those (where administrators were responsible for

[12] "The Center Eclectics: John Wilkinson," *Center Report* (Santa Barbara, Calif.; Center for the Study of Democratic Institutions, 1970), pp. 26–27.

the decision) whose ideas or activities created "image" problems for the college and those (where faculty made the decision) whose unconventional techniques or charismatic appeal to students led colleagues to the conclusion that they were not adequately "covering the material," and even one person who was terminated on the basis of a manifest inability to communicate sensibly to students or colleagues (it being difficult in the circumstances to determine whether he was brilliant or muddleheaded). Taking the lots at large, my rejects would be more intense, more committed, more exciting, more innovative. And to my faculty of losers I should probably add those who acquired tenure only after a bitter, knock-down-and-drag-out battle in which student power may have been decisive.

I suspect that mediocrity is systematically rewarded because the process itself is corrupting. The first persons to be corrupted by peer evaluation are the mediocre themselves. Not that mediocrity is inherently the enemy of excellence, as conservative critics of equality have always tried to instruct us. They have always meant to say—or should have meant to say—that the mediocre, when their noses are rubbed in their relative inferiority, resent the airs and pretenses of the relatively more competent. But, whether they react in that way surely depends on the ways in which they are reminded of their own mediocrity. If the relatively more competent get their kicks out of taking the Hobbesian view of life as a race "which we must suppose to have no other goal, no other garland, but being foremost; and in it . . . continuously to outgo the next before is felicity, and to forsake the course is to die,"[13] it is hardly surprising that the relatively incompetent pleasure themselves by resenting their superiors or, it might be added, by imagining themselves to be superior when the opportunity is afforded. Thus, one should not be surprised by the fact—if, as I believe, it is a fact—that the most vehement insistence on the necessity for collective peer judgment tends to come from highly placed, secure, and semiretired mediocrity.

If to this Hobbesian view of life is added Calhoun's cosmic rationalization that progress is entirely attributable to the pressure

---

[13] T. Hobbes, *The Elements of Law, Natural and Politic*, p. 1, Chap. 9, Para. 21.

of "those in the rear ranks to press forward into the front,"[14] we should not wonder that the resentment of the losers may extend to the ideal of excellence itself. There may even be more than psychological satisfaction in the protection of mediocrity by the mediocre, for, after all, judged by any meaningful standards of excellence, we are all mediocre.

The more competent are also corrupted by the parallel tendency to confuse their performances with standards of excellence and to assume that the pursuit of excellence requires that their competence be collectively recognized and rewarded. Evaluate, criticize, suggest—we owe that to ourselves—but "judge not, that ye be not judged." Equality, and the compassion which informs it, distinguishes evaluation from judgment. As Paul advised the Galatians, "But if you bite and devour one another, take heed that you be not consumed of one another." This admonition is more than an appeal to enlightened self-interest; it reflects the principle that, in contrast to evaluations of merit, judgments of worth belong only to God, and men undertake them at peril of their own corruption. The belief in God, political scientist Thomas I. Cook used to say, had performed an inestimable historic service by dissuading men from confusing themselves with Him. A genuine commitment to excellence, we might argue, might dissuade men from imagining that their own competencies must be translated into invidious measurements of human worth. Meanwhile, as long as people are motivated by the status (and incomes) associated in the status system with excellence, rather than by their own models of excellence, we should not be surprised to see their judgments corrupted by the sin of pride.

The strength of recent attacks on tenure is understandable. On the one side students, who suffer most directly from the incompetence of faculty, have joined the attack. This is an especially curious phenomenon since very often the same students are simultaneously leading the attack on punitive grading. Having attacked the grading system, often successfully, on behalf of equality, dignity, and community; having challenged the idea that education is a

[14] J. C. Calhoun, *A Disquisition on Government,* in R. K. Cralle (Ed.), *The Works of John C. Calhoun* (Boston: Little, Brown, 1851), Vol. 1, pp. 56–57.

competitive process; and having thereby come to appreciate the value and to demand the fruits of tenure for themselves, the same students are sometimes engaged these days in political pillow talk with reactionary politicians to abolish tenure for faculty. But if their attack on the grading system reflects more than self-interest, one might hope that the vision of a learning community which informs it might even come to include faculty.

The case is different with those who oppose tenure on ideological grounds. Here we confront the curious fact that education, where the psychological theories underlying competitive inequality are most obviously untenable, should be the area where they are most vigorously pressed. These pressures will not be countered by appeals to academic freedom or by denials that tenure protects incompetents. We must find ways of making the subtle but vital point that the same values which protect incompetents make possible for all the endless pursuit of excellence. As other chapters note, if tenure were to be abolished, faculty likely would assure themselves of job security through unionization. A cynic might predict that such an outcome, rooted in self-interest and achieved by bargaining power, would be seen by many current critics as more "American" than claims for tenure, rooted as it is in professional commitment and justified by considerations of community and mutual growth.

The basic issue in the battle over tenure goes far beyond the question of academic freedom. At issue is professionalism—that vague but lofty ideal of a calling whose rewards are intrinsic and whose members are bound together in a community of dialogue, whose members are motivated by internalized models of service and of excellence and whom society can therefore trust to function without the carrots and the sticks that characterize the competition of the market place. The very notion of a profession threatens to become a casualty to the voracious ethic of the market. The issue is excellence, but the problem is to protect standards from the assaults of those who confuse the pursuit of excellence, happily open even to the mediocre, with the struggle for position and status in a meritocracy.

Tenure is important primarily because it is compatible with a view of ourselves that makes the endless pursuit of excellence open to all. Ironically, however, the promise of tenure in this regard remains beyond our reach as long as we insist on imagining that tenure is simply an academic variant of the competitive ethic, marginally adjusted to meet the demands of academic freedom. The time has come to say plainly that the intellectual life, at least, is neither a racetrack nor a business and that it is not "American" or democratic or even useful that it should be.

Chapter 5

Tenure System at the University of Utah

Arvo Van Alstyne

The Commission to Study Tenure at the University of Utah was established in November, 1970 by action of the Executive Committee of the University Senate as a response to repeated proposals by community leaders to abolish tenure in higher education in Utah. A bill to accomplish this was introduced—but not enacted—during the 1971 general session of the state legislature. Most of the attacks upon tenure emphasized that tenure was an outworn relic which

This chapter is based upon the Final Report of the University of Utah Commission to Study Tenure, filed in May 1971. The author, professor of law at the University of Utah, served as chairman of the commission. The commission report, and hence this chapter, embodies the unanimous views of the eleven commission members. The other commission members were: faculty members—B. G. Dick, J. L. Clayton, S. Gustavus, D. Hanson, L. D. Spicer, and the late S. W. Angleman; student members—S. Gunn, M. Monroe, and C. Myntti; and citizen member—D. K. Watkiss.

served no useful purpose in the modern academic world and which operated principally to provide lifelong job security for incompetent faculty.

Mythology of Tenure

The Commission concluded early in its investigation that most, if not all, of the popular criticism of tenure reflected deeply held but often erroneous assumptions as to the purposes, meaning, and operation of the tenure system at the university. A survey of the popular literature confirmed the view that the local antipathies were, to a large degree, manifestations of a broad contemporary mythology. Before constructive efforts could be mounted to deal with some of the problems of the tenure system, therefore, it was deemed essential that the basic fallacies at the root of the general criticisms be stripped away. Briefly summarized, five major themes dominate the prevailing misconceptions about tenure.

(1) The prevailing mythology regards tenure as a special privilege of guaranteed employment uniquely enjoyed by college and university faculty members. The fallacy in this view lies in the pejorative implications of the terms *special privilege* and *guaranteed employment*. In fact, nothing in the theory or practice of the tenure system precludes the dismissal of a tenured faculty member for adequate cause. This principle, which merely requires assurance that appropriate grounds exist for terminating legitimate expectations of continued employment, represents a rule of fair play and justice which is not unique. It clearly does not guarantee employment, and it surely cannot accurately be described as a special privilege. Some analogous form of tenure is characteristic of most employment relationships in our society, whether described as a merit sytem for government employees, a seniority or job security plan for employees covered by a collective bargaining contract, a profit-sharing and stock-option program for business executives, or a license to practice one of the learned professions (medicine, law).

(2) The prevailing mythology assumes that a professor may acquire tenured status by mere passage of time in his position, without regard for professional competence or academic responsibility. In fact, it is not easy for a new faculty member to acquire tenure;

he can do so only by demonstrating over an extended probationary period (ordinarily five years) that he is qualified, on the basis of teaching effectiveness, scholarly achievement, and university service, to be retained by the university. The burden of demonstrating that he has the qualifications for tenure is squarely upon the individual. A significant number of faculty members are dismissed during their probationary period and thus fail to achieve tenure. Others leave the university voluntarily as they perceive the unlikelihood that they will obtain the requisite favorable recommendation. At the conclusion of the probationary period, a professor who fails to achieve tenured status must be dismissed; university policy forbids extension of an academic appointment beyond the probationary period for nontenured professors.

(3) Current mythology assumes that nearly all university faculty members enjoy tenure. In fact, when all instructional personnel are taken into account without regard for rank, the number (461) of tenured faculty members at the University of Utah, as of February 1971, amounted to only 19 per cent of the total (2,434). When teaching assistants are excluded, only 24 per cent of all faculty members at the university hold tenured positions. And even when attention is directed solely to regular teaching appointments in professorial ranks—thereby disregarding all faculty members not holding appointments in tenure-producing ranks (lecturers, instructors, clinical and research professors)—the figure increases only to 51 per cent.

(4) Current mythology contends that a faculty member with tenure cannot be dismissed from his position for incompetence. In fact, the adequate cause which the tenure system requires to support the dismissal of a tenured faculty member includes a broad range of grounds that may, for convenience, be described as incompetence or irresponsibility. Indeed, the tenure system recognizes that the university retains broad discretion, within constitutional limits, to define for itself the standards and criteria of accountablity for professional performance expected of its tenured faculty and merely insists that they be applied in a manner consistent with academic freedom and procedural due process. While the formal mechanics of the tenure-dismissal procedures (involving the service of a formal statement of charges and formal hearings by the University Committee on Academic Freedom and Tenure) are seldom used, tenured

faculty members have been removed from university employ through informal methods leading to voluntary resignation.

(5) The prevailing mythology assumes that tenured professors enjoy lifelong job security without corresponding obligations to maintain professional competence or acceptable standards. In fact, under applicable university regulations, every tenured faculty member has a duty to maintain personal competence as a teacher and faculty member and to refrain from conduct which demonstrates lack of ability or willingness to meet his academic responsibilities. The authoritative "1940 Statement of Principles on Academic Freedom and Tenure" promulgated by the American Association of University Professors and the Association of American Colleges specifically declares that the professor has a "special position in the community" which "imposes special obligations." A comprehensive guide to these special obligations was set forth in the "1966 Statement on Professional Ethics." Here again, it bears repeating, the university has broad discretion to define in its published rules the standards of personal responsibility to which its faculty are expected to adhere, consistent only with recognition of the principles of academic freedom and personal civil liberties.

Tenure as a Shield for Academic Freedom

It is abundantly clear from the history and practice of academic tenure that its predominant function is to safeguard the public welfare by protecting academic freedom while assuring academic accountability. A rational assessment of the tenure system thus presupposes understanding of both the meaning and significance of academic freedom and the procedures associated with tenure. While it is difficult, if not impossible, to formulate an unambiguous and completely satisfactory definition of academic freedom, the basic interests to be protected and their relationship to university tenure can be identified in general terms.[1] The central concern of academic freedom is the promotion of the common good

---

[1] The literature on academic freedom is extensive. The present statement relics heavily upon F. Machlup, "On Some Misconceptions Concerning Academic Freedom," in L. Joughin (Ed.), *Academic Freedom and Tenure* (Madison, 1969), p. 177, and S. McMurrin, *"Academic Freedom,"* in *Encyclopedia of Educational Research,* p. 1.

by ensuring the absence of, or protection against, external and institutional influences that may inhibit scholarly freedom to seek, expound, and disseminate ideas. Freedom in research, freedom in teaching, freedom in publication, and freedom in learning are all postulated as indispensable to the ultimate objectives of the educational institution—the advancement of truth, strengthening of cultural integrity, cultivation of critical intelligence, and improvement in the quality of personal and social life of the community at large. "Conceived positively, academic freedom is the encouragement to adventurous, creative, and innovative thought, the condition and inspiration for genuine intellectual and artistic achievement."[2]

Society's commitment to the educational enterprise necessarily demands that the university assume the responsibility for continued examination and appraisal of the validity of accepted values, established theories, and traditional practices. But this function of the university may create tensions and conflicts between the academic community and discrete elements within the larger community which it serves. Viewed in this context, academic freedom is a safeguard which the academic community has developed in order to protect its own, as well as society's, long-range interest in free critical inquiry from the chilling effects of censorship and reprisal. Uninhibited exploration of ideas cannot thrive in an atmosphere of intimidation and potential repression of ideas which are bold, challenging, and unpopular. The university cannot discharge its appointed role if its faculty are constrained to seek either the safety of silence or the ambiguity of indecision in matters of intellectual concern. Academic freedom thus embodies society's rejection of coerced conformity and its acceptance of intellectual diversity as a primary instrument of educational policy.

Although the primary focus of academic tenure is the protection of academic freedom, certain collateral advantages of the tenure system should not be overlooked. Stability of employment expectations, for individuals of demonstrated competence, tends to enhance the attractiveness of the teaching profession and may induce highly qualified persons to pursue a teaching career in lieu of more lucrative pursuits. (Indeed, academic freedom itself, with

[2] McMurrin, p. 2.

its associated atmosphere of intellectual ferment and unfettered inquiry, can be a powerful incentive for qualified scholars to enter academic life.) Tenure, as a visible manifestation of university commitment to the faculty member, offers an assurance of career continuity which facilitates reciprocal faculty commitment to the long-term study and research programs by which the frontiers of knowledge are expanded.

Implicit in the principle of academic freedom are certain corollary responsibilities for those who enjoy that freedom to employ it in ways that advance its objectives. Incompetence, indolence, intellectual dishonesty, serious moral dereliction, arbitrary and capricious disregard of appropriate standards of professional conduct—these and other grounds are fully recognized as "adequate cause" for dismissal or other disciplinary sanctions against faculty members. In addition, since academic freedom, like other freedoms, can be abused, the faculty has a collective obligation to take effective action against those individuals within its ranks who are derelict in discharging their professional responsibilities. At the same time, the faculty has an equally important obligation to resist as vigorously as necessary all attempts, from whatever source, to violate academic freedom. Simply stated, academic freedom and academic responsibility are interdependent; the role of tenure is to protect the former while nurturing the latter.

Acceptance of the social utility of academic freedom does not lead inevitably to approval of the tenure system. It seems reasonably clear, however, that the tenure system is well adapted to the tasks of identifying during the probationary period those particularly competent faculty aspirants who deserve tenured status and eliminating faculty members who become incompetent or irresponsible after achieving tenure. The system is calculated to provide maximum protection for only those faculty members who are judged capable of exercising the privileges of academic freedom in a responsible manner. This relationship between academic freedom and tenure practice is implicit, for example, in the essentially typical tenure system of the University of Utah.[3]

---

[3] Tenure at the University of Utah generally adheres to the standards and procedures advocated by the AAUP. The Utah system

Faculty members can achieve tenure only after annual reviews of professional competence, academic performance, and general suitability during an extended probationary period. University administrators, faculty colleagues, and student evaluation committees participate in these review procedures, but the burden of demonstrating eligibility for retention and tenure is upon the probationary faculty member.[4]

Near the conclusion of the prescribed period, tenure is affirmatively granted if the candidate survives a final comprehensive evaluation. If tenure status is not then conferred, the faculty member must be dismissed. As indicated, the award of tenured status means simply that the faculty member has been judged to possess the requisite qualities of academic competence and responsibility in sufficient degree to warrant expectation of continued employment. In effect, he is accorded the benefit of the doubt in the event the institution later seeks his dismissal, coupled with an assurance that the presumption of fitness can be overcome only by evidence adduced by the institution in conformity with appropriate standards of academic due process.

Thereafter, if charges deemed adequate cause for dismissal or other disciplinary action are brought against a tenured faculty member, they must be considered by an appropriate faculty committee after due notice and full and fair opportunity for hearing and introduction of relevant evidence. The committee's judgment must be transmitted to and considered by the administration and governing board of the university before a final decision upon the charges is made.

---

has statutory support in the Utah Higher Education Act of 1969 (see 1953 Utah Code Anno., § 53-48-25, repl. vol. 1970), as implemented by official university regulations approved by the State Board of Higher Education.

[4] University of Utah records disclose that from 1965–1970, inclusive, 278 faculty members achieved tenure, while 32 (approximately 10 per cent) were denied tenure at the end of the probationary period. These figures, which demonstrate that tenure is far from automatically conferred, understate the actual experience of the university because they fail to include faculty members who voluntarily resign upon perceiving the likelihood that they will not obtain a favorable tenure recommendation at the conclusion of probation.

The committee hearing procedures, with their trappings of academic due process, are the functional core of the tenure system. The reasons for this are somewhat complex but clearly reflect the primary relationship between tenure and academic freedom.

First, these procedures are calculated to insure, so far as possible, a fair determination of the basic facts: did the individual in fact conduct himself in a manner contrary to accepted standards of professional responsibility as defined by institutional rules? The disposition of courts in recent years to insist upon procedural fairness in governmental decision-making affecting significant private interests (including employment decisions) illustrates a general antipathy toward unchecked and unreviewed exertions of power. In tenure cases, as well, an appropriate hearing and fact-finding procedure improves the rationality and integrity of the dismissal proceedings by reducing the risk of both mistaken or uninformed action (with resulting injustice) and arbitrary or prejudiced administration.[5]

Second, academic due process is conceived as a primary defense against lack of institutional candor in the prosecution of charges leading to potential dismissal. Charges of academic incompetence or irresponsibility sometimes may be lodged for ulterior purposes; grounds for dismissal can be asserted in formal terms that mask real but unexpressed reasons in violation of the individual's academic freedom. Such risks are minimized when tenure procedures rely upon the responsible judgment of a faculty member's peers. Even when, as rarely happens, the issues are not obscured by ambiguous and conflicting factual data, they may be complicated by the inherent difficulty of applying in specific factual contexts the general concept of academic freedom. That concept incorporates the full range of responsible intellectual freedom as a standard of

[5] Recent Supreme Court decisions illustrating the growing importance of procedural due process include *Connell v. Higginbotham,* 403 U.S. 207 (1971) (public employee dismissal); *Bell v. Burson,* 402 U.S. 535 (1971) (driver's license suspension); and *Goldberg v. Kelly,* 397 U.S. 254 (1970) (termination of welfare assistance). For a thorough analysis of the importance of procedural techniques for assuring fairness of administrative action, see K. C. Davis, *Discretionary Justice* (Baton Rouge: Louisiana State University Press, 1969).

judgment. Accordingly, the accumulated experience, professional sensitivity, and mature insight of the academic community (as represented in the membership of the faculty review committee) provide elements of expertise and objectivity in appraising the propriety of the charges. In this connection, the designation of tenured faculty members to serve on the committee provides protection against "command influence" or other improper administrative pressures, while multiple membership and a relatively high level of campus visibility tend to minimize the likelihood that intolerance and personal bias will infect committee deliberations.

Third, due process operates as an important check against administrative excess in the assignment of sanctions for academic infractions. An adequate evidentiary hearing can expose to the committee's view the full panorama of relevant considerations, including not only the individual faculty member's derelictions but also his contributions to the university and the community and the degree of deprivation which may result from dismissal as compared with less drastic alternatives. The fitness and acceptability of the sanctions may thus be assessed by the collective wisdom of the committee rather than the relatively idiosyncratic and perhaps less sensitive insights of administrative officers beset by institutional and political pressures. In this respect, the tenure system postulates a procedural regime in which academic freedom is safeguarded in dismissal proceedings not merely by scrupulous regard for criteria and methodology but also by concern for compassionate and humanistic values.

Although nothing in these procedures—other than the necessary allocation of administrative effort to comply with them—precludes the invocation of sanctions against errant or incompetent faculty members, it appears to be a fact of academic life that formal disciplinary proceedings are seldom, if ever, initiated against tenured faculty members. The formal existence of such procedures, however, provides the university with powerful leverage for terminating the employment of an unsatisfactory tenured professor through informal means. Prescribed procedures at the University of Utah, for example, contemplate that charges of misconduct, incompetence, or irresponsibility will be explored first in private discussions between the faculty member and the administration, in an effort to secure a mutual settlement. When substantial factual disputes appear to exist, the president may appoint an ad hoc committee of faculty members to conduct a private investigation and give him advice and counsel. Informal proceedings of this kind, according to evidence submitted to the Utah commission, have produced voluntary resignations or early retirements in a number of cases in which the university indicated its determination to press formal charges.

The existence of clearly defined formal dismissal procedures, of course, contributes to the efficacy of informal techniques since, from the viewpoint of the faculty member in question, "voluntary" withdrawal avoids the notoriety, embarrassment, and possible disgrace, as well as the mental distress, which may attend formal dismissal action. For the same reasons, however, the threat of formal charges may exercise an unduly coercive influence upon an innocent faculty member, thereby negating both due process and academic freedom. To forestall this circumstance, University of Utah regulations specifically provide that any resignations may be appealed by "any faculty member" to the University Committee on Academic Freedom and Tenure, for review and report to the University Senate. The disapproval of any protested resignation by either the committee or the senate must be taken into account by the president and governing board of the university before any final decision on the resignation is made.

Alternatives to the System

The tenure system at the University of Utah, as here briefly described, appears to provide maximum protection for academic freedom while, at the same time, minimizing the risk that incompetent or irresponsible faculty will enter the ranks of the tenured. A faculty survey, conducted on a confidential basis by the commission,[6] as well as other evidence brought to the commission's atten-

---

[6] Responses to the Utah commission's questionnaire indicated that a significant segment of the faculty perceived the existence of faculty members guilty of improper conduct or failure to discharge professional commitments in a satisfactory manner, professional in-

tion, indicated, however, instances of tenured incompetence, unacceptable academic performance, or failure to observe professional standards of behavior. While such instances are relatively few, their infrequency is not grounds for complacency. The interests served by the university, and the delicacy of its relationship to its several publics, demand that every conceivable step be taken to provide assurance that abuses of tenured status will be dealt with in a reliable and effective fashion.

Two alternatives seem feasible: abandon tenure and seek means better adapted to eradication of professional inadequacy (which provide at least equal protection for academic freedom); strengthen the tenure system by modifying existing practices to assure greater effectiveness in dealing with abuses of tenure.

Nearly all alternatives to tenure incorporate, in substance, one or another of these three approaches: elimination of tenure, with faculty employment left to the pleasure of the university administration, adoption of terminal contracts with fixed periods of employment (possibly for periods ranging from three to five years), subject to renewal from period to period; and implementation of collective bargaining between university officials and faculty association representatives. Although each alternative has some merit, the Utah commission found them all objectionable in certain respects

---

competence, and inadequate student or departmental relationships. Approximately 30 per cent of the respondents indicated a personal belief that one or more members of their departmental staffs should be dismissed. This figure, however, must be viewed with caution, since no departmental identification is possible (due to the confidential manner in which the questionnaire was structured and administered). It seems likely, for example, that many of the affirmative responses may have come from different members of a few departments, representing a consensus of departmental opinion about the same individual or individuals. The fact that 70 per cent of the responding faculty identified no one in their departments as deserving dismissal may be a more significant measure of faculty perceptions of the faculty quality, since incompetence, poor teaching, inadequate scholarship, and other derelictions appear to be widely understood as grounds for dismissal. It should also be noted that responding faculty expected that some of those deserving dismissal would, in fact, leave the university, and that the continued employment of about half of those not dismissed would be due to factors other than tenure.

and, in particular, less protective of academic freedom than the tenure system.

Elimination of tenure. It has been suggested that, in earlier times, the tenure system may have been essential to the preservation of academic freedom. Academic freedom is said to be so widely and uniformly accepted, institutionally implemented, and judicially protected that tenure is no longer necessary to its preservation. Elimination of tenure, the argument runs, would deny incompetent and irresponsible faculty members a form of job security which they do not deserve and expand the flexibility with which the university administration could improve the quality of education by upgrading the quality of the faculty.

While the objectives of this proposal deserve support, it is regarded as an inherently unsound means for achieving those ends. Its unstated assumption that the tenure system serves primarily as a job security device is inaccurate and misleading. As shown above, the tenure system is designed, both in theory and in procedural arrangements, to prevent incompetent and irresponsible individuals from achieving tenure and to eliminate from tenured ranks those few unqualified professors who elude the screening process or who retrogress after entry. While the system may not have functioned with complete efficiency, it would be irresponsible to abolish it without the strongest possible assurance that the positive values which it serves will not thereby be impaired and that its deficiencies cannot be remedied by less radical methods.

The academic community shares the concerns of the critics of tenure, but a substantial portion of that community finds little basis for the complacent view that academic freedom has matured to the point of axiomatic invulnerability.[7] Court decisions document the fact that freedom of expression, of which academic freedom is a part, is under attack on many fronts;[8] experience at major colleges

[7] The commission's faculty survey disclosed that a substantial percentage of the faculty regarded tenure as a protection for academic freedom and academic freedom as insecure without tenure.

[8] See W. Van Alstyne, "The Constitutional Rights of Teachers and Professors," *Duke Law Journal* 1970, 841; "Developments in the Law—Academic Freedom," 81 *Harvard Law Review* 1968, 1045. A more general analysis of the recent cases on freedom of expression is

and universities provides convincing evidence that the principles of academic freedom are far from universally respected.[9] Contemporary efforts to curtail the free investigation of ideas on university campuses by excessively restrictive policies which limit the choice of speakers demonstrate the essential fragility of intellectual liberty.[10]

The history of past attacks upon academic freedom provides no basis for optimism that the future will be any different or that academic freedom will survive unless firmly supported by the general public and the academic community. As the President's Commission on Campus Unrest observed in its report of September, 1970, the time of rapid cultural, social, and technological change in which we live generates pressures which polarize and politicize the university community. Because "both external and internal threats to academic freedom have increased as the nation has become more sharply divided," the commission urged the academic community to devote increased "resistance to pressures toward conformity" and "to combat dogmatism, intolerance, and condescension, as well as attempts to suppress divergent opinions among its members."[11] The tenure system provides an established and effective framework for implementing these objectives.

The suggestion that the judicial system can provide effective

---

found in F. Strong, "Fifty Years of Clear and Present Danger: From Schenck to Brandenberg—And Beyond," *Supreme Court Review* 1969, 41.

[9] See, for example, the recent reports of the AAUP Committee A on Academic Freedom and Tenure, 57 AAUP *Bulletin,* 1971, *57* 35–57; *id.,* 1970, *56,* 387–439.

[10] A. C. Emery, *An Oath of Freedom,* 35th Annual Reynolds Lecture, University of Utah, Feb. 16, 1971. See also, R. Hofstadter and W. Metzger, *The Development of Academic Freedom in the United States* (New York: Columbia Univ. Press, 1955). See also, A. Morris, "Academic Freedom and Loyalty Oaths," *Law and Contemporary Problems,* 1963, *28* 487. See R. S. Brown, *Loyalty and Security* (New Haven: Yale University Press, 1958); V. Countryman, *Un-American Activities in the State of Washington* (Ithaca, New York, Cornell University Press, 1951); D. Gardner, *The California Oath Controversy* (Berkeley, California, University of California Press, 1967).

[11] Report of the President's Commission on Campus Unrest, 1970, pp. 188–189.

protection for academic freedom seems dubious. While the United States Supreme Court has begun to examine the constitutional implications of academic freedom, the law in this regard is still in its formative stages.[12] It is reasonably clear that both faculty and students are entitled at least to a minimal degree of constitutional protection against interferences by public officials with their freedom of expression, but it will probably require many years for the courts to develop a reasonably comprehensive and reliable jurisprudence of academic freedom.[13] Moreover, it is far from certain that judicial machinery can effectively replace the more sensitive instruments of internal self-government as an acceptable means for striking a rational balance between the sometimes competing claims of institutional improvement and intellectual freedom.[14]

In any event, the judicial system can be expected to provide only peripheral support for a system of academic freedom which is adequate to educational needs. Costly and time-consuming litigation is an inherently inefficient process for resolving the kinds of disputes likely to arise within educational institutions committed to academic freedom. Abolition of tenure would undoubtedly transfer many claims of violations of academic freedom, arising from dismissal and

[12] See *Epperson v. Arkansas,* 393 U.S. 97 (1968); *Pickering v. Board of Education,* 391 U.S. 563 (1968); *Keyishian v. Board of Regents,* 385 U.S. 589 (1967).

[13] See Board of Regents v. Roth (U.S. Supreme Court, Docket No. 71–162, decided June 29, 1972) and Perry v. Sindermann (U.S. Supreme Court, Docket No. 70–36, decided June 29, 1972), indicating that all faculty in state educational institutions are constitutionally protected against dismissal for exercise of their freedoms of expression or association under the First and Fourteenth Amendments, but that only tenured members are entitled to the notice and hearing procedures associated with due process. See also W. Van Alstyne, *Duke Law Journal* 1970, 841; National Education Association, *Protecting Teachers Rights,* 1970, 841.

[14] To the extent that judicial protection for academic freedom emanates from the First and Fourteenth Amendments such protection will be principally available only at public colleges and universities, since neither of these constitutional limitations is applicable to private institutions. The concept of academic freedom, however, is one which permeates the entire system of higher education and is not limited to state colleges and universities.

nonretention cases, from the less cumbersome administrative processes of the university to the courthouse. The resulting detriment to the educational process—as faculty and administrators divert their energies from educational concerns to pretrial discovery proceedings, conferences with counsel, and attendance at trials—could be significant.[15] Reliance on court procedures would vest the power of judgment over professional educational issues in the hands of judges and jurors who lack in the specialized experience and insight necessary to informed decision-making in such matters.[16]

It is equally questionable whether other institutional arrangements of a quasi-legal nature could match the capacity of the tenure system to provide protection for academic freedom. This conclusion in no way disparages the role of the American Association of University Professors (AAUP). As the principal national agency for the protection of academic freedom, the AAUP enjoys both the membership strength and national visibility commensurate to its chosen task. The AAUP, however, regards the tenure system as essential to the preservation of academic freedom and exerts its primary influence by insisting upon scrupulous adherence to academic due process as institutionalized in prevailing tenure systems.

It is a practical certainty that abolition of tenure at the University of Utah would be regarded by the AAUP as necessarily entailing a significant impairment of academic freedom. An AAUP determination to this effect could seriously cloud the academic status of the university, potentially impairing its ability to recruit and retain faculty members of superior ability, as well as its capacity to attract federal and foundation grant support. While certain private educational institutions may not find formal tenure essential for

[15] The potential volume of court actions should not be underestimated. The chairman of the AAUP Committee A on Academic Freedom and Tenure, for example, recently reported that nearly 750 formal complaints were received by the AAUP during the 1969–1970 academic year. W. Van Alstyne, *supra* note 8. During the two succeeding years, the comparable figures increased to 880 and 1139, respectively. *Academe,* 1972, 6:3, 2.

[16] See C. Byse and L. Joughin, *Tenure in American Higher Education* (Ithaca, New York: Cornell University Press, 1959), pp. 142–147.

faculty recruited primarily from denominational ranks, the reputation for academic freedom is widely regarded as indispensable to maintenance of a distinguished faculty.

Furthermore, the abolition of tenure would be regarded by many university faculty as a deliberate refutation of existing reciprocal commitments between the university and its faculty. This could motivate faculty members to devote attention to the development of their status and reputation in professional circles outside the university as a means of assuring employment mobility. It also seems likely that abolition of tenure would intensify already strong pressures for faculty to organize into professional associations (that is, unions) to achieve the same protection which formerly had been available through the tenure system.[17]

A proposal to abolish tenure which empowered the administration to dismiss a tenured faculty member without assigning cause and without the obligation to establish rational academic grounds for its action would be widely regarded as little more than an assault upon academic freedom. On the other hand, if the abolition proposal asserted an intention to protect academic freedom through faculty review committees, where dismissals could be contested, it would necessarily imply shifting the burden of proof to the faculty member.[18] That burden would be insurmountable in many cases. Defending against an unwarranted charge of incompetence is inherently more onerous and difficult than proving such a charge.

The allocation of the burden of proof is an absolutely vital feature of the procedures which protect academic freedom. Abolition of tenure would mean that faculty dismissals could in fact be predicated on grounds unrelated to appropriate academic concerns and insulated from effective challenge by an insurmountable burden of proof. The resulting erosion of academic freedom and accom-

---

[17] See S. Kadish, "The Strike and the Professoriat," in W. Metzger (Ed.), *Dimensions of Academic Freedom,* (Urbana: University of Illinois Press, 1969), p. 34.

[18] The implication would be a "necessary" one, because the protective function of tenure dismissal procedures centers upon the allocation of the burden of proof to the administration. One way to abolish tenure would be to shift the burden of proof to the faculty member.

panying loss of loyalty, commitment, and unity, would be seriously detrimental to the quality of education.

Fixed-Term Renewable Contracts. As another alternative to the tenure system, the university might issue fixed-term contracts providing that faculty employment would automatically terminate at the end of the contract period (perhaps three to five years) unless a new contract were offered by the administration following review of the individual's competence and responsibility.[19]

Assuming that the fixed-term contract is nonrenewable unless the faculty member establishes grounds for continuation of his employment at the end of each contract term, let us examine the significant practical problems of this procedure. Without an increase in personnel, it is doubtful that the administrative officers in a large institution, such as the University of Utah, could review all faculty members for retention at the end of their respective contract terms. Because it would seem both imprudent and impolitic to increase administrative staff at the expense of the educational budget, the task of performing the necessary contract reviews would presumably fall on the faculty (as it now does under the tenure system). However, if all faculty were nontenured, as the proposal contemplates, those engaged in contract renewal judgments would experience a substantial conflict of interest, since they would be exposed to like review within a short period of time, possibly by the very persons whom they review. The propensity for toleration of incompetence here seems greater than in the tenure system, under which tenured faculty members can evaluate their colleagues according to objective professional standards without fear for their own economic security.

The contract system thus appears to include most of the deficiencies of abolition of the tenure system and, in addition, would seem difficult to administer in an equitable fashion. This proposal, however, has merit in one respect. It offers a constructive approach to the problem of dealing with incompetence or irresponsibility that develops after acquisition of tenure. It postulates the need for an

[19] Term contract systems of this sort are apparently being tried experimentally at a few institutions, including Hampshire College, Franklin Pierce College, and Johnston College of Redlands University. See *Wall Street Journal,* April 16, 1971, p. 1, col. 1.

ongoing and critical review of faculty performance, with an eye to improving the quality of instruction and intellectual production wherever possible, and in extreme cases initiating ad hoc proceedings for removal of those professors who fail to achieve at professionally acceptable levels. This constructive feature of the proposal undoubtedly could be implemented effectively within the framework of the existing tenure system.

Unions and Collective Bargaining. Efforts at faculty unionization to facilitate collective bargaining on matters of job security and academic freedom, in the judgment of the commission, inevitably would follow abolition of the tenure system. Indeed, a movement toward faculty unionization is moving rapidly ahead, and facilitating legislation has been enacted in several states (see Chapter Nine). In the judgment of the Utah commission, unionization and collective bargaining are undesirable substitutes for the tenure system at the University of Utah. It seems doubtful that the bargaining process can protect the community's interest in academic freedom, and, in times of stress or crisis, it may be particularly susceptible to pressures inimical to educational objectives. Although collective negotiations in industry have traditionally focused upon the economic incidents of employment, it seems inevitable that, were tenure abolished, issues relating to both job security and academic freedom would be introduced into the academic bargaining process.[20] The principles of academic freedom are far too important to be the subject of negotiation. Responsible judgments with respect to professional competence and academic freedom ordinarily can, and normally should be, made only in a quasiadjudicative setting involving individualized charges and issues rather than in the more generalized and less focused process of bargaining. Such judgments, moreover, can be expressed most competently and reliably when they are a response to academic due process made by a committee of professional peers. A collective bargaining process also might produce relatively fixed salary scales, with periodic increments based

[20] An AAUP statement, "Policy on Representation of Economic and Professional Interests," *Bulletin*, 1969, *55*(4), 489, contemplates that collective bargaining contracts will seek to include "explicit guarantees of academic freedom and tenure."

upon length of service or other criteria, thereby reducing the flexibility with which the university administration can reward excellence and provide incentive to effective faculty performance.

Finally, experience in related areas suggests that collective
bargaining procedures may polarize viewpoints, rigidify tactical
positions, delay resolution of disputes, politicize faculty and students,
and induce resort to "pressure" tactics, such as strikes, picketing,
slowdowns, and boycotts, in an effort to influence negotiations.
Although such tactics seem inconsistent with traditional academic
ideals, professional attitudes may yield to the requirements of tactical
expediency if the incentives become great enough.

Conclusions and Recommendations

When the misconceptions are dispelled, the practical implications evaluated, and the alternatives analyzed, the tenure system
emerges as an institution calculated to promote academic freedom
with appropriate accountability. The quality of a university largely
depends upon the commitment of its faculty and staff to the achievement of educational objectives. Intellectual aspirations, however, are
not enough; sustained public support for the university requires
that institutional commitment be communicated by word and deed
to students, taxpayers, and public officials alike. Properly understood and effectively implemented, academic freedom and tenure
can play an indispensable role in demonstrating that the university
community shares the concerns of its constituencies, including their
impatience with academic incompetence and irresponsibility, but is
determined to achieve accountability in these matters without harm
to the basic values of educational freedom.

The Utah commission thus recommends that the tenure system be retained at the University of Utah, but that efforts be
undertaken to initiate specific reforms. First, the commission recommends that the university initiate proceedings leading to the promulgation of a code of faculty responsibilities.[21] As noted above, faculty

---

[21] The AAUP has suggested the desirability of formal statements of faculty obligations. See "A Statement of the Association's
Council: Freedom and Responsibility," AAUP *Bulletin,* 1970, 56-4,
375.

obligations are presupposed by the tenure system; but the exact content of such obligations is largely undefined, except in general terms, and appears to be imperfectly understood by some faculty members as well as many private citizens. Such a code could assist in defining the legitimate expectations of the university as to acceptable standards of faculty performance.[22] Although the code should be adaptable to a broad range of contingencies, it should incorporate a reasonably specific basis for identifying acts and omissions deemed to be grounds for dismissal or other disciplinary sanctions. It should also provide sufficient clarification of faculty obligations to dispel the kind of administrative inertia, rooted in claims of ambiguity and uncertainty as to applicable standards, that tends to resist initiation of disciplinary proceedings.

Second, the commission recommends the creation of a comprehensive career development program for all faculty members. While the pre-tenure review and screening system appears to function with reasonable efficiency, more attention should be devoted to the problem of post-tenure decline. "Incompetence" among some tenured faculty—although partially the result of ineffective probationary review procedures in the past—is, and is likely to continue to be, largely a manifestation of arrested career development rather than of inherent lack of intellectual capability. Rational explanation of declining professional adequacy may be found in a variety of complex and interacting factors which relate to the psychology of teaching, nature of academic commitments, level of professional aspirations, quantum of physical and intellectual vigor, and unique personal influences. It seems probable that self-renewal is feasible, if appropriate institutional assistance is provided. Perhaps more important is early identification of factors likely to diminish teaching effectiveness and intellectual progress. Identification could provide the basis for preventive measures designed to arrest the process and, hopefully, reinvigorate individual academic potential.

The university decision to employ a professor on a probationary basis and its subsequent decision that he should receive

[22] Illustrative of the kinds of codes here contemplated are the statements of faculty responsibilities recently promulgated at the University of California (Berkeley), Stanford University, and the City University of New York.

tenured status involve mutual commitments between the professor and the institution. In most cases, these commitments are honored fully by both parties. When the professor begins to fail in his obligations, often through no intention on his part, the university should undertake to provide rehabilitative and correctional aids in the interest of both parties. Longevity of service is clearly not irrelevant in this connection; the revitalization of a declining, though experienced and intellectually capable, faculty member who has devoted an extended part of his life to the university is a far more humane approach than dismissal. In addition, the effort, if successful, may well prove to be both educationally and economically sounder than to replace a mature faculty member with an inexperienced teacher of unknown potential.

While an effective career development program may be an exceptionally difficult objective to institutionalize, the effort surely should be made.[23] The educational establishment can hardly plead incompetence in the field in which it professes expertise.

Third, the commission recommends the development of effective and visible means by which alleged violations of faculty responsibility can be efficiently and fairly screened, evaluated, and adjusted. Maximum effort should be directed toward amicable and informal resolution of student and citizen grievances involving faculty members. A strengthened procedure for investigating and processing complaints also would assist in the effective administration of the proposed code of faculty responsibilities.

Evidence brought to the Utah commission's attention indicated that many members of the university community, as well as citizens at large, are inadequately informed as to the availability of disciplinary procedures which may be brought to bear against faculty members who fail to meet their professional commitments. Indeed, much criticism of the tenure system appears to reflect a sense of frustration on the part of individuals who perceive the

[23] The most comprehensive treatment of college faculty career development programs is undoubtedly found in recent publications of K. E. Eble, emanating from the Project to Improve College Teaching, of which he was national director. See K. E. Eble, *Professors as Teachers* (San Francisco: Jossey-Bass, Inc., 1972); K. E. Eble, *Career Development of the Effective College Teacher* (Washington, D.C.: AAUP, 1971).

existence of grounds for complaint against particular faculty members but who believe (often erroneously) that "nothing can be done about it." Improvements in substantive criteria and expectations relating to faculty performance would remain vulnerable to criticism, however, unless the university also undertook to establish adequate procedures by which departures from accepted standards could be formally investigated and acted upon.[24]

Because procedural formalities can be so time-consuming and cumbersome as to be counter-productive, a well-structured procedural system should emphasize institutional mechanisms at a preliminary administrative level for informal processing of grievances, reconciliation of misunderstandings, and rectification of inequities. Often, for example, private discussions between student and faculty member may be all that is required; in other instances, problems can be effectively mediated by a department chairman or dean. While these techniques should be encouraged, a need appears to exist for an agency at which informal screening and adjustment of complaints could take place without the appearance of "command influence" and in a setting of assured confidentiality.

Certain complaints against faculty members could not be satisfactorily investigated or adjusted without disclosure of the identity of the complainant to the professor in question or to his department chairman or dean, thereby involving a risk of retaliation. It seems likely that apprehension of retaliatory measures could be significantly alleviated by providing a neutral and autonomous complaint officer with whom complaints could be lodged for investigation and processing.

The complaint officer, as conceived by this commission, would be a university ombudsman,[25] with broad powers to investi-

---

[24] The Scranton Commission concluded that establishment of "procedures for dealing with grievances is an aspect of university governance that deserves special attention, since escalation of emotional issues on campus often is exacerbated by absence of adequate communications." See *Report of the President's Commission on Campus Unrest,* 1970, pp. 204–206.

[25] The ombudsman concept, drawn from Scandinavian experience, is discussed—with comprehensive citations to the voluminous literature—in R. Aaron, "Utah Ombudsman: The American Proposals," *Utah Law Review,* 1967, 32.

gate, mediate, conciliate, and adjust complaints against faculty members, but without disciplinary authority. In his investigatory role, complaints against faculty members could be screened to determine validity and provide a measure of protection against "witch-hunts." Valid complaints could be pursued along informal channels to produce reliable verification or refutation. When the facts appear to be without dispute, the ombudsman would attempt to work out an informal and amicable disposition of the grievance. If the matter is not handled to his satisfaction at the informal level, the student should have the right to initiate formal proceedings against the faculty member, leading to possible disciplinary sanctions. Formal adjudication, however, must conform to the requirements of academic due process.

It seems evident that the shot and cannister currently aimed at academic tenure are misdirected. The call to abolish tenure is the identification of a convenient target for a variety of dimly perceived educational ills for which tenure properly bears little or no responsibility. Critics of tenure, however, have provided a major public service in directing attention to the system and the need to improve its operation so that results correspond more closely to aspirations. Properly understood, tenure emerges as the shield and buckler of academic freedom; those who seek its demise have reason to pause and ponder the likely consequence of the success of their efforts. Those who preside at the wake of tenure may well find themselves guests at the funeral of academic freedom as well.

Chapter 6

Tenure and Teaching

Kenneth E. Eble

⌇⌇⌇⌇⌇⌇⌇⌇⌇⌇⌇⌇⌇⌇⌇⌇⌇⌇⌇⌇⌇⌇⌇⌇⌇⌇⌇⌇⌇⌇⌇⌇⌇⌇⌇⌇⌇

Academic tenure is defended chiefly on the grounds that it is vital to academic freedom. Its defenders see the professor threatened by a public often hostile to new or strange or unpopular ideas and offer a plenitude of examples, beginning with Socrates, to support their argument. On the other hand, attacks on tenure generally focus on the protection the system supposedly affords the incompetent professor. Usually the professor is perceived in only one of his roles that of teacher—and often he is stereotyped by images of sloth and aging incompetence. There is some truth to both contentions—more to the former than the latter, however. The connection between academic freedom and tenure has been examined often and amply documented in the light of both specific incidents and theory. Jefferson's claim that the spirit of freedom is kept alive by effective exercise argues that freedom will never be secured and tucked away, that one cannot grow tired of claiming freedom except as he would lose it. Any examination of particular infringements on academic freedom occurring throughout the country every year (and increasingly in the past decade) would warn against a casual attitude toward academic freedom or tenure's role in preserving it.

By comparison, the precise relationship between teaching and tenure has hardly been examined at all. We can talk at length to individual professors who will testify that tenure gives a measure of job security and bolsters the personal courage important to their functioning as teachers. We can find, on the other hand, examples on almost every campus (and in almost every human enterprise) of individuals whose competence is marginal but who are not likely to be dismissed. Two recent studies attempt careful assessments of faculty attitudes toward tenure. The University of Utah study (see Chapter Five) found that "a substantial percentage of the faculty regards tenure as a protection for academic freedom, and academic freedom as insecure without tenure." In the same questionnaire, 70 per cent of the responding faculty believed no one in their departments deserved dismissal. The 30 per cent who thought some individuals should be dismissed generally represented clusters of reponses from particular departments, probably pointing to the same individual or individuals. The commission's conclusion was that "the number of faculty members deemed deserving of dismissal may, in fact, be relatively small."

A broader national study, done by Jerry Gaff and Robert Wilson for the Project to Improve College Teaching, provides another sample of faculty attitudes. The largest number of faculty respondents find tenure a mixed blessing, citing its important effects on academic freedom but raising the question of protecting incompetence. A number almost as large felt that tenure had no effect upon teaching, and only a small number of faculty expressed the conviction that tenure had either adverse or beneficial effects on teaching.

In my work with the Project to Improve College Teaching, I have discovered no meaningful correlations when examining ratings of professors relative to their standing as tenured or untenured faculty members. Good and bad teachers may be found among the tenured as well as the untenured and in about the same numbers.

Among its general effects, tenure provides a probationary period during which skill in teaching can manifest itself. All beginning teachers do not attain tenure. At the University of Utah during the past six years, about 10 per cent of those undergoing formal tenure review procedures did not receive tenure. Evidence indicates that nationwide a much larger percentage are not retained during the probationary period or voluntarily resign before a tenure decision is reached. Any given sample of experienced teachers (most of whom would have tenure) probably has a higher level of professional competence than a comparable sample of inexperienced teachers (most of whom would not). But accurate comparisons of teaching effectiveness between tenured and untenured faculty, are difficult to make. It is conceivable that measures of teaching competence could be agreed upon; weighting could be accomplished in accordance with numbers, age, health, and other factors; matching samples might be possible; and continuing study over a period of years could obtain valid and important data. In advance of such analysis, however, it seems premature to blame tenure for poor teaching or to suppose that summarily firing those who are identified as incompetent would improve teaching. Clearly, there is need for substantiating evidence.

Essentially two arguments support the claim that tenure affects teaching adversely. The first is that security breeds incompetence or invites decay; the second that teaching suffers if an institution cannot fire its incompetents. The first argument challenges the whole direction of modern social organization. Livingston (Chapter Four) effectively examines that argument, which often maintains that the welfare state has sapped the vigor of all societies it has fastened upon. The marginal truth to the second argument can be acknowledged at once. There is not likely to be any strong argument that keeping incompetent teachers is beneficial to teaching. (Livingston's argument is not so much in favor of incompetence as it is against the ill effects of a system which bases its values on competitive superiority.) The important question, however, is not whether incompetent teachers should be removed, but how one should go about it.

The most efficient way, obviously, is for one person to become convinced of someone else's incompetence and to dismiss him

forthwith. But that will hardly do in a democratic society, and
tenure in American universities is closely connected with ideas of
democratic freedom and justice. The arbitrary decision, the un-
founded accusation, the unproved charge, the unsubstantiated dismissal—these all run counter to the American sense of justice. What
tenure basically insists upon is the following out of due process in a
dismissal for cause. If incompetence is charged, then evidence must
be brought forth, and the person accused of incompetence be given
an opportunity to be heard. To be sure, dismissal proceedings seem
to face administrators with insuperable obstacles: evidence to be
obtained; witnesses to be found; and proceedings to be gone
through. I do not see, with or without tenure, any other choice. It
is probably not so much *tenure* as *time* which makes dismissal proceedings difficult. In any occupation, time served increases the claim
one has on a job. The untenured faculty member is easier to remove,
not because he lacks tenure but because he lacks the years of affiliation with an institution which create relationships, complicate
judgments, and presume institutional satisfaction. The conclusion
seems inescapable that abolishing tenure would do little to make a
just dismissal for cause any easier than it is now. While one might
agree that protecting incompetence is, in general, a bad thing, how
a democratic institution goes about ridding itself of incompetence
remains the vital question.

   If I have been persuasive in arguing against arbitrary dismissals, I may have shifted the argument to the commonly held
opinion that the attainment of tenure removes the professor from
further evaluation of his services. The facts of academic life are
quite otherwise. The process of moving through the academic ranks
entails annual review of all faculty members until they achieve full
professorial rank. Nor does evaluation stop when one achieves this
rank. Salary decisions remain important throughout a person's
career and, as financially pressed as most institutions are, such
decisions can never be made perfunctorily. In addition, the full
professor remains under the scrutiny of his students and colleagues
in important ways. Formal administrative structures are the norm
for institutional operation. And one can add to these forces the
extrinsic and intrinsic pressures the professional disciplines place
upon their members.

The responsibility for continuing evaluation of the professor resides largely, though not exclusively, in the faculty. The protection tenure affords is often cited as the reason for being unable to upgrade an entire faculty, either within a college or a department. Colleague judgments can deliberately maintain the mediocre, for it is the incompetent who makes the mediocre look good by comparison. This complicates the task of upgrading a department, and administrators who have a sure sense for spotting incompetence are impatient with such complications. Nevertheless, I see no more logic, justice, or wisdom in arbitrarily dismissing a large portion of a department than in arbitrarily dismissing a single faculty member. Instead of dwelling upon the injustice of the tenure system, the vexed administrator might welcome the restraint it places on his acting injudiciously. The problem of the mediocre department, like that of the teacher of diminished effectiveness, is not to be remedied by abolishing the tenure system, however. The faults that arise from departmental autonomy can best be remedied by establishing administrative mechanisms independent of departmental judgments and action. It is primitive operational strategy to rely upon culling out the undesirables as the only means of improving a department's strength. Institutions use both internal and external teams to analyze departmental performance and to suggest means of improving performance aside from or in addition to either hiring or firing faculty. Administrative action alone, quite apart from tenure, has proved capable of ministering to departmental as well as individual faculty ills. The point is that though tenure may be involved in these matters, the problem is far more complex.

The conclusion I reach is that abolishing tenure and the system's supposedly baneful effects would in itself do little to improve teaching. Nor would the task of hiring and firing academic personnel be any less complex or difficult without the tenure system. I think academic freedom would suffer greatly, for tenure even as it is, and supported in particular cases by the courts, does not insure academic freedom. The critics of tenure, as O'Neil's analysis points out (see Chapter Ten), do not attack it because it inadequately protects academic freedom. Nor are they coming forward with plans that include strong safeguards. In the situation in which the academic community currently finds itself, tenure is essential to freedom, however short it may fall in being able to protect and preserve the teacher's freedom everywhere and at all times.

I have dwelt briefly on the vital relationship of tenure to academic freedom because freedom is a necessity for excellence in teaching, a necessity which manifests itself in a number of ways. First, freedom is the basic condition for man's learning. I cannot see teaching going well in any subject where the expression of ideas, the exposure of new theories, or the advancing of knowledge is involved if the teacher does not feel free. Moreover, the individual who is not engaged in such teaching can hardly be said to be engaged in higher learning.

Graduate education is often mundane, often dreary, but surely it succeeds in some measure as it asks a student to seek out something new or to combine the old in new forms, to uncover evidence, to sift and weigh it, and to reach conclusions which may not have been reached before. This grounding of teaching in the free inquiry of scholarship makes the positive exercise of freedom a necessary condition for teaching, for giving a scholar something to profess.

We demean teaching, particularly in the lower schools, by regarding it chiefly as an act of transmission working safely within a received body of important skills and useful information. That attitude is wrong as regards teaching of any kind. It is clearly wrong when teaching is connected with the discovery of truth, the expansion of knowledge.

American values rest so securely upon assertions of freedom that it is unnecessary to review either our basic documents or our continuing history. When higher education talks about academic freedom, it is describing within the contexts of teaching and learning the basic American belief. As Louis Joughin writes (*Academic Freedom and Tenure*, University of Wisconsin Press, 1967), "Academic freedom and tenure do not exist because of a peculiar solicitude for the human beings who staff our academic institutions. They exist, instead, in order that society may have the benefit of honest judgment and independent criticism which otherwise might be withheld because of fear of offending a dominant social group or transient social attitude."

Surely one cannot regard the present time as one in which

criticism is not needed or one in which vital criticism is not likely to offend a dominant social group. Civil rights is only the largest problem that has faced a dominant majority, and academic freedom cases in the South as reflected in AAUP files increased almost in direct proportion to the rise of civil rights action there in the sixties. The seeking of solutions to urban problems demands involvement of college and university teachers with expertise in relevant fields. What they study and necessarily bring before their students has a high potential for offending various segments of the public. Even teachers in the sciences, usually at some remove from the public, are likely to be involved in controversies related to pollution, population control, public health, and the like. One hesitates to say freedom of expressions is more necessary at one time than at another. Yet the present time is desperately in need of vigorous criticism, even as dissent in the universities has aroused public resentment and attempts to stifle it.

Second, teaching is a process, and as much as a teacher must be free to pursue that which he will profess, he must also be free in the ways he goes about teaching. Much of teaching as I have seen it, much of my own teaching, stays in routine ways. The times change, the students change, but we proceed as before. If we abridge a teacher's freedom, even in small ways, we add to those natural inclinations to establish and stay safely within routines.

We forget too easily in our abstract considerations of teaching and tenure that teaching goes on in a heavily regulated context. Class hours, credits, assignments, grades, administrative structures, all impose limitations. If we do not have the security which underlies the act of or the argument for breaking out of inhibiting contexts, teaching suffers. Among the charges specifically and seriously made by administrators in academic freedom cases before the AAUP are: a teacher "had his students purchase a book as outside reading without notifying the college bookstore"; a teacher "attempted, without consulting her department head, to effect a change in her teaching schedule directly through the registrar"; a teacher used "inappropriate language in the classroom"; a teacher did not always "use good taste in the selection of teaching materials"; a teacher "used questionable teaching methods"; a teacher "failed to seek approval for library requests."

The case of an untenured instructor dismissed at Indiana University for burning a flag in class has more far-reaching implications for teaching practices. The complexities of the case, reported in the AAUP *Bulletin,* Spring 1970, cannot be explored here. The bare details are that a young teacher in an English composition class burned a small American flag as a way of illustrating the difference between concrete objects and symbols of abstract values. A faculty hearing committee questioned his judgment but did not recommend dismissal. The president and the board dismissed him nevertheless. No one can deny this was an extraordinarily powerful teaching device, nor would many disagree that his judgment was questionable. "The academic freedom of a teacher in the classroom," the AAUP report commented, "includes the right to use techniques which, on hindsight, may on occasion appear to be unwise." But, the subsequent events involving students, faculty, administrators, the board of trustees, and the public testify to the importance of the lesson he was trying to teach. If we are to develop a body politic which can separate the concrete from the abstract, can recognize the power of symbols, and can uphold the distinction between the expression of ideas and the commission of physical acts, we must have these lessons taught and in dramatic ways.

As I have gone around the country and have observed teaching in many classrooms, I think teachers' want of imagination and enterprise is more serious than the infrequent occasions when a teacher's imaginative act rises to public attention. It would be tidy if imagination always coexisted with good judgment, if the necessaries of teaching were always consonant in substance and in language with the institutional or public idea of what is acceptable. But neither life nor language takes on these constraints, and teaching which does not come across to students as related to the lives they live, the world they occupy, risks the grave offense of being ignored.

Third, a teacher must have freedom to criticize existing practices, to experiment in the face of possible objections or failure, and to strike out in new directions. Such freedoms are especially important for the young. I have little rebuttal for the charge that the probationary period which precedes tenure fails to give the young teacher needed protection. I defend the probationary period on other grounds, discussed later in this chapter. I also think the period should be short and that its existence places great responsibility on tenured professors both to protect and encourage the untenured professors whose views on teaching as on other matters are not in conformance with established ways.

For tenured and untenured professors alike, one kind of academic security resides in always playing it safe. There is no need for tenure for the professor who is never critical of the courses or methods or curriculum which prevail in his department or of the instructional policies or practices of the institution at large. A preferable kind of security can be defined as being able to oppose established routines without fear of institutional reprisal. Books, assignments, ideas will probably always provoke complaints from some members of the outside community. Tenure does, indeed, give protection from such attacks. It also can protect an individual from attacks from within. The tenured university professor risks some damage to his career whenever he departs from conventional academic pursuits, even, say, to commit himself to undergraduate teaching or, much more, to undergraduate teaching of an innovative kind.

An example of the subtle constraints the professoriate places upon its teachers, against which tenure affords little enough protection, emerged in drafting this chapter. One of my professorial colleagues objected to the emphasis in the last paragraph on the risks of departing from conventional academic ways. "All potentially true," he wrote, "but isn't it really the *way* the person does it? If he disregards or belittles what has been done, he will invoke censure. If he is gracious and courteous and prudent, censure will be rare—unless the whole climate is acrimonious." Is that the price one has to pay to function as a teacher? If so, the students may be right, in substance and in language, when they say to their supposed teachers, "Up yours."

It is not that grace and courtesy and prudence are not admirable qualities, but surely they cannot circumscribe teaching without doing it harm. Teaching needs the vigor and daring that may offend. The individual protection tenure affords makes a specific contribution to the exercising of freedom in the act of teaching. Equally important is the part tenure plays in creating a climate of freedom which encourages exciting and imaginative teaching and which supports the restless, innovating, unconventional teacher. For unless we feel that teaching has arrived at both the truth and the way to truth, we must use to full advantage those vital energies which still keep searching for both.

Marvin Bressler, in the *Annals of the American Academy of Political and Social Science* (July 1971), mentions another possible effect of tenure on the competitive market—the tendency for tenure to check the movement of all the best professors to the best universities. "Thus," he writes, "the tenure system, for all its injustices and rigidities, has the effect of assuring that some able teachers will walk with students at the rear of the academic procession. In this respect, the maintenance of tenure is, so to speak, in the service of the liberal ideal of fostering equal educational opportunity through a random distribution of faculty talent."

My own argument in this respect has to do with internal competition within the academic world. During the affluent years just past, an open market for academic services probably had adverse effects upon teaching. The most successful professors seemed to be those who went where the salaries were highest, the teaching load lightest, the disciplinary opportunities greatest. One might give thanks for whatever tenure did to modify this kind of academic free enterprise. The visibility of such types everywhere but in the classroom in recent years has been among the forces causing the public to charge the profession with the neglect of teaching. The highly competitive market for the nonteaching professor has been a major reason for a value system generally unfavorable to the classroom teacher. Tenure has remained as an assertion of values other than determination of rewards by a competitive market. Its force may not have been great, but it may have provided that reasonable measure of security which enabled some professors to opt for an academic career rather than a more remunerative one outside, or to opt for teaching within a collegiate institution rather than seeking a university post.

In a competitive market, institutional loyalty may also play a part in keeping valuable and highly mobile faculty members at institutions where they derive great satisfaction from teaching. For an administrator, the other side of getting rid of the deadwood is keeping faculty the institution needs. Tenure may be damned for protecting deadwood, but it must be praised for what it does to strengthen institutional loyalties. Although too many loyal, deeply-rooted faculty may be the mark of a provincial institution, a transient faculty is not likely to build teaching excellence either. On balance, the job security deriving from tenure may protect both the public and the profession from the effects of a strictly competitive market and higher education from the internal competitive forces which work against teaching.

Finally, the probationary period is an important part of tenure, with potentially important consequences for teaching. The probationary years clearly should be viewed as years of development, not merely as extended time for screening. It would seem better to put money and imagination into developing teachers early in their careers than into quality control schemes stretched over a professor's entire life.

One of the practices most ruinous to building respect for our profession is the up-or-out policies maintained by many large and prestigious universities in a time of expanding enrollments. Under such policies, many beginning teachers are hired with the intention of keeping only a few at the point of tenure. Little effort goes into developing competence among new teachers; the emphasis instead is placed upon personal competition to do the winnowing. The process may single out excellence in teaching, but it tends to encourage conformity to the established ways of the department, the scanting of teaching in favor of research, and the currying of favor with powerful members of the senior staff. Tenure is not to blame for abuses of the probationary period, nor does it minimize the necessity of selecting teaching personnel carefully. But respectable tenure policies both limit the time spent in a nontenured position (the AAUP recommends no more than seven years) and recognize the need to use that period for developmental purposes.

In the course of the Project's two-year study, I was unable to locate even one thorough-going institutional system for faculty development which paid serious attention to the development of teachers. Graduate programs give very little attention to preparing teachers, and effective in-service programs for assisting new staff members are not widely established. And yet, there is no shortage of ways in which a new faculty member might be assisted in developing as both teacher and scholar. These are not just the individual's responsibility but the institution's as well.

If we are to defend the probationary period as a part of tenure, proper regard must be given to the period (including dropping the term *probationary*). Foremost, institutions must make serious efforts to help develop individual competence in both teaching and scholarship. The threats of nonretention—up-or-out, produce or perish, conform or go elsewhere—must be replaced by an attitude which regards the pretenure period as helpful to both the individual and the institution in finding out about each other without prejudice to either if a permanent relationship does not result. As Gaff and Wilson clearly point out, effective teaching depends greatly on a reasonably congenial teaching environment. Students, colleagues, and working conditions are the most important aspects of this environment. One does not learn about these matters in catalogs or through a one- or two-day visit. As a period of association which increases the likelihood of continuing favorable relationships between individual and institution, the pretenure period serves a necessary purpose.

Looking back on what I have written, I acknowledge the speculative character of much that has been said. But teaching is not an exact science, and trying to ascertain what favorably affects the teacher's practice is certainly a speculative inquiry. What seems central is the feeling of being free, which a strong system of academic freedom and tenure help to create and maintain. It is not that a teacher wants to stir up the populace constantly, though the necessity to intrude an idea into a student's mind may call for disturbance now and then. Socrates was rightly called a gadfly, and no teacher succeeds unless he can stir the learner from his passive state. Teaching is not a static activity; it demands the energetic application of imagination and intelligence. It cannot prosper except in a climate of freedom, a climate that stimulates thought and gives opportunity for curiosity to flourish, a climate that dares us to confront received opinion and to challenge students to do likewise.

Self-confidence is as important for a teacher as the mastery of subject matter. The measure of security and the investment in a person which tenure implies may be useful to maintaining self-confidence. The converse is also important. And to some degree, the tenure system reduces the exaggerated self-consciousness that may result from being subject to constant surveillance, the unwillingness to confront institutional limitations when one is under a threat, and the negative reactions that coercion can arouse. Dismissing the incompetent may have less value than trying to reduce the possibilities for incompetence in the first place and working with those conditions which may lead to incompetence. A wise institution, in fact, might have as its major goal the development and maintenance of a high level of teaching competence. If such were the direction, the instances of egregious incompetence should be sufficiently small to permit the institution to carry them without great harm.

Tenure is rightfully identified with the establishment these days. There is something stuffy about the concept and its connection with academic tradition. Yet, at a time when students are zealous in speaking against the establishment, it exerts a strong influence in letting their voices be heard. Tenure does add some encouragement to professorial pomposity, which leads to many sins against teaching. It also may seem to encourage sloth, although self-indulgence may be a more apt description of the malady. But I take some stock in a college president's plea to "make 'deadwood' an honorable office; find room for the good, honest, lazy man."

Plans for modifying tenure, with the exception of those which would extend it to the nontenured, do not aim primarily at teaching. The contract system does not appear to offer any great improvement over tenure and promises to be more cumbersome. All the same problems remain—the necessity of judging competence and acting on that judgment foremost among them. Though the fixed- or sliding-term contract seems to work against certain ill-effects of life-long tenure, it appears to encourage conformity among teachers. Spelling out objectives may be a useful exercise; it may also cause a man to opt for those teaching objectives which look good on a contract but which lock him into a defined pattern.

The relationship between tenure, effective teaching, and the individual teacher is altogether too little understood to make tenure the central issue in improving teaching. And, insofar as the abolition or reform of tenure might deceive institutions into thinking something favorable was being done for teaching, the effects might be as harmful as assuming that such abolition or reform would benefit academic freedom.

Much needs doing if teaching is to be improved, but few of these improvements have much to do with tenure: (1) Identifying teaching talent early and developing that talent in graduate schools. (2) Establishing institutional programs which develop the teaching potential of faculty members at various stages in their careers. (3) Adopting ways of evaluating teaching which are searching, fair, and based upon data from various sources. (4) Using evaluation not only for making judgments on teaching competence but toward developing competence. (5) Incorporating teaching into the reward system in tangible ways. (6) Increasing institutional flexibility to take advantage of the varying skills and interests in teaching found within a faculty and in an individual faculty member throughout his career. (7) Working to revise the reward system within institutions and the profession in order to gain a strong commitment to teaching from the existing professoriate and to make use of a range of talent the reward system now discourages and excludes. We need to look as closely at tenure as at our other accepted routines and practices, but reform of tenure is no key to improving teaching. If in the examination of tenure, we perceive something of what needs to be done about developing teachers, then teaching might well be served.

Chapter 7

Faculty Reward and Assessment Systems

Harold L. Hodgkinson

It is common knowledge that a growing concern over tenure exists both on the campus and in various sectors of American society. This is matched by increasing concern over accreditation procedures in higher education,[1] and the two areas have much in common. Both systems of evaluation ("accrediting" persons for tenure and institutions for accreditation) are totally immune from public review, at a time when the public is paying sizeable amounts for higher education. Neither system has developed indices of measuring teaching or institutional effectiveness that are persuasive to those outside higher education. The statement that the best teachers get tenure and the best institutions get accredited must be accepted or rejected on faith, as no data exist which could test the performance of either evaluation system. Indeed, by keeping the criteria vague,

[1] Accreditation will be a major concern of the second report of the Newman Task Force (in press).

those in charge of both systems avoid the issue of accountability. Neither system has a reward component, except in the sense that getting tenure or accreditation could be called rewarding. Beyond this, what? Some individuals with tenure are stronger teachers, contribute more, and progress more rapidly than others, yet tenure casts all in the same mold. Similarly, some institutions make spectacular strides in getting tenure while others squeak by, yet each is treated identically.[2] After receiving tenure or accreditation, some individuals and some institutions rest on their laurels, while others vigorously engage in personal and institutional advancement. At this crucial point, no reward system is in operation.

Although there are time-and-motion studies that tell us how many hours a week a teacher engages in various professional activities and studies of the academic marketplace, departmental organization, and faculty participation in campus-wide governance,[3] very little literature exists on faculty aspirations, on how they set their goals, or on what they would like to be doing twenty years from now. The questionnaire format, used in most of these studies, does not lend itself to this kind of analysis. In these studies faculty emerge as hollow men; we learn nothing about them as persons. Cottle (see Chapter Two) gives more information on what it's like to be a faculty member than I could find anywhere else, with the exception of Kingsley Amis' *Lucky Jim*.

The point is vital in terms of constructing a viable reward system, in that one has to know what *reward* means to those who are involved with the system. In rewarding people, instead of raising the ante or increasing the carrots, one might also discover what

[2] It should be mentioned that the Federation of Regional Accrediting Commissions of Higher Education (FRACHE) has set up a special commission to study the problem of regional accrediting.

[3] N. Sanford, *The American College* (New York: Wiley, 1962); L. B. Mayhew, *The Literature of Higher Education 1971* (San Francisco: Jossey-Bass, 1971); P. L. Dressel and S. B. Pratt, *The World of Higher Education* (San Francisco: Jossey-Bass, 1971); R. Wilson and M. Hildebrand, *Effective University Teaching and Its Evaluation* (Berkeley: Center for Research and Development in Higher Education, 1970); T. Parsons and G. Platt, *The Academic Profession: A Pilot Study* (Washington, D.C.: National Science Foundation, 1968).

people feel threatened by and try to minimize those factors. The literature is not very helpful either in terms of what threatens faculty, although it is common knowledge that they are protective of the status quo. When change does take place, as Hefferlin notes, it is by accretion.[4] Snyder's work at MIT sheds some light on the topic,[5] but it would be difficult at present to work systematically toward reducing the areas of threat that inhibit faculty willingness. to change, as we simply do not know enough. Whatever these threats are, many faculty appear to find more security within a collective negotiation organization than a professional one, if recently expanding faculty unionization is any criterion.

Many of the problems of faculty assessment parallel those related to reward structures. The exact practices and procedures used in assessing a teacher's fitness for tenure are seldom clearly stated. When they are defined, there is seldom any specific statement of *how* such assessment will be made. In many school systems (and some community colleges) the problem is handled chronologically; that is, three years of service will move a teacher from step three to step four. This system is easy and understandable, though it dodges the central issue of making competence-based assessments and thus is essentially non-professional in character.

Another approach to the assessment problem is that of gauging a teacher's ability to carry out behavioral objectives. In terms of skill acquisition, behavioral objectives have helped teachers to gain greater specificity of goal-setting and assessment, but it can also encourage them to avoid the harder questions of inculcating values and attitudes, which can be central to a teacher's task. The behavioral objectives movement has gained strength in public schools and in some community colleges, but much less in four-year colleges and universities, where faculty find the work of detailing what students can *do* as a result of taking a course both unprofessional and demeaning.

Neither the simple solution of chronological step systems nor

[4] JB L. Hefferlin, *Dynamics of Academic Reform* (San Francisco: Jossey-Bass, 1969).

[5] B. Snyder, *The Hidden Curriculum* (New York: Knopf, 1971).

behavioral objectives is adequate for a system which assumes that teaching excellence comes in many sizes and shapes. (The research *does* show that there is no one ideal teacher type—good teachers can be young or old, aggressive or shy, theatrical or calm. Good teachers spend no more time on preparation, reading papers, committees, etc., than those nominated as poor teachers. Faculty and students generally pick the same people as good teachers, but for extremely different reasons.)

Assessment procedures are frequently over-simplified, the chief manifestation of this characteristic being superficial attention to the individual. It is important to remember, for example, that individuals change through time, that aspirations as well as competence vary with time, and that these considerations should become part of the assessment system as well. For example, certain stages exist in any professorial life cycle: neophyte graduate student, inexperienced instructor, first political involvement with department, tenure, chairman of a major committee, full professor, officer of a national association in his field, department chairman. In addition, "developmental tasks" parallel professorial cycles, such as the conflict between demands of getting tenure and home and family, of making peace between aspirations for prestige within his discipline and service to the campus, of getting his own children through college, of adjusting to retirement, etc. Ideally, an assessment system will take into account both professional life cycle and developmental task changes.

Beyond the importance of such considerations to the individual, a word might be added about their importance in an organizational context. Almost every organization needs to reward people for two very different characteristics—competence and loyalty.[6] As organizational imperatives change, new individuals with new skills must be incorporated and allowed to develop leadership for particular situations. As time passes, however, these individuals give way to others, who then become the "front line." It is vital that persons who are no longer at the cutting edge of competence

[6] W. J. Goode, "The Protection of the Inept," *American Sociological Review*, February 1967.

can be redeployed without either damage to the ego or to the institution. Any effective reward and assessment system will take into account the needs of both individuals and organizations.

Goals for Assessment and Reward

Let me now suggest some of the desirable ingredients of any reward system. As I have said, evaluation should be designed to assist the person in improving his performance. *Be that person a student or a teacher.* My impression, however, is that most current evaluation systems work primarily to reject people rather than help them attain improved performance. Clear performance criteria would be helpful, although they alone do not usually allow for much individual style or uniqueness, which is important in both teaching and learning. Assessment must be available continuously: when the person (teacher or student) thinks he needs it. This means that year-end or term-end assessment is less constructive than assessment used in time to warn of potential weakness. A system set up to encourage maximum feedback as continuously as possible is ultimately of most value to both individual and institution.

Any reward system should also be based on intrinsic rather than extrinsic motivation. The individual should be encouraged to develop his own criteria for increasing his competency and should be helped to understand assessment feedback in terms of his own goals. Rather than encouraging leading from strength, reward and assessment systems might encourage the person to improve on his weaknesses. (Student grading systems frequently drive students away from unfamiliar areas in which they might not do well and toward continuing in areas where they have already succeeded). The development of weak or new areas will be impossible if the system seems designed to punish rather than encourage the individual to develop more clear-cut assessments of his own strengths and weaknesses.

Collaboration among colleagues can also improve teaching. When colleagues are set against each other—by means of such artificial devices as teacher-of-the-year awards—this sort of collaboration is hindered.

Assessment and reward systems must reflect in specific ways the educational objectives and styles of both the individual teacher and his college or university. Although there will be departmental differences in this regard, the essential relationship between the institution's objectives and the methods of assessing faculty and student performance should be consistent. Finally, there is need for a person skilled in a variety of assessment procedures (clinical as well as statistical) on many campuses to help interpret evaluation results for both teachers and students.

Any system which attempts to assess and reward teaching competence should be flexible and individualized. The currently uniform approach to the defining of teaching competence is at the heart of the issue. We know that some people are very good at lecturing and very poor at advising, and vice versa. Few institutions, however, have dared try the option of a flexible load: evaluation is based on that area in which each teacher performs best. In the public schools, much interest has been shown in the notion of differentiated staffing, which works with great efficiency in some schools by capitalizing on the talents of the entire teaching staff. In similar fashion, team teaching often results in greater student gains than two teachers could produce by working independently. Some people are now managing to think about the educationally unthinkable—the notion that much of what a student learns in college is not learned in a classroom. Students tell us that one thing they want from the institution is some system for helping them integrate the insights they are getting outside the classroom with regular instruction. Related to this is new interest in the advisory role of the faculty member. Although extremely hard to assess, some institutions have concluded that the advising of students is an essential component of the faculty member's role.

In general, it appears that assessment *only* for the purpose of tenure decisions is giving way to the idea that assessment should be used to help improve teaching performance, whether or not the individual has tenure. This means that tenured faculty (if the institution maintaining tenure) should go through exactly the same assessment process as the nontenured faculty member, in order that his teaching may be improved as well. The assessment system should be based primarily upon the notion that *all* teachers want to improve and that the institution has a vital stake in facilitating such improvements.

Growth Contract

Some institutions are now turning to the concept of individualized learning contracts as an effective way of helping the student define his objectives and assess attainment. Contracts are written both at the individual course and at the four-year program level. At the course level, the instructor indicates what resources can be made available to help the student reach his goals and concurs on procedures for evaluating the student's progress. At the end of the quarter or semester there are no questions about evaluation, as the procedures were written into the contract earlier. Various high schools and junior colleges have been using this approach for several years, both within a single course structure and as a device for planning a student's entire program. (At Ottawa University, the New College at the University of Alabama, at Empire State in New York, and at Hampshire, students work with a "primary advising committee" made up of faculty, another student at times, and outside experts in the student's field, to develop an over-all program. They also have individual course contracts in certain areas.)

The next step, now being tried at a number of institutions, is growth contracts for faculty. This device is designed to undercut the traditional view that once tenure is granted the institution expects no further improvement in teaching effectiveness. Under this system, every faculty member states, at four- to five-year intervals, his personal goals for the next interval. There are no one-year initial appointments; the new faculty member is given three or four years in which to accomplish the goals indicated in his initial contract. Even when used concurrently with a tenure system, faculty growth contracts intrude a vital new dimension: the institution *expects* faculty to grow and change during their stay, and helps them accomplish it.

There are a number of interesting dimensions to this approach. Rather than pulling the faculty apart, as the traditional tenure system often does, the growth contract and its evaluation should operate to pull the faculty together since *all* participate as colleagues in the best sense (partners in a joint enterprise).

Also, this practice can be instituted without waiting for settlement of the tenure debate, as it is not a substitute for tenure and could be made compatible with any existing system. (It would be hard to imagine a tenured professor objecting to a request by the institution paying his salary for a statement of both what he would like to do during the next five years of his professional life and how his progress in these areas should be evaluated.) Indeed, there are many departments already operating in the contract mode for both junior and senior faculty, in which the chairman discusses with each member of the department what he would like to accomplish in the next period, states what objectives, as well as what evaluative procedures might be effective given his individualized pattern of aspirations and goals. The document becomes an agreement by both parties, subject to mutually agreeable modification. In many respects, too, the system can be implemented more quickly and easily at the departmental rather than the institutional level, allaying any anxiety that the new practice is another administrative plot.

In addition to such matters as developing materials for a new course, faculty often mention the desire to acquire more skills in group processes, devising student evaluation procedures, or in taking courses in areas they have never studied. It appears that faculty members are open to the prospect of designing a "five-year plan" dedicated to *their* individual growth. Nothing is being forced on the faculty member; his only new obligation is to the concept of planning for personal and professional growth. And, of course, when he does so those responsible for the development of the institution will acquire a better base for their own planning, will have a clearer notion of faculty goals and expectations, and can work to meet them on a systematic basis.

One final virtue of the contract idea is that it tends to undercut the "squeaky wheel" style of campus governance, in which the needs of those who make the most noise are met. Instead, everyone is encouraged to make his wishes known and to develop a plan for attaining at least some of them. Early indications suggest that the approach has genuine promise and deserves to be tried out at a number of institutions. It is one of the few procedures in which the techniques of assessment are consistent with educational objectives.

There will undoubtedly be problems with this new approach. It will be easier to implement in small schools and departments than in a major university department of over one hundred persons. In addition, it would seem to be in conflict with the American Federation of Teachers (AFT) contract, which has little or no concern for differences in goals or practices within the union. It is not yet known whether the growth contract arrangement could be established in a college or university engaged in collective bargaining, groups like the American Association of University Professors (AAUP), who might consider such an approach professionally demeaning. My own feeling is that the widespread adoption of something like the faculty growth contract might help convince the public that college and university teachers really *do* want to improve their professional competence.

At times, the debate over whether or not to continue tenure seems unproductively "academic," in the worst sense of that term. The battle lines, as drawn, polarize everyone. In my opinion, however, tenure has had little effect, for good or ill, on the quality of teaching in American colleges and universities, and we will probably maintain some sort of job security system in higher education. But American society is beginning to ask, "What is being done to improve the quality of teaching in colleges and universities?" To answer that there is nothing to be done, that the tenure system is as far as we can go on quality control, is absurd. The quality of anyone's teaching can be improved in a variety of ways. The enormous impact of management information systems on the classroom teacher has yet to be felt, but it will clearly set up some operational imperatives regarding the "value-added" notion that the faculty member should be doing better the longer he stays. If the professoriate will not tackle this issue because of fear that tenure is the only issue that matters, then academics can be justly accused of lecturing on navigation while the ship is going down.

Chapter 8

Promotion and Good Teaching

Joel G. Magid

The contemporary university, if I may paraphrase Sir Thomas Browne's description of man, is a great amphibian, living in divided and distinguished worlds. Browne's worlds were heaven and earth, soul and body. The worlds of the university are those of abstract intellect, contemplation, and scholarly research, on the one hand, and, on the other, the very mundane classroom world that conveys intellectual values and skills to undergraduates of excellent to average or poor academic backgrounds.

Unfortunately for the student, for the community, and for our society at large, the faculties, and indeed the very structure of many American universities, recognize the fact that they live in divided worlds without recognizing the fact that the second world, the world of teaching, is as distinguished and as important and as necessary for wholeness and integrity as the first world, the world of scholarship. Many academicians trained in scholarship fail to

120

recognize the intellectual and human challenge of working in this second world. For some perverse reason, probably their conditioning in graduate school, many faculty members actually resent being asked or expected to operate as teachers as well as scholars. These faculty members argue for an expansion of the first world, for greatly increased graduate programs, and for relief from the demands of teaching undergraduates, particularly undergraduates with poor academic backgrounds.

Our colleges have recently been forced to recognize their responsibilities to the under-educated and poorly educated. Many of our students—regular or special entrance—come from urban and rural communities whose educational systems are poor to awful. Other students, who come to us from excellent suburban high schools, seem to be increasingly skeptical about the intellectual values traditionally espoused by our colleges. To teach both kinds of students well requires a commitment in time and emotional and intellectual energy, a willingness to experiment with new ways of organizing the classroom experience, an openness to the redefinition and reorganization of subject matter, and, perhaps most importantly, a belief that teaching these students is a worthwhile, distinguished profession. It is difficult, although not impossible, for a teacher to feel this commitment, willingness, openness, and belief when he operates in a system that denies the value of this job by failing to recognize and reward it. In too many of our schools, no matter what official policy may say, no matter what pious senior faculty may repeat, it is made clear to junior faculty that the way to promotion must be paved with publications, that spending too much time on or with students is a form of occupational suicide.

In a system in which promotion usually means the granting of tenure, there is a natural desire on the part of those making promotion decisions for some kind of certainty, some evaluation or measurement process that can be deemed reliable and objective. This striving towards certainty, towards a system of evaluation that can be based on some sort of measurable evidence, is a bureaucrat's wet dream of paradise; such a striving runs counter to almost every significant development in twentieth-century intellectual life, from Heisenberg's uncertainty principle in physics to the new novel to studies in linguistics and educational theory. We need a system of evaluation that depends on personal knowledge of a candidate, a system that doesn't mistake the measurable for the significant, a system that seeks out those contributions that will indicate the candidate's ability to grow and develop in an uncertain and changing academic world.

The following recommendations aim at implementing already existing policy in many universities by defining ways of recognizing the importance of teaching and service for promotion. These suggestions do not attempt to denigrate the world of scholarship and its values; they do attempt to give equality and strength and more representation to the minority group on campus that considers teaching its primary responsibility. My proposals, however, are not limited to matters concerning promotion; most of my suggestions are oriented towards an improvement in the quality of education provided by our undergraduate colleges.

(1) College appointment, reappointment, and promotion committees should be stacked in favor of good teaching. Since there is bound to be disagreement about what good teaching is, the committee should be open to differing voices selected by different constituencies. Suggested methods of stacking: the dean, who usually appoints some members of such committees, should appoint faculty on the basis of their reputation as good teachers (in the hope that good teachers will recognize other good teachers); students should elect faculty to the committee from a slate drawn up by the student government; if politically possible, and on many campuses it isn't because of irrational faculty fears, students should elect their voting members to the committee; faculty should elect their representatives to the committee. Each of the interested groups—administration, students, and faculty—should choose an equal number of committee members. In addition, the dean should have the right to appoint up to two additional members to the committee if he is convinced by the petition of a group of faculty (women, blacks) that the committee needs additional voices to reflect the opinions of faculty who have usually been bypassed by the committee. By broadening the composition of such committees in this manner, a college can at once democratize the evaluation process and assert its commitment to recognizing and rewarding good teaching.

(2) Each candidate for promotion should be invited by the

promotions committee to submit a written brief in his own behalf. Such a brief would give the candidate a chance to define his own strong points, some of which his department may have ignored in making its recommendations. The candidate would be expected to demonstrate his intellectual vitality (including unpublished as well as published efforts), his service to department and college, and his contributions to teaching (both in his classes and in his department); more on this below.

(3) When evaluating candidates for reappointment or promotion, the college committee should publicize the names of all those being considered that year and should request confidential letters from all members of a candidate's department as well as from any other faculty who may wish to express an opinion on a candidate. Such letters will democratize recommendations, will force faculty to define criteria for such recommendations (a formula letter will be, I hope, unimpressive and unconvincing), and will minimize the influence of those faculty opposed to a candidate for personal or political reasons. To minimize the chance that such letters would be leaked and cause personal animosities among the faculty, the letters should be destroyed at the end of each academic year if no review proceedings have been instituted. Similarly, the names of all candidates for reappointment or promotion should be publicized in the student newspaper with students invited to write to the committee about any teacher being considered. As in (1) above, by allowing for as many evaluators as possible, the college will focus attention on the evaluation process and on the effectiveness of a teacher among his students and colleagues.

(4) As a matter of simple courtesy and human decency, the aura of secrecy which surrounds promotion recommendations must be ended. Candidates for promotion should be informed of any decision—by the department, by the college committee, or by the administration—within a week after that decision has been made. The candidate should also be entitled to a formal statement of the reasons given for any negative decision.

(5) A truly good teacher should have an impact on his colleagues as well as on his students. All colleges should regularly publish an inexpensive, mimeographed newsletter-journal for faculty in which faculty could share ideas about teaching. Although this

publication could also reprint articles from other journals, it would operate primarily as an internal organ dealing with practical, psychological, and theoretical discussions of teaching at the college. Faculty could also use this opportunity to test out theories and articles they might later want to submit to national journals. Publication of such a newsletter-journal could do much to improve teaching and would certainly help faculty get to know each other better. Candidates for promotion could use publication in this journal as evidence of their qualities as students of education and as teachers. The promotions committee should certainly consider such evidence in their deliberations on a candidate.

(6) In addition to publication in the journal described above, candidates can also be judged by their contributions to student journals. This does not mean that faculty should usurp space in either student magazines and newspapers or both. It does mean, however, that faculty should actively contribute to intellectual life out of the classroom by contributing to student publications that request such contributions. Too often publication is aimed at a distant and unknown audience. When a faculty member publishes on campus, both students and faculty know where he is to found and can discuss his work with him. This can be exhilarating for both author and reader, and can serve to foster a greater sense of community on campus. Faculty members who make such contributions to campus intellectual life should have those contributions recognized by the committee on promotions.

(7) Many faculty members think an ideal teaching schedule is one that allows them to be away from the campus as much as possible. A college that values *and rewards* teaching should expect faculty whose primary responsibility is teaching and working with students to be on campus at least four days a week, thus enabling the faculty member to schedule additional office hours for student conferences and to attend and participate in more campus activities and meetings.

(8) Scholarly work and the intellectual vitality of the faculty should be reflected on the campus as well as in scholarly journals or books. Every department should be expected to have fairly regular faculty seminars in which faculty can present to their colleagues work they are engaged in or, simply, reflections on the state of their

discipline. Similarly, a lecture series for students and faculty will enable faculty to share their interests with others, and the pressure of presenting one's interests to a live audience will defeat the stultifying triviality of much that passes for scholarship. Such lectures would also give senior faculty an opportunity to evaluate the quality of mind and intellectual vigor of a nontenured colleague. It should be remembered, though, that a lecture need not draw a large audience to be successful; a university should not be governed by Nielsen ratings.

(9) In order to prevent a faculty member from becoming repetitive and overly specialized, departments should discourage teachers of undergraduates from teaching the same advanced course for more than three consecutive years. Teachers, in fact, should be encouraged to teach outside of their immediate field of specialization. The excitement of learning, of working up a new course, will enable the teacher to grow intellectually and will prevent him from forgetting what the problems of learning are for someone who hasn't spent years studying a subject. Teaching outside of his specialty, a teacher should naturally come to rely more on his colleagues' knowledge and experiences—thus fostering better communication, more intellectual exchange, and a greater sense of community among faculty. In evaluating a candidate for promotion, both the department and the committee on promotions can give considerable weight to the number and kind of courses a teacher has taught, particularly those he may have originated.

(10) Students should have the right to evaluate their teachers, and that right must be respected by teachers and administrators. Student evaluations, though, should not be used absolutely; such evaluations should be a part of the evidence considered by departmental and college committees on promotion. Since literature on the efficacy of various methods of student evaluations is readily available, I will express only some brief reservations about some of these methods. Reliance on evaluations of graduating majors in a department does not provide for recognition of the teacher who works well with beginning students. Since our colleges are accepting more and more special entrance students, teachers who can work well with these students must be encouraged and rewarded. Reliance on evaluations of honors students does not recognize that teacher

who can reach the average student, a far more difficult task than reaching the better student. Computerized and formal evaluations have some validity, a validity that is, however, minimized by the controlling effect of the language in which the questions are presented to a student. But a carefully-written annual evaluation form for all students is probably the fairest and most accurate gauge of student opinion.

One possibility for student evaluation that has not received much discussion, probably because it is an administrative nightmare: every year the committee on promotions should request from each student a letter defining the good and bad points of any teacher he may have. The advantages of such a system: students who take the trouble to fill out such a form are probably those most interested in educational questions and therefore should have more thoughtful opinions; responses are individualized so that every student will be forced to think about and define his own educational values; teachers whose popularity is based primarily on easy grading, a sense of humor, a failure to make intellectual demands upon the student, and so forth, will not come out as well in letters as in a formal questionnaire.

(11) Universities should augment their education programs significantly. So many communities need so much help that an education program oriented towards these needs and using the local secondary school system as a laboratory should be of the highest priority. If such a program realistically faces the problems of teaching, it will serve to improve teaching quality in the whole school by helping the rest of the faculty to find ways of teaching students from such an environment. A competent education department should be educating the faculty as well as the student body.

Since teaching is learning, departments, in conjunction with an expanded education department, should establish programs in which students can earn academic money—credits—by teaching in special programs in the local school system and in the college's own remedial or introductory programs. (This does not imply that teaching remedial or elementary courses is work for amateurs; rather, students in such programs need as much help as they can get, and this help should come from other students as well as from faculty.) Even tutors, for instance, can learn a lot about education if they keep a journal of their tutoring experiences and if they meet regularly with a faculty member to discuss the problems of teaching.

(12) Every department should maintain an updated reading list on problems in and suggestions for teaching in general and in that department in particular. This list would be particularly valuable for new teachers, but most faculty could also benefit from it. One of the greatest ironies of the academic world is that it is made up of and produces scholars who have little or no knowledge of the scholarship on teaching in their own field. As director of freshman English, I asked the members of my department on three separate occasions for titles to include in such a bibliography; I received one response from a department of over forty. And administrators have been no better than teachers in encouraging discussion of teaching; when I circulated among freshman English staff a little booklet I had written about teaching our required course, I was told that I was the first director of freshman English to be interested in the psychology of teaching instead of busying himself exclusively with administrative details.

(13) Intelligent and creative administration of an academic program is a major scholarly act of teaching and research and should be recognized as such. "Creative" administration of a freshman English program, for instance, would include publication of a bibliography and guide for teachers, circulation of ideas about teaching composition, supervision and advice to teachers, informing teachers about programs in other schools, innovations in the program to meet the needs of students entering the school through special programs, and encouraging communication and cooperation among teachers working in the program,

(14) Every year the president should expect the dean of the college to report on what the college has done to promote good teaching and the problems it still faces. The dean, in turn, should expect every department chairman to report to him annually on what has been done within the department to improve teaching and other student services. If the administration of the school honestly calls for such reports on the status of teaching in the academic community, the department chairmen and the committee on promotion will begin to recognize and reward those teachers whose primary commitment is to teaching.

The above proposals will have meaning only if the administration provides a dynamic and creative leadership that makes it clear that working in the classroom and academic community is as important as working in the scholarly journals. Such a commitment to education must be more than a paper commitment, more than a holy incantation of the virtues of good teaching; it must reward those who put their time and emotional and intellectual energies into the job. Although most colleges and universities claim to be interested in scholarly objectivity, many of these schools have refused to face the difficult problem of evaluating and rewarding good teaching. Measuring a scholar's bibliography has been easier, less demanding intellectually, than measuring a teacher's effectiveness. The above proposals suggest several kinds of evidence that can be used in evaluation of teaching; I hope that more colleges, in recognizing their obligation to teach whoever is there to teach, will begin to meet the intellectual challenge of defining criteria for the evaluation of teaching and of making value judgments based on those criteria.

Chapter **9**

Faculty
Unionism

William F. McHugh

‌

It was Holmes who observed that the lifeblood of the law is experience.[1] This is true of the collective bargaining process. While there are emerging patterns, experience in college and university collective bargaining is meager, and conclusions about its impact on tenure are necessarily speculative. It is simple enough to set out in a few conclusive pages an assessment of the impact. However, there is merit in treating the question in a more generalized context in order to establish a logical pattern and to lend a perspective of understanding that will stimulate the reader to relate the general conclusions to his own experience and institution. To that end this chapter is divided into three parts. The first focuses on the causes of faculty unionism and its recent trends; the second upon the elementary and relevant characteristics of both the collective bargain-

[1] O. W. Holmes, *The Common Law* (Boston: Little, Brown, 1938), p. 1.

ing process and a tenure system; the third develops conclusions relating to the dynamics between the collective bargaining process and tenure.

Causes

Whereas the decade of the sixties was a time of student confrontation, the seventies will be the hallmark for increased tension in faculty-university relationships. Depending upon the circumstances, this tension could result in a mass movement toward unionism akin to the spread of schoolteacher unionism.

For the past thirty years or so our colleges and universities[2] have been undergoing a remarkable reformation,[3] resulting in a fundamental shift of emphasis in terms of what is expected of today's academic institutions, their purposes and responsibilities. While there are many equally significant forces at work, only two specific factors which have given rise to increased tensions in faculty-institutional relationships will be emphasized here: first, the full-scale assumption by the universities of government-sponsored research and social action programs which have been directly related, perhaps at times subservient, to the needs of government and business and a fast changing society; and second, the full-scale egalitarian commitment to the ideal of mass higher education resulting in large concentrations on campus of undergraduate and graduate students with heterogeneous backgrounds, needs, and life-styles. These two factors have been instrumental in bringing about over the past few decades a truly phenomenal change in our academic institutions. Sponsored research and the development of institutional public service capabilities have directly integrated the academic institution with society with the result that the institution

[2] Caution should be used throughout: "Colleges and universities" include a wide variety of institutions, ranging from community colleges and technical schools to large urban universities. Therefore, the reader must ask what type of institution is meant, given the context of discussion.

[3] R. Nisbet, *The Degradation of the Academic Dogma,* (New York: Basic Books, 1971), p. 13. This superb book brings a clear historical perspective to problems in higher education.

has taken on some of the characteristics of business and governmental enterprises.

Today's colleges and universities engage in such diverse
activities as: research on wild duck diseases; learning abilities of
preschoolers; continuing education programs for the unemployed;
pest control; medical and space research; advising federal and
local government on air pollution; training programs for corporate
executives; operational affiliations with teaching hospitals; governmental programs for the disadvantaged; joint programs with foreign
universities; student study groups in Washington; educational TV
programs; sustaining performing arts troupes; maintaining museums;
or operating the equivalent of a modest-sized publishing house.
Perhaps the seed was sown by the Morrill Act,[4] passed under
Lincoln's administration, which gave rise to the land-grant colleges
and their agricultural extension programs. Chemistry and economics became relevant to the agricultural interests seeking to
modernize and adjust to the prospect of feeding a fast-growing and
technically oriented society. Today an academic institution might
be responsible for operating an agricultural extension service, hotel
school, or an industrial labor relations school as a part of its public
service function. University professors draw up regulations for
public agencies, sit on governmental agency boards or research
corporations, periodically hold governmental positions, or serve in
advisory roles to business corporations. They run, coordinate, or
work in university-sponsored research programs. Such programs
and the complexity of the institution itself have brought upon the
campus large numbers of auxiliary specialists or nonteaching professionals, ranging from financial experts; TV technicians; coun-
selors; admissions, computer, and financial aid specialists; research
technicians; and many others.

Barzun said: "No adequate idea of the incessantly buzzing
and booming academic grove, the harsh orchestration resulting
from the disparate purposes carried on there can be derived from
generalities. . . . Nothing short of enumeration will suggest the
size of the structure or the complexity of the effort. And even then,

[4] Act of July 2, 1862, Ch. 130, 12 Stat. 503 (now U.S. Code
1964, Title 7, §301 et seq.).

the very act of setting items down on paper introduces an order which falsifies the inevitable confusion."[5] And Kerr named the new and distinctive multi-purpose institution the "multiversity."[6] There are hybrid institutions which fall somewhat short of the multiversity because of limitations in size and capabilities, which have firmer roots in the undergraduate liberal arts tradition. Yet even these have broken in part from the more traditional academic model and share many of the multiversity characteristics. Other institutions have retained their strong undergraduate and liberal arts character and have changed relatively little over the years. But the faculty in even these last two classes of institutions have been influenced by the multiversity.

Add to Kerr's multiversity another institution which could be labeled a megaversity: a pluralistic multicampus system. With the exception of the University of California the notion of a state megaversity system comprised of a variety of institutions in a multi-campus structure and under the influence of a single or multiple governing board arrangement has gained acceptance in only the last decade or two. New York, Illinois, Missouri, and Florida are examples, and to a lesser degree and still in developmental stages are systems in Connecticut, Pennsylvania, Massachusetts, Wisconsin, and Maine. The State University of New York system under a single board of trustees has a faculty of fifteen thousand, almost a quarter of a million students, two thousand programs, twenty thousand course offerings, and includes agricultural and technical campuses, university centers, liberal arts colleges, and medical centers. Variants on this theme can be found in the multi-campus systems of community colleges in Chicago or systems of state teacher and liberal arts colleges in Illinois, New Jersey, and Pennsylvania.

These institutions are a product of not only large-scale commitment to sponsored research and social action programs but the egalitarian commitment to mass higher education—in the broad sense of providing advanced career training, research experience, and other self-development goals—*in addition to* traditional schol-

[5] J. Barzun, *The American University: How It Runs and Where It Is Going* (New York: Harper and Row, 1968), p. 13.

[6] C. Kerr, *The Uses of the University* (New York: Harper and Row, 1963), Chap. 1.

arly preparation and academic pursuits. This national commitment to individual self-development is expressed in Gardner's dictum that "we must seek excellence in a context of concern for all"[7] and has brought to the nation's campuses a staggering host of students with multiple needs on a scale which would have been nearly unthinkable thirty years ago. It has been evidenced by tremendous financial commitments by the federal government with respect to building, scholarships, and other programs. Many states have allocated Midas-sized budgets and capital expenditures to their public universities to meet exploding enrollments. Financed in whole or in part by state, city, and county governments, community colleges unrooted in any tradition, have multiplied like hamsters.

The rapid change which has taken place in the contemporary academic scene has caused in some institutions an ungluing of traditional relationships and created serious distortions. One observer has remarked that it requires little gift of prophecy to be able to imagine a future of almost limitless dislocation of academic structure, rules, functions, and authority.[8]

Conflict and Confrontation. Due in part to the academic reformation, the last decade has seen practically an institutionalization of conflict within the nation's academic institutions. The politics of confrontation has bred attitudes of mistrust among the constituent parts, and the persistent demands for evangelistic commitment to causes and reform have not nurtured attitudes of congeniality or tolerance. There has been violent discord over matters ranging from curriculum ("relevance"), student "rights," and research to fundamental governance and indeed the very uses of the university itself. The *New York Times* has displayed photos of Columbia professors unceremoniously lowering themselves from the office windows of "liberated buildings." Despite high-minded matters of academic freedom, some campuses during the roaring sixties were more dangerous on occasion than walking the freeway at midnight. Perhaps a redeeming feature has been the unintentional wealth of Marx Brothers comedy on campus.

[7] J. W. Gardner, *Excellence: Can We Be Equal and Excellent Too?* (New York: Harper and Row, 1961)
[8] Nisbet, p. 17.

The profound shift from Gemeinschaft to Gesellschaft has been accompanied by a cult of individual authority, with everybody "doing their thing." The academic community seems no longer bound together by a value system centered on scholarship and teaching but by interests with inflated talk of student power, women's power, faculty power, and so on. There has followed in the wake of sit-ins and riots a deluge of student rights court cases. Due process has been more popular than sex. It is not uncommon today for student governments and organizations to retain lawyers for the express purpose of challenging institutional policies on matters ranging from admissions and expulsions to the use of institutional funds. The spirit of confrontation is not new to younger faculty whose major experience with academic life was in the sixties. Nor is it new to those who were graduate students and are now entering the academic ranks.

Why are some shocked at faculty unionism on the grounds that it is conflict oriented? Admittedly, times have calmed, but the sixties left an endowment of collective attitudes amenable to systems designed for adversary relationships.

Has the temper of our times ordained the democratization of today's university? The notion of higher education as a privilege tempered the nature of the proprietary sense in it once held by the students. However, when education is viewed as a right of the citizenry and directly related to the economy and social mobility, it features a totally different view of one's place and role in the institution. This is manifest in the increased student pressure for participation in academic senates, departmental affairs, curriculum matters, and, in some cases, the heretofore jealously guarded faculty evaluative process itself. This egalitarian spirit, embalmed in phrases like "participatory democracy," has created a fundamental tension with the aristocratic university tradition, rooted in medieval times and so long associated with our great academic institutions.[9] The concept of faculty as an autonomous guild, and privileged enclave with special rights and prerogatives, is implicitly challenged by the premises underlying the student movement. I speculate that many

[9] Nisbet, Chap. 1, pp. 87, 101.

of the older faculty view student participation as an intrusion upon faculty prerogatives. Consultation yes, but formal structuring into academic committees as equals, no!

It is no doubt an understatement to say that the older and more traditional forms of governance and communication, so dependent upon a consensus of shared values, broke down in face of the needs and stresses triggered by the student confrontations of the sixties. Substantial restructuring of traditional governance models became an addiction, and the general thrust has been in the direction of senates or assemblies representative of the entire academic community: faculty; students; paraprofessionals; blue collar; administrators; and so on. On some campuses student participation has been increased to almost fifty-fifty in the academic councils or senates. There have been efforts at ombudsman arrangments and even extending formal student representation to boards of trustees. This revamping has usually been accompanied by the elimination of the older forms and structures; they have not always been matched by effective substitutes. At some institutions the indiscriminate tinkering with traditional faculty governance machinery has left the faculty qua faculty, without a university-wide forum for policy expression unencumbered by nonfaculty. In other institutions, where there has been some success at restructuring governance, the glue is not yet dry, and it remains to be seen whether they will work under stress. One of the paradoxes of faculty unionism is that while it is democratic in one sense, it has many of the guild features associated with traditional faculty organization. Because it is based upon interest group representation, it leaves out students, who do not share a community of interest with the faculty. In this sense, it meets the student challenge to faculty autonomy. It concerns itself with economic and policy considerations tied particularly to faculty interests and provides a well-defined forum for expression of faculty "rights," which are expressly hammered out in a contract. A review of organizational campaign literature bears this argument out with its emphasis upon job security, control over faculty personnel matters, consultative rights in university decision-making, departmental autonomy, etc.

Thus, unionism may well appeal to the more conservative

and traditional elements of a faculty[10] as a reaffirmation of the faculty guild concept in the face of student pressures. Faculty unionism may result in a collision course with the newly emerging tripartite governance patterns, and avoidance of this possibility will be a priority when unionism comes to campus.[11]

Another element of the attack on faculty autonomy is suggested by O'Neil (see following chapter): the disenchantment of the general public, state legislatures, and alumni with the professoriate is a factor to be reckoned with. It is not fair to say this is purely reactionary or punitive. Prestigious national commissions on student unrest have emphasized the need to tighten up university administration and eliminate peripheral service activities.[12] They have criticized the autonomous baronies of schools, faculties, and centers for not having fulfilled fundamental responsibilities to undergraduate education.[13] The notion that teaching has suffered at the expense of grantsmanship or that universities have become staging areas for faculty careers has currency both within and without the academy.[14] There is increasing pressure for curriculums more responsive to the size and multiple needs of today's student body. There is criticism that undergraduate education has suffered at the expense of graduate education with too many irrelevant courses and restrictive curriculums. There is mounting pressure to improve teaching methodology and to develop a system for assessing teacher performance and teaching accountability. There is emerging a widespread reevaluation of, if not attack on, faculty tenure.

This general disaffection is shared by students, legislatures, educators, parents, and the general public. Under certain circumstances, these factors may well be manifested by punitive external attacks on vested faculty interests, driving faculty allegience to the

[10] I have been impressed with the large number of older men in the leadership positions of the various faculty unions during the election period at SUNY.

[11] See W. McHugh, "Collective Bargaining and the College Student," *Journal of Higher Education*, 1971, 62(3), pp. 175–185.

[12] See *Cox Commission Report on the Crisis at Columbia*, pp. 33–34.

[13] *Cox Commission Report*, pp. 23, 32, 33, 35.

[14] *Cox Commission Report*, p. 31. See also the *Scranton Report*, conclusion sections, and Nisbet, pp. 71–111.

external organizations willing or able to resist them. The willingness of faculty to unionize in defense will be in proportion to the severity and character of these attacks.

Economic Restrictions and Pressures to "Manage." Another cause of faculty unionism, and perhaps the most significant, is the current economic condition of our institutions. Hardly a day goes by when one doesn't hear about the need for greater productivity and accountability. For the first time in recent memory there is a movement toward major academic program retrenchment. The lowering of graduate enrollment projections in certain fields and the corresponding program cut-backs, together with the shrinkage of faculty positions on a large scale, place further tension on faculty-university relations.[15] For the first time in almost two decades job security is of major concern to many faculty. Reallocation of resources and decisions affecting program cuts will become increasingly critical. There is a growing popular belief that to provide the proper balancing of equities and the best use of resources in order to serve the public, universities will have to be "managed" like the industrial giants, like big government.

The increased financial responsibility for public higher education assumed by state and local governments has created a trend toward structuring an orderly and rational approach for allocating resources. Hence, the recent consolidation of existing institutions and the creation of master boards with budget and planning supervision over regular or multi-campus governing boards, or central governing boards with direct authority over day-to-day operations. This has paralleled the "efficiency, economy, and planning" movement in state and local governments[16] where the effort is to establish management and fiscal control of state agencies. The upshot of all this is a partial shift in the locus of decision-making to not only the university or college governing board but to other levels of public managerial authority in the executive and legislative branches. These offices, of course, may greatly influence or even

[15] Overextended teacher education programs at state teacher colleges which are in transition to liberal arts colleges with some graduate expansion.

[16] M. Moos and F. Rourke, *The Campus and the State* (Baltimore: Johns Hopkins Press, 1959), pp. 68, 43–69.

dominate educational issues and major budgetary considerations.

In private institutions, institutional survival may well depend upon a greater type of managerial control over the internal decision-making and budget process customary in a business enterprise. The authority to do this is ready-made, for the organic statutes and charters for most colleges and universities provide for the establishment of boards of trustees and allocate to them the *legal power* to make all major policy decisions and to appoint and dismiss faculty personnel. Improperly handled, the management psychosis can widen the growing gap between faculty and administration and create some interesting nonsequiturs. "If you are going to treat us as mere employees, we must unionize to prevent it."

The current fiscal crunch will force a reexamination of some fundamental premises behind faculty-university relations which have been taken for granted over the past decades. The pressures of mass higher education and current economic realities have now aroused talk of the open university, degrees by examination, dramatic changes in time necessary to satisfy degree requirements, increased individualized off-campus study programs. Plans for such programs are sometimes accompanied with implicit attacks upon traditional academic schemes in which the faculty have vested interests. Pursued on a large scale, new programs will call for greater use of TV, tapes, and cassettes; supervision of off-campus study programs with greater emphasis on interdisciplinary cooperation; new schemes of faculty compensation and incentives; redefinition of workload, curriculum content, and admission standards and requirements. These projects are already being undertaken, but the pace and scale will increase.

The contemporary academic institution has emerged as a powerful influence, if an unpopular and expensive one, with a substantial concentration of resources and multipurpose capability. It has become a major producer, wholesaler, and retailer in the knowledge industry and is inextricably related to national growth and the well-being of society.[17] It has become, too, a major instrument

[17] Kerr, p. 114. Kerr quotes (p. 126) Whitehead's observation: "In the conditions of modern life, the rule is absolute: the race which does not value trained intelligence is doomed. Not all your heroism, not all your social charm, not all your wit, not all your victories on

of social purpose. The yoke of technology and the requirement of responding to government programs have placed a premium upon administrative and institutional adaptability. Pressures by a now-heterogeneous student body for supermarket offerings tailored to individual needs add to the burden. The tremendous size of the states' financial commitment to public institutions combined with economic restrictions has resulted in an increasing tendency for governmental control over the university decision-making process and the allocation of its resources, especially in the case of state-operated multicampus systems. These economic forces will call for dramatic changes. Institutional responses to these various pressures are likely (depending upon their character) to be viewed by faculty as an attack on faculty sovereignty and its heretofore favored status. It is likely to encourage faculty at some institutions to seek unionism as the major means of protecting and representing their interests.

External Organizations and Right to Bargain. In a recent survey,[18] 60,477 faculty members were asked their opinion of the following statement: "Collective bargaining by faculty members has no place in a college or university." The results showed that 19.1 per cent agreed strongly, 23.5 per cent agreed with reservation, 33.7 per cent disagreed with reservation, and 20.4 per cent disagreed strongly. Thus, 54.1 per cent of those surveyed believe that collective bargaining by faculty members has at least some proper role in a college or university. As of July 1, 1971, faculty were unionized at approximately 130 colleges and universities;[19] the majority of these were public community colleges.

The rapid growth of collective bargaining in some of the

---

land or sea can move back the finger of fate Today we maintain ourselves. Tomorrow science will have moved forward yet one more step, and there will be no appeal from the judgment which will be pronounced on the uneducated." Kerr concluded: "These are the uses of the university."

[18] These figures are from an unpublished survey conducted as part of a project of the Carnegie Commission on Higher Education. Part of the survey was reported in the *Chronicle of Higher Education,* April 6, 1970.

[19] Course materials distributed at the Conference on Faculty Unionism, Institute of Continuing Legal Education, University of Michigan, Ann Arbor, September 1971, p. 292.

nation's public institutions suggests a spread of epidemic proportions to other institutions across the land. For example, New York's Taylor Law authorized collective bargaining by public employees in the fall of 1967. In three years, thirty-two of thirty-eight community colleges in New York were operating under negotiated contracts. Chicago's junior college system operates under a city-wide collective bargaining agreement, and nearly all of the community colleges in Michigan are organized. But this is not restricted to community colleges. In June 1972 the full- and part-time faculty together with the nonteaching professional employees of the City University of New York comprising thirteen institutions, seven of which are four-year liberal arts institutions, voted to have one bargaining unit represented by one bargaining agent to replace the previous agreements with the National Education Association (NEA) for full-time professionals and with the American Federation of Teachers (AFT) for part-time professionals. The new bargaining agent, the Professional Staff Congress, is the result of a merger of the NEA affiliate legislative conference and the AFT affiliate. New York State's Public Employment Relations Board ordered a system-wide representation election for all the professional staff in the state's system of higher education, the State University of New York (SUNY), which was won by the NEA-backed Senate Professional Association. A state-wide contract was negotiated effective August, 1971. The twenty-six SUNY campuses and their fifteen thousand professionals will be governed by the system-wide collective bargaining agreement. A collective bargaining agreement (NEA backed) has been negotiated for New Jersey's multicampus state college system, and the Rutgers University faculty (AAUP) negotiated a salary package with the Rutgers administration. Central Michigan University has completed its second contract with its faculty bargaining agent (NEA backed). The faculty of Oakland University in Michigan elected the AAUP as its bargaining agent; negotiations stalled with a strike in September 1971, but agreement was reached by early 1972. A representation decision from the Michigan Employment Relations Commission involving Wayne State University faculty and professional staff resulted in a victory by the AAUP (615 to 586) over the AFT.

Pennsylvania's law giving public employees the right to

bargain became effective July 1, 1971. A state-wide October 1971 election has already been won in the Pennsylvania state teacher college system by an NEA affiliate. Knowledgeable observers are watching Temple, Pittsburgh, and Penn State to see if the faculties there will opt for unionism. Organizational efforts are already underway in many of Pennsylvania's community colleges.

The recently-passed Hawaiian statute specifically authorizes collective bargaining in Hawaii University's multicampus system, and observers there speculate that an election is likely in late 1971 or early 1972. Although Illinois does not as yet have a comprehensive collective bargaining statute for public employees, there has been organizational activity at Northern Illinois University and Southern Illinois University. But as of September 1971 there has been no election. Legislation in Florida permitting public employee collective bargaining, including the faculty in Florida's University system, barely missed passage in 1971.

Before turning to the private experience, some general observations on the public institutions are in order. The majority of negotiated contracts and the spread of faculty unionism have taken place in states which have passed laws authorizing public employee bargaining and in states where state or local public employees, especially school teachers, have in fact organized. While there are no specific comparative studies, there seems to be a definite carry-over from school teacher unionism to college faculty unionism, especially to community college faculty. Some observe that gloomy predictions of the deprofessionalization of school teachers have not been borne out. On the contrary, the argument is that school teacher unionism has resulted in increased professionalism through greater participation in educational policy matters heretofore reserved to the school boards. Moreover, the economic gains achieved by school teachers through unionism have been substantial. Another argument is that public faculty unionism is a matter of practical necessity in order to insure a faculty base for maintaining an equitable distribution of resources among competing public employees. If state workers in other public agencies are organizing, shouldn't faculty organize to protect their own collective interests?[20]

[20] This argument was frequently advanced in faculty discus-

If limited experience indicates that the passage of laws authorizing bargaining in public institutions has promoted unionism, it is reasonable to assume that the recent assertion of jurisdiction by the National Labor Relations Board over nonprofit colleges and universities will have a comparable effect upon private institutions. The landmark decision (involving nonfaculty staff at Syracuse and Cornell universities) now authorizes collective negotiations under the National Labor Relations Act by faculty in private colleges and universities across the nation. The NLRB decision does not cover public institutions, which are specifically excluded under the National Labor Relations Act and governed by state laws. The Cornell decision was quickly followed by similar decisions at C. W. Post and the Brooklyn Center of Long Island University and at Fordham University.[21] These decisions dispel any doubt that faculties in private colleges and universities have the right to unionize. The Brooklyn Center is presently negotiating with AFT. St. John's University has already negotiated a collective bargaining agreement with AAUP and an independent faculty association. Scranton University of Pennsylvania has negotiated an agreement with its faculty.

The spread of faculty unionism, as should be obvious, has been due in part to the efforts of three national external organizations (AFT, AAUP, NEA) which have actively promoted unionism. For a faculty considering unionism, external organizations have a practical appeal. In the main, they are better equipped to organize and promote collective bargaining than are local senates or traditional governance organizations. As previously noted, some senates are comprised of students or employees who do not share a community of interest with faculty in a collective bargaining sense. Labor relations acts are tied to employment status and will not permit representative organization unless there is a community of interest among those to be represented. Where faculty have no organizational forum, they will frequently turn to an external organization.

Most important, external organizations have money, trained

sions on collective bargaining in SUNY and was a theme in organizational campaign literature.
    [21] *Syracuse and Cornell University*, 183 NLRB 41; *C. W. Post*, 189 NLRB 109; *Long Island University*, 189 NLRB 110.

staff, lawyers, and the other resources necessary to organize, campaign, and utilize the legal machinery of labor acts. Organizing for collective bargaining requires skill, is strenuous, rough and tumble, with a lot of administrative headaches. Independent organizations frequently falter simply because the leadership hasn't the time, expertise, money, or the stomach lining. This is less true of small colleges where the scale of the effort is manageable. External organizations may also choose to stake an internal organization to staff, campaign costs, and other services. Once certified, the in-house organization may either formally affiliate or develop a working relationship. For practical purposes, however, such affiliates become external organizations in the sense the term is used here. That is, they are no longer part of the organic governance structure of the institution.

Finally, external organizations as bargaining agents are willing to represent the particular cause of an individual faculty member. Governance or faculty council machinery is frequently oriented toward achieving group consensus and not to redressing specific individual problems. Many academic institutions simply have no grievance machinery at all.

To oversimplify for a moment, consider the case of X public institution. The campus administration, under intolerable budget and accountability pressures, is frequently placed in the position of having to disseminate "now-hear-this" budget directives. Circumstances are such that it is politically unrealistic for the administration to take pro-faculty positions. Tactics may require maintenance of a low profile with ambivalent public positions while utilizing persuasive behind-the-scenes skills and hard logic with the political decision-makers. To the casual observer on campus, leadership occasionally appears marble-mouthed, if not hare-brained. The upshot is an undermined authority image. Along comes the external organization with a clear, perhaps simplistic faculty-oriented position. If there is a cause celebre on campus involving an individual faculty member (there usually is) all the better; any organization worth its salt will confront injustice.

Initial organizational efforts serve as a catalyst for two or three other organizations on campus, and the affair quickly becomes a matter of organizational one-upsmanship. The litany of the organizational campaigns is clear and to the point. All organizations represent the following to X's faculty with varying emphasis:

We are geared to lobby for the good of education and faculty in the state and national legislative halls and to protect your interests against bills which unilaterally attempt to increase workload, eliminate tenure or sabbatical leaves.

We will guarantee due process in dealings with the administration and preserve academic freedom.

We will see to it that the faculty will be consulted where appropriate and insist upon participation in the institutional decision-making process.

For the first time you will have a meaningful grievance procedure guaranteeing *your* right to challenge arbitrary administrative acts against you with final decision by an impartial third party thereby eliminating unilateral administrative decisions.

We will guard against unreasonable workloads.

Your salaries will be competitive and at the very least keep pace with the cost of living.

Fringe benefits and retirements must be raised to compete with patterns in industry and state government. A man who devotes his entire life to his institution is at least entitled to that.

Facilities, office space, and secretarial services will be improved commensurate with your professional status and standing, etc., etc.

These general themes are played in a barrage of campaign literature, meetings, and seminars and applied to X's particular problems and weaknesses. All of this, of course, is calculated to appeal to X's largest number of faculty. The levels of expectation are quickly raised and, after the past decade of affluence, seem imminently reasonable. The university administrators, busy balancing the budget, are suddenly confronted with the question of whether or not to launch a no-bargaining campaign. (Fordham was one of the first universities to launch such a campaign.) The question may already be answered when X is in a labor state, was the governor's bill, and state policy supports public collective bargaining as a means for promoting stability in public employment. Besides, who can be against academic freedom, better salaries, and participatory democracy, and yes, due process. Finally, the eternal verity is always there: faculty are faculty and cannot be effectively "managed" without a high level of voluntary cooperation, motivation, and professional responsibility. Attempts at antiunion campaigns in some institutions can be disastrous and self-defeating over the long pull if interpreted by the faculty as an antifaculty posture.

These are some of the causes of unionism: a confluence of factors involving institutions with dislocated structures, roles, and authority patterns in dynamic transition, its constituent parts conflict-oriented; attacks upon the professorial guild from within and without; serious economic restrictions involving cut-backs, poor job markets, and external pressures to centralize and manage; the crucial fact of legal authorization and promotion of collective bargaining by external organizations.

Characteristics of Bargaining Process and Tenure System

Bargaining Process. Collective bargaining is a process designed to resolve conflict arising from an employment relationship. It includes two elements: the negotiation of a written contract, and the subsequent establishment of a sound faculty-university relationship. This includes administration of the contract grievance provisions, which are designed to resolve differences over meaning and application in particular instances. But more important, it entails problem oriented consultation and cooperation with the faculty bargaining agent on a number of matters which go beyond the negotiated contract but are germane to the goodwill of the bargaining agent and the support and morale of those it represents. For example, the contract may give the university authorities the unilateral right to cut academic programs and to lay-offs. As a general rule, it would be short-sighted not to consult with the faculty's bargaining agent in a timely manner on such a planned action.

There are four general characteristics of the bargaining process which should be kept in mind. First, it clearly contemplates an *adversary relationship* and assumes a divergence of faculty and institutional interests, raising the possibility of a power struggle. In private and public institutions in states where the strike is authorized (Pennsylvania and Hawaii) the ultimate weapons are the threat of strike, on the one hand, and the willingness to take a strike on the other. In most public institutions where the strike is not authorized, the weapon is more typically the threat of confrontation by resort to an impasse mechanism, culminating in a public fact-finding report which may gain public political support, an important factor in public sector labor relations. Or it may even come to an illegal faculty strike.

Second, implicit in the adversary relationship is the assumption of a *bilateral relationship*. Quite simply, the NLRA and most state collective bargaining laws increase the faculty's legal status by *requiring* the university to recognize the exclusive representative status of an elected faculty bargaining agent and to bargain with it in good faith. This does not mean agreement has to be reached. Accordingly, there is implicit in this bilateralism an assumption of a contractual relationship between the faculty and the university. Thus, many incidents of the faculty-university relationship and, indeed, the general tone of that relationship will be established in a contract. This is in distinction to the by-laws or promulgated policies of the board of trustees which in the past have been, in a de jure sense, *unilaterally* established by the college governing board.

This bilateralism also assumes a dichotomy between the faculty and the administration. This is based upon the theory that it is "management's" responsibility to set and pursue institutional objectives. The bargaining agent's objective, whether rationalized on the basis of what is best for the institution or not, is to further the collective interest of the faculty it represents. It is reasoned that this interest may be at odds with the character of the tasks and the institutional objectives and priorities established by the institution in the name of the whole. This premise is well summarized by Hoffer:

> *The allegiance of the manager is to the task and the results. However noble his motives, he cannot help viewing the workers as*

*a means to an end . . . and it matters not whether he does it for
the sake of profit, for a holy cause, or for the sheer principle of
efficiency . . . when it can plan and operate without having to
worry about what the worker will say. . . . Any doctrine which
preaches the oneness of management and labor—whether it stresses
their unity in a party, class, race, nation or even religion—can be
used to turn the worker into a complaint instrument in the hands
of management. . . . Our sole protection lies in keeping the division between management and labor obvious and matter-of-fact.
. . . Thus it seems that the worker's independence is as good an
index as any for measuring the freedom of a society.*[22]

This raises the transcendent issue in the college and university collective bargaining process: the problem of dichotomizing the
management rights function and the professional responsibility of
the collective faculty. This in turn raises a key issue in collective
bargaining with faculty. The NLRA and the majority of state
public employment relations acts permit collective negotiation with
respect to salaries, wages, hours, and other terms and conditions of
employment. The question is what constitutes "terms and conditions
of employment" with respect to faculty in a college or university.
What is the scope of the collective bargaining process?

The view widely held by faculty in today's colleges and
universities is that they should have wide discretion in the conduct
of their professional activities. It is reasoned that faculty should
have some form of "shared authority" by participating in the
governance or formulation of the institutional policies and rules
which govern the performance of their duties. This notion, peculiar
to the faculty-university relationship, has gained momentum over
the past twenty years during the golden age of faculty autonomy.
But it is more than professionalism, for it has historic institutional
roots reaching down to the medieval guild and the universities'
corporate status which enjoyed a *liberty* in medieval times; the
faculty have historically evidenced a proprietary sense in the institu-

[22] E. Hoffer, *The Ordeal of Change* (New York: Harper and
Row, 1963).

tion and have lived in it as a community.[23] This view is also embedded in broader concepts of academic freedom tied to institutional autonomy. If faculty autonomy is indiscriminately pursued, it projects into the bargaining relationship a much wider spectrum of matters[24] than customarily associated with industry or public sector collective bargaining where the distinction between the employees' and management's function is more clearcut. So it is that the bilateralism characteristic of the bargaining process introduces a fundamental tension which, if not properly understood, can foster a polarization.

A study by the American Association for Higher Education found:

> *Our field studies do not indicate that economic factors per se have been an important consideration underlying recent expressions of faculty unrest. . . . A meaningful application of the concept of "shared authority" should involve a wide variety of issues. The issues include educational and administrative policies; personnel administration; economic matters ranging from the total resources*

[23] Nisbet, p. 62 and Chap. 4 generally.

[24] CUNY contracts, articles I, V, VII. In the State University of New York representation proceeding before the New York Public Employment Relations Board (PERB), Kugler, president, New York State AFT College and University Council, testified that the following subjects would be the subject of negotiation: merit increases, number of students, promotions, compensation for extracurricular activity, TV and radio tape residuals, research staff, office space, secretarial services, travel funds, academic calendar, evening and extension assignments, sabbatic leave, leaves of absence, maternity and sick leave, tenure policies, grievance procedures, general regulations pertaining to campus affairs, consultation on educational matters, curriculum, admissions, student activities, choice of administrators (including deans, chairmen, presidents), pensions, health benefits, life and disability insurance, salary policy, moving expenses, tuition waiver for dependents, central faculty authority, master plan formulation, educational policy governing entire university, establishment of new campuses, intercollege agreements, and finally, but not least, selection of the chancellor and other central administrators. While it is something more than charitable to say this list is self-serving, it cannot be said it is modest.

*available to the compensation for particular individuals, public
questions that affect the role and functions of the institutions; and
procedures for faculty representation in campus governance.*[25]

Accordingly, faculty organizations espouse in their campaign
literature a concept of negotiable issues covering a range of matters
touching on admissions, class size, workload, calendar, procedures
for budget formulation, participation in planning and allocation of
resources, and procedures for the selection of certain administrators
and department chairmen, as well as the more traditional economic
items.

A recent policy expression on the matter by the AAUP
recognizes the "significant role which collective bargaining may
play in bringing agreement between faculty and administration on
economic and *academic issues*" (emphasis added). The AAUP
policy recognizes that the negotiation of a collective agreement may
"provide for the eventual establishment of necessary instruments of
shared authority." Recently negotiated contracts manifest this
trend (see Chapter Twelve). It is too early to tell whether or not
this trend will continue, inducing a polarized response from boards
of trustees and state governments toward a "management's rights"
psychology,[26] and in the long run become self-defeating from a
faculty standpoint; that is, in the sense of trading off prebargaining
rights by conceding them as management rights in exchange for
salaries and job security. I suspect this will occur at some institutions. Unfortunately, it begs the ultimate question of whether it
will be good for higher education.

Third, the collective bargaining process is premised upon a
collective relationship: organizations of employees sharing a community of interest represented *exclusively* by an elected representative. Other organizations may thus be excluded from negotiating
with the institution (including possibly an academic senate), and
competing organizations are relegated to a back-seat status on major
institutional issues. It is a democratic process in the sense that

[25] American Association for Higher Education, *Faculty Participation in Academic Governance* (Washington, D.C., 1967), p. 1.

[26] M. Lieberman, "Professors Unite!," *Harpers,* October 1971,
p. 61.

everyone in the bargaining unit has the opportunity to vote upon who the bargaining agent shall be or whether or not there shall be bargaining. It is an egalitarian process in the sense that the agent is dependent upon and must be responsive to the majority of those it represents with no legal obligation to make distinctions within its own organization based, for example, upon such matters as academic rank or senior faculty status. Trustees' policies frequently confer certain legal recognition to such status among faculty themselves. This collective relationship stresses the dynamics of politics and organizational behavior which become major factors in faculty-university relations and which may reach beyond the campus. This is especially true of an elected bargaining agent affiliated with national or state organizations possessed of legal, financial, and other staff organized and financed to confront institutional or court action.

The character of faculty leadership is likely to change as a result of this collectivism. It will require considerably more investment of time with emphasis upon an institutional perspective of faculty-university relations. Leaders will not be called upon to lead the city-states but the nation. Leadership will require political abilities in individuals attuned to the public. Where there is an affiliation between the local faculty bargaining agent and an external organization, the local leadership of the agent and its constituents will no doubt be influenced by and oriented to the organizational policies of such organizations (that is, AAUP, AFT, NEA), and perhaps even administratively meshed with them.

Fourth, most systems for resolving conflict depend upon *third party neutrals* when efforts at mutual accord break down. The bargaining process is no exception and relies upon mediation, fact-finding and arbitration to resolve impasses during actual contract negotiations or grievances arising from the administration and application of the contract. In theory, the objective of a third-party mediator is to persuade the parties to resolve their differences by reopening negotiations. He oils the negotiations machinery.

Third party neutrals are usually selected by the parties themselves or appointed by a public employment relations board, conciliation commission or service, from panels of experienced mediators and arbitrators. Private institutions are likely to resort to the Federal Mediation Service or the American Arbitration Association while public institutions are likely to be dealing with state board-controlled conciliation services.

Arbitration is a more formal adjudicatory proceeding resulting in a determination on the merits of the impasse issues. It has the indicia of a legal proceeding, and the written decision may serve as a precedent for comparable future issues. Experience and arbitration decisions serving as precedents in analogous situations may influence the arbitrator's decision. Arbitration decisions in schoolteacher cases or the arbitrator's personal experience in schoolteacher matters may influence decisions in community or four-year college faculty-university disputes.

Binding arbitration, as contrasted to advisory arbitration, means that the parties will be bound by the arbitrator's decision. Binding arbitration is relatively common as the terminal step in a grievance system (grievance arbitration) but less commonly used to resolve impasses arising during the negotiations themselves (interest arbitration) especially where there is the right to strike. Why be bound by an arbitrator when you can strike or are willing to take a strike? Fact-finding is for practical purposes the same as advisory arbitration and most frequently authorized in the public sector in cases of negotiation impasses where the strike is not authorized. On the other hand, in both Hawaii and Pennsylvania the public bargaining laws authorize binding arbitration of negotiation impasses. The theory behind fact-finding is that publication of the fact-finder's report clarifies the issues and informs the public and legislative decision-makers. It gives the parties an opportunity to assess the public reaction to their respective positions. Since the legislative body frequently makes the ultimate decision, the theory is that while the fact-finder's report is not binding, it places public and political pressure on the parties to settle their differences or on the legislative body to accept the fact-finder's report.

Where they exist, academic grievance systems are likely to involve informal review by joint faculty-administrative committees which make recommendation to the dean, president, or trustees, depending upon the type of case, whose decision is then final. The emphasis is on informality and behind-the-scenes consensus; the purpose is to adjust individual problems (not collective or institutional matters) and rarely involves outside third parties.

Collective bargaining grievance is quite different. The negotiated grievance system characteristic of the industrial model[27] is the one contained in almost all of the negotiated academic contracts public and private. Typically designed in three or four stages of progressive formality, the final decision is subject to binding arbitration by the outside impartial arbitrator(s). From the union point of view, the main purpose of the grievance system is to provide a means to challenge management decisions or actions and to watchdog the contract. It involves not only individual grievances, therefore, but also institutional or collective grievances. The particular interpretation placed upon a key contract provision or the manner by which it is implemented can affect basic faculty-institutional relationships, entail a substantial increase in cost factors, or involve basic institutional policy. These general observations are qualified by the specific negotiated grievance system at a particular institution. Thus, not all have binding arbitration; others have a limited definition of grievance referring only to board or institutional policies. Much depends, too, on what is contained in the entire contract, especially where grievance is defined as a violation of the contract. In other cases a grievance is broadly defined to include the grievability of board policies or other institutional policies.[28] The major movement in college and university bargaining agreements is toward adoption of the industrial grievance model with binding arbitration.

Tenure System. Hutchins said that academic freedom comes and goes because of some conviction about the purpose of education on the part of those who make the decisions in society. This thought

---

[27] *Industrial model* may be a somewhat misleading term. There is no distinct and single industrial prototype, and there is, in fact, a great deal of variety in the way the collective bargaining process is applied in private industry depending upon the locale and industry. Grievance procedures are somewhat more standard in general form.

[28] For example, Central Michigan has the tighter grievance definition; St. John's has the broader.

is implicitly paralleled in Hofstadter and Metzger's[29] observation
that the modern idea of academic freedom has been developed by
men who have absorbed analogous ideas from the larger life of
society. Modern science's notion of the empirical search for truth
fostered by freedom of inquiry verified by objective processes is an
example. From commerce has come the notion of free competition
of ideas. From the politics of the liberal state has come the idea of
free speech and free press essential to perspectives in a pluralistic
society. Most significant, from religious liberalism and the "taming
of sectarian animus" has come the spirit of tolerance:

> *The essentiality of freedom in the community of American
> universities is almost self-evident. No one should underestimate the
> vital role in a democracy that is played by those who guide and
> train our youth. To impose any strait jacket upon the intellectual
> leaders in our colleges and universities would imperil the future of
> our Nation. No field of education is so thoroughly comprehended
> by man that new discoveries cannot yet be made. Particularly is
> that true in the social sciences, where few, if any, principles are
> accepted as absolutes. Scholarship cannot flourish in an atmosphere
> of suspicion and distrust. Teachers and students must always remain
> free to inquire, to study, and to evaluate, to gain new maturity and
> understanding; otherwise, our civilization will stagnate and die.*[30]

While it is true that academic freedom is associated chiefly
with the concern of the professor in his professional capacity, the
more inclusive elements just referred to are broadly analogous to
academic freedom and provide its historical matrix. It is in this
context that the term *academic freedom* is used here, and not in
the sense of a license for privileged social status regarding matters
unrelated to intellectual pursuits.

There is by no means a uniform tenure system in higher

[29] R. Hofstadter and W. P. Metzger, *Development of Academic
Freedom in the United States* (New York: Columbia University Press,
1955), pp. 61–62.
[30] *Sweezy* v. *New Hampshire,* 354 U.S. 234, p. 250; 1 L. Ed.
2d 1311, 77 S. Ct. 1203.

education.[31] Some community colleges, technical institutes, and teacher colleges have no system of tenure at all. Some institutions have tenure policies which have developed through practice and custom, while others have highly detailed policies with elaborate notice requirements, and still others have simply endorsed and imported the AAUP policies. In some public institutions, such as state teacher colleges, the matter of tenure may be detailed in statutory law which forms part of the tenure system prescribed for school teachers. In other public institutions, however, the governing boards are given authority to set and establish their own tenure system. (This is generally the case in the major public institutions.) Accordingly, the following generalizations must be qualified with these facts in mind.

There are three coordinate elements in a tenure system. First, tenure enables a faculty member to teach, study, and act free from a large number of restraints and pressures which would otherwise inhibit independent thought and action. In this sense, tenure is part and parcel of academic freedom. Second, it is a means for providing job security to promote institutional stability and loyalty and to reward individual service and accomplishment. Third, tenure represents acceptance into the professorial guild; acceptance by one's peers. In a larger sense, it entails an affirmative obligation, as in the ministry or priesthood, with a corporeal allegiance to the deferential honor inherent in teaching and scholarship. This aspect of tenure presently seems in eclipse, save for a few first-class liberal arts colleges and a handful of great universities.

There are two basic academic appointments relating to tenure. These are term appointments, which confer security against dismissal for a fixed term, and a continuing appointment, conferring such status for the life of the professor while at the institution. Many institutions promulgate by trustee action policies which outline the tenure system at that institution. These might require a tenure decision after a prescribed period of time; for example, after seven years service. Where this is the case, term appointments

[31] C. Byse and L. Joughin, *Tenure in American Higher Education* (Ithaca, N.Y.: Cornell University Press, 1959), Chap. 5.

may not be indefinitely piggybacked to the detriment of the individual and to the tenure system itself. Institutional policies or regulations also frequently tie prescribed notice of nonrenewal requirements to term appointments: the longer the service, the longer the notice. An example might be six months notice for two-year appointments or a year's notice for three or more years of service. In some cases, written policies of the institution will establish broad criteria such as teaching, scholarly research, mastery of subject matter, university service. Faculties and individual departments supplement and apply such criteria to the particular tenure review case. The tenure appointment review process characteristically entails a pyramid of reviewing committees originating in the academic department and culminating with a recommendation for tenure to the president, who presents it to the governing board for approval. The campus-wide committees reviewing departmental committee recommendations usually include deans or academic vice-presidents. Once a budgeted position is established, the de facto decision of appointment, reappointment, or tenure is, as a practical matter, a faculty decision. Nonetheless, in the American university the de jure authority to grant appointment and tenure is almost always vested in the trustees by statute, charter, or bylaws, depending upon whether the institution is public or private. Despite this ultimate legal control, rejection of faculty recommendation is the exception rather than the rule. Frequently, trustee policies or bylaws will expressly delegate an advisory or consultative role to the faculty in the appointment and promotion process. In some institutions, faculty might even be delegated authority by the board to establish and apply the criteria upon which tenure is awarded.

It is necessary to digress for a moment to note the distinction between the tenure review process just described and a dismissal proceeding. There is a fundamental difference between a tenure review resulting in the expiration of a term appointment and separation from the institution, on the one hand, and, on the other, dismissal from an institution. In the latter, the institution brings a charge of inadequate performance of duties, incompetence, or misconduct with the clear design of ridding itself of an undesirable. Such a proceeding may be brought during the term appointment or against a tenured faculty member. It typically requires notice and a formal adjudicatory hearing, usually with right to counsel. The hearing is frequently before a faculty committee which makes findings and recommendations to the president or board. It is likely to be an adversary proceeding concerned only with the issues raised by the charges. In comparison, a tenure review is concerned with whether or not to grant tenure in light of the departmental or academic program needs, the economics of the situation, and the qualities of the particular candidate. It obviously never applies to a person who already has tenure, whereas a dismissal proceeding could. Separation from an institution because tenure was not granted theoretically carries no professional stigma; dismissal for cause clearly does. One of the purposes behind a dismissal procedure is to protect the academic freedom of tenured faculty and those on term appointments. A dismissal proceeding insuring due process is a fundamental element in any academic tenure system but should not be equated with the tenure evaluative review process. Serious implications arise when administration and faculty confuse the two, especially where circumstances serve to further confuse the issue, as the following discussion will demonstrate.

There is a twofold purpose behind a term appointment which establishes a fundamental tension between the individual and the grantor[32] of the appointment. One purpose is simply to get a particular job done at a certain time. Second, the appointment clearly provides an opportunity to evaluate or test a potential candidate for tenure. These two aspects of a term appointment will, of course, receive in any given case varying degrees of importance depending upon intentions of the parties at the time of initial appointment, length of service, the type of institution, school, department, or program within which it was given. One view characterizes a term appointment as fundamentally a contractual obligation on the part of the institution in return for services rendered by the faculty member. Admittedly, an individual may be considered for a continuing appointment at some future point, but this view holds there is no implied expectancy of continuing employment nor

[32] "Grantor" of the appointment can be confusing. Precisely, it is the faculty, usually through the department itself (given an approved budget line), who decides to appoint. It is also the university which in a de jure sense must approve it and officially grant it.

even a moral obligation inherent in the term appointment relationship guaranteeing it will mature into a continuing appointment. It says the individual is fully protected where there are notice requirements and where a tenure decision is required after a prescribed period of service. When an individual receives notice that his appointment will not be renewed upon expiration, it does not necessarily follow that he is inferior, lacking, or has done something wrong. On this reasoning there is no obligation to give written reasons to the individual for failure to renew.

This traditional approach to the term appointment emphasizes a strict contract relationship: the appointment was voluntarily agreed upon between the individual and the institution to terminate at the expiration of the fixed term, subject only to institutional policies requiring a tenure decision after a prescribed period of service. This is rationalized on the basis that it facilitates the pursuit of institutional excellence by insuring flexibility to react to economic realities and desirable market conditions, permitting access to higher quality faculty, and shifting emphasis in academic programs. From the faculty point of view it gives job security for a fixed term and the opportunity for self-development by leaving open the opportunity for promotion to a continuing appointment (tenure), and provides security against arbitrary or unlawful dismissal during the term of the appointment.

This view of the term appointment has been attacked by many faculty and certain employee organizations as subjective, elitist, institutionally oriented, and with no provision challenging nonrenewals founded upon unlawful, capricious, subjective, or punitive reasons. To some extent, there lies behind this position an underlying view that emphasizes the probationary aspect of the term appointment, the job security aspect. Assuming a term appointment is in effect a probationary appointment, it is reasoned that the individual is on a tenure track leading to a continuing appointment at the institution from the moment he is appointed. The argument is that where the university has policies relating to notice requirements and requires a tenure decision after a prescribed period of service, it follows that an initial term appointment may create an institutional obligation to grant tenure if certain conditions are met. This view says there is an implied obligation on the part of the institution to grant tenure, provided the individual does not do something wrong or does not fail to measure up to expressly articulated institutional standards. It is further argued that in cases of nonrenewal denying tenure, the burden should logically shift to the institution to show the reasons for nonrenewal or to state reasons which will show where the faculty member has failed to measure up to expressed institutional criteria and therefore denied a continuing appointment otherwise available. It is not suggested that the two views are always mutually exclusive; the emphasis will shift depending upon the circumstances. For example, a person arriving at his seventh year may well have a greater claim or expectancy of tenure, especially where there has been a pattern of promotion and a series of salary increases. In the latter case, nonrenewal raises the presumption in the mind of some that there was a wrongful reason behind the nonrenewal.

Some even consider failure to give reasons and nonrenewals in certain cases as tantamount to dismissal for cause but depriving the individual of due process normally provided in a dismissal proceeding. This argument is frequently made in cases where an institution or faculty appears to be ridding themselves of a "troublemaker" by merely waiting out the expiration of the term appointment or where the particular candidate is controversial.

Because of the complexity of this problem and alleged abuses in time of stress, there is a growing trend to resolve the matter by imposing a review committee to insure that institutional "procedures" used in reviewing a candidate are properly followed. Thus, a candidate who feels wronged can trigger a review of the matter before an impartial committee, which presumably limits its scope of review to whether or not the appropriate evaluation procedures were followed.[33] The following hypothetical case demonstrates all of the views we have considered, capturing the flavor of the complexities in some tenure dispute cases.

Smith is an associate professor of political science at X University. Having served at X for four years, he was given another

---

[33] See the elaborate review procedure endorsed by the AAUP in its *Statement on Procedural Standards in the Renewal or Nonrenewal of Faculty Appointments* in the Summer 1971 AAUP *Bulletin*.

three-year term contract expiring August 31, 1972. Under X's bylaws, Smith is entitled to a year's notice in case of nonrenewal, on or before August 31, 1971. X's bylaws also require a decision to either grant tenure or to nonrenew after seven years of service. Smith has been an exceptionally outspoken and controversial fellow, especially over the past two years. He has been rated as better than average as a teacher and has written two articles in an avant-garde journal. He has been a member in ACTION, a campus organization composed predominately of graduate students and young faculty. ACTION has been highly critical of the university and has initiated numerous peaceful demonstrations. In May 1970, ACTION interrupted a trustee meeting and articulated a set of demands through its spokesman, Smith. The issue at stake was the extent of X University's commitment to a particular program for disadvantaged students. This event received unusual news coverage, especially Smith's characterizing X's board chairman as "an uninformed fat head."

X University is in financial difficulties and has declared a freeze on the creation of all new positions and has instituted a modest retrenchment program. Each department was asked to reduce its budget by 2 per cent.

Because Smith was approaching his seventh year and the bylaws required a year's notice in nonrenewal cases, Smith was reviewed by the political science department's appointments committee in February 1971 which voted five to four, chairman abstaining, to nonrenew his appointment. The collegewide appointments committee, which includes the dean and is chaired by the academic vice-president, concurred six to one, noting that the departmental vote was close and therefore there was no clear majority requesting that Smith get tenure.

Smith was given due notice in June 1971 by letter from the president that his appointment would not be renewed. No reason was stated. Smith says he should be given a written reason why he was nonrenewed and an opportunity to confront the grounds for nonrenewal before an impartial body of peers. X refuses to state the reasons in writing. Subsequently, the political science department met and reversed its decision by a vote of five to four after Smith had presented his case to the department and showed them student evaluations of himself he had kept over the past three years. A group of students also appeared in his behalf. The department then requested the president to grant Smith tenure. The department chairman objected by separate letter saying the latter vote was out of order, he had not attended the meeting, the original decision should stand, and he had orally told Smith the department could do better and needed a man with an interest in European political theory. The arguments are summarized below.

Smith says the five to four departmental decision was capricious and arbitrary since the five voting against Smith were senior faculty whose own records of achievement were not as good as his own in light of the two promotional criteria, teaching and research, contained in X's bylaws. Smith's record far exceeded his four nontenured colleagues who received renewals, two of whom were rated as "teaching disasters" by the students. On what basis does "X" think it can do better, what are the credentials of the "phantom candidate" to replace Smith. Smith has been rated above average as a teacher and has written two articles. The revote of five to four shows the department has changed its mind.

X replies that Smith is just average, the majority of the department feels it can do better in the current buyer's market, qualifications of senior faculty are irrelevant, Smith's nontenured colleagues were given new term appointments and not tenure, the department wishes someone with an interest in European political theory compared with Smith's interest in American politics.

Smith says that there can be no economic basis for the decision since he has information showing the department intends to fill his position.

X replies that the department agreed to trade two instructor lines in order to keep Smith's line, cites the University's new policy that all new appointments are to be limited to one year, and points out the establishment of a committee to study the feasibility of freezing future tenure appointments as demonstrating X's economic crisis.

Smith contends he was nonrenewed because of exercising his First Amendment right of expression and lawful assembly, citing an alleged remark by X's chairman of the trustees to the effect that "Smith would be better off earning a day's pay in the library or classroom than parading around the administration building with the rest of those bearded adolescents."

X replies that no such statement had been made and that the review process and the decision not to grant tenure supported the first departmental decision.

Smith says the procedures and criteria were not followed in his case and points to the new AAUP policy on procedures to review nonrenewal of term appointments. He argues that he is at least entitled to due process, which should include written reasons and an opportunity to present his case before an impartial review committee to ascertain if procedures and criteria were followed. Smith requests his personnel file for review to see if all proper materials were available to the departmental tenure committee and collegewide committee to insure proper application of the criteria set forth in X's bylaws. He further points out that the nonrenewal process in his case was tantamount to a dismissal since the underlying and unspoken reasons were his lawful demonstration activities and exercise of First Amendment rights. He is thus entitled to a hearing. Smith says this must be so in view of X's reluctance to give him reasons and because he is obviously otherwise qualified.

X replies that such a review would set the stage for attacking the peer evaluative process in a formalistic and adversary forum. X argues that it is impractical to limit the scope of review of the hearing committee to the sole question of whether procedures were followed. The review would result in a consideration of the whole affair on the academic merits of whether Smith should have tenure. It would be the first long step to instant tenure since every nonrenewal would be challenged and require an involved review procedure. X says if it gives reasons to Smith and a review committee, it will have to do it for everyone. In practical effect, it would circumvent departmental decision.

This summary of the arguments illustrates the problem. Moreover, there have been a rash of court cases raising many of the issues presented here hypothetically; two of these cases are now pending before the Supreme Court of the United States.[34]

[34] *Roth vs. Board of Regents,* Case 18490, 446 F2d 866 (7th Cir. 1971); *Sinderman vs. Perry,* 430 F2d 939 (5th Cir. 1970). See

There are some points to keep in mind with regard to the tenure system which have a direct bearing on its relationship to collective bargaining. I speculate that there are a sizable number of faculty members who look upon tenure principally in terms of job security and who are sympathetic to Smith's position. This sympathy stems in part from the egalitarian tone prevailing at many institutions and from the present unpopularity of the traditional aristocratic styles allegedly manifest in subjective and perhaps "clubby" tenure review procedures where control is vested in senior faculty.

There seems, too, a sense of mistrust and suspicion in the aftermath of the sixties and a corresponding need felt for formality and due process. There seems to be an air of suspicion that the establishment is ridding itself of the unorthodox. This feeling is exacerbated by the insecurity caused by changing economic conditions. Institutions have rapidly moved away from the era of affluence and rapid expansion of faculties when tenure was relatively easy to obtain. Faculties are now faced with a poor job market and poor job mobility at a time when institutions are undergoing serious financial constrictions.

There is a growing awareness of loose evaluative procedures and the courts are increasingly scrutinizing faculty allegations of nonrenewals based upon unconstitutional grounds. The challenge to the traditional view of a term appointment and the call for due process review is in the main a challenge to the traditional peer evaluation system. For, in most cases, the challenge is to a departmental recommendation. It is also an attack upon informal and sloppy evaluative systems, the result of rapid expansion and affluent times. In an egalitarian sense, it says that each individual must be treated objectively and equally; learned elders notwithstanding. In another sense it is a resistance, perhaps a breakdown, of traditional authority schemes and a further assertion of individual "rights".

We have traveled a tortuous path through the causes of unionism, the basics of the bargaining process, and the profile of

also *Lucas vs. Chapman,* 430 F2d 945 (5th Cir. 1970); *Greene vs. Howard University,* 412 F2d 1128 (U.S. App. D.C. 1969); *Jones vs. Hopper,* 412 F2d 1323 (10th Cir. 1969); *Bolmar vs. Keyes,* 162 F2d 136 (2nd Cir. 1947).

the tenure system with some of its current problems. What general conclusions can be drawn in relating unionism to tenure?

Collective Bargaining

Matters relating to job security are well within the definition of terms and conditions of employment under most collective bargaining and employment relations statutes. Generally speaking, scope of *negotiations*[35] has been liberally construed to include a wide variety of matters in the bargaining process. This definition is buttressed where experience between the parties has, in fact, resulted in certain classes of issues being negotiated. Thus, scope of negotiations is determined in part by practice and experience. Written contracts are not coterminous with scope of negotiation. Contracts do represent accessible documentation in the absence of surveys or other studies on the practice in a given field. So far, negotiated agreements at the community college, four-year institutions, and university level indicate that faculty are pursuing a tenure system with some or all of the following elements: a systematic means of awarding term appointments with prescribed notice requirements; specification of evaluation criteria; an evaluation procedure including committees and composition; location and character of the materials upon which a decision will be made for promotion and tenure (access to and content of personnel files); a means for challenging institutional violations of tenure policies; a dismissal for cause procedure; and an institutional commitment to principles of academic freedom, usually contained in general contract provisions at the beginning of the agreement.

For example, in New York as of January 1971, twenty-two community college agreements demonstrate a clear trend to prescribe a definite probationary period after which a tenure decision is

[35] The Pennsylvania Public Employment Relations Board has rendered a decision which limits scope of negotiation somewhat in school-teacher bargaining. The Hawaiian Public Employment Relations law places limitations on scope of negotiation. Whether these would limit negotiations on tenure is questionable at best. Even in these states the likelihood is that some elements of a tenure system would be negotiable.

required and to provide for evaluative criteria or some other provision regarding the evaluation process. Some college agreements provide for access to a faculty personnel file and make specific reference to principles of academic freedom.

Similarly, a 1969–1970 survey of the negotiated agreements of twenty-four Michigan community colleges indicates that many have provisions for written evaluation, fixed probationary periods, and statements on academic freedom. New York and Michigan provide the majority of community college contracts to date. Chicago's community college system also establishes an employment and tenure policy in its contract with the AFT. In community colleges, tenure systems will be a major negotiable issue. This emphasis should be especially true of colleges which have no system of tenure, where there is an authoritarian administrative style, or tenure rights are limited to informal practice. Where there already exists a tenure system in the governing board's policies, efforts will be made to import them into the negotiated agreement.

Experience in the four-year colleges and universities is not extensive and therefore perhaps less reliable than community college experience. The following negotiated agreements were analyzed: SUNY, CUNY (two agreements—part-time and full-time), New Jersey State Teacher College System, St. John's University, Central Michigan, Rutgers, and Scranton University. Rutgers and Scranton make no explicit comprehensive provision for a tenure system in the contract itself. The other agreements, in practical effect, include many of the elements referred to above, namely, access to personnel files, promotional criteria, notice, required tenure decision after a prescribed period, and academic freedom provisions. They are not appreciably different from the community college experience. CUNY and New Jersey both provide for academic rank ratios.

Although tenure provisions might not appear in the contract itself, existing board tenure policies might, for practical purposes, be effected by other means. For example, a union might exert pressure to negotiate a tenure matter and force the institution to change its own policy as a trade-off for the removal of tenure demands from contract negotiations. Such action, however, is probably the exception rather than the rule.

The scope of negotiations raises basic questions concerning management's rights and prerogatives. In academic negotiations, this question is further complicated with problems of governance. Management rights provisions are illustrated by Genesee Community College in New York: "The legislature and the trustees, separately and collectively, hereby reserve unto themselves all powers, authority, duties and responsibilities, and the adoption of such rules, regulations, and policies as they deem necessary in the management, direction, and administration of all operations and activities of the college . . . limited only by the specific and express terms of this agreement." SUNY's contract states: "Except as expressly limited by other provisions of this agreement, all of the authority, rights, and responsibilities possessed by the State are retained by it."

To what extent such provisions could or would be used to encroach upon currently acceptable faculty prerogatives concerning tenure matters is not clear from experience. Such a question is likely to arise, if at all, in a retrenchment situation[36] where the contract makes no provision for retrenchment; or it might arise in refusal to fill vacancies.

Speaking in terms of the scope of the bargaining relationship as compared to the scope of contract negotiations, the latter will probably involve a wide range of complicated and subtle relationships relating to tenure between the union and the university during the administration of the agreement. Take, for example, student or senate involvement in evaluation and promotion committees or guidelines, personnel file guidelines, departmental committees, or college-study committees on tenure; these will somehow have to be related to the contract and the broader bargaining

[36] *In the Matter of City School District of the City of New Rochelle;* Cases U-0240, U-0249, U-0251. New York PERB held that the decision of the school superintendent involving budgetary cuts with concomitant job eliminations is not a mandatory subject of negotiations between the union and employer. However, the employer is obligated to negotiate with the Federation on the impact of such decisions on the terms and conditions of employment of the employees affected.

relationship. The union will play a prominent part in the latter, if not the former.

Academic-freedom language, frequently couched in ambiguous terms, takes the following line at Dutchess Community College in New York: "All parties to this agreement recognize the importance of academic freedom to the fulfillment of the college's educational purposes and therefore endorse the 1940 Statement of the American Association of University Professors on Academic Freedom." At Fulton-Montgomery Community College in New York: "It is the policy of the college to maintain and encourage full freedom within the law, of inquiry, teaching and research. This freedom shall include the right to belong to any legal organizations and to promote such organization, and to hold and make public any view or opinion involving, but not limited to, social, economic, political and educational issues." At St. John's University in New York: "The parties incorporate herein by reference the 1940 *Statement of Principles on Academic Freedom and Tenure* of the American Association of University Professors in accordance with the endorsement of the Board of Trustees of the University on January 15, 1968."

It is also important to appreciate the interrelationship between the negotiated agreement and the existing written tenure policies of the governing board. Thus, the collective-bargaining agreement can, in practical effect, freeze into the contract those portions of the board policies relating to tenure (for instance, the St. John's contract), or possibly be interpreted to require reopened negotiations on board tenure policies when such policies are intended to be changed by the trustees (for instance, the SUNY contract), or incorporate by reference certain provisions relating to tenure, such as academic freedom provisions (for instance, the Rutgers contract). Practically all of the aforementioned agreements attempt, by expressed negotiation in the contract, to preserve the existing institutional policies concerning tenure or to negotiate aspects of the tenure system which are contained in the trustee policies, or both. An open-ended provision allowing considerable latitude and favorable to faculty is illustrated by the following quote (from a negotiated agreement of St. John's) which seeks to freeze an ill-defined status quo and portions of the trustee bylaws or policies. "The parties agree to continue all practices of the administration currently adhered to by it. 'Practices' refers to those practices of the office of president, offices of the vice-presidents, offices of the deans, based upon written policies of the board of trustees and the university senate. . . . All of the provisions of the statutes presently in effect relating to tenure and promotion remain in full force and effect with the following modifications . . . [then follow contractual provisions which qualify the foregoing]." In sum, the majority of contracts in community colleges, four-year colleges, and universities include tenure matters and seek to freeze existing trustee tenure policies.

Almost all of the negotiated contracts seek to subject to the contract-grievance system both tenure matters negotiated in the contract or the application of written board policies relating to tenure. As a practical matter, there is little difference between the two. Some contract grievances permit binding arbitration but seek to limit the arbitrator's scope of review to whether there were procedural violations in the evaluative process vis-a-vis the academic merits of the decision itself (CUNY, SUNY, St. John's). The St. John's agreement requires written reasons for nonrenewal. Other colleges provide for review of procedural violations in evaluations but keep the review before an in-house committee with no provision for arbitration (Central Michigan). The New Jersey State College contract expressly attempts to exclude from the grievance procedure "decisions involving the nonreappointment of probationary or nontenured personnel." However, the New Jersey contract contains detailed promotion procedures, personnel file procedures, and promotional criteria which could arguably come within the contract grievance definition on the theory that violations of procedures, as opposed to substantive "decisions," are grievable because they fall within the definition of grievance as an improper application of the "terms of this agreement."

There seems to be some resistance to hashing out the academic merits in the grievance machinery which, as pointed out earlier, can become rather formal and adversary. The practical rub occurs when evaluative procedures become so detailed or cumbersome that attempts to follow them almost guarantee their violation, to say nothing of the time, record-keeping, and so forth. Furthermore, the hypothetical Smith case demonstrates that the practical distinction between procedure and decision itself is indeed blurred. For example, was the initial failure of the department to consider student evaluations of Smith a fatal procedural error? A hearing committee or arbitrator might wish to see the students' evaluation and assess to what extent and how the department evaluated Smith's teaching per the teaching criteria in the board policies. Or, assume there was an applicable academic freedom provision, would not departmental colleagues be questioned whether Smith's demonstration activities influenced their decisions? Would not such questions be rebutted by showing the academic grounds and other reasons on the merits as to why the decision was made to nonrenew? Hearing committees and arbitrators (especially those inexperienced in academic ways) are likely to permit matters relating to academic qualifications, perhaps indiscriminately, into the record. Considerations of these matters means bringing in department members to testify on both sides concerning the grievant's academic qualifications, potentially setting in motion a Kafkalike hearing and encouraging personal enmities among "colleagues." Initial experience (inexperience) will probably result in substantial confusion and investment of time because of this problem.

The difficulty in hewing the line between a review of evaluative procedures and the merits of the nonrenewal decision itself is compounded where the scope of grievance review includes findings as to whether in a tenure decision there were "errors of fact, gross prejudice, capricious action, or factors violative of academic freedom." Difficulty also occurs when a review board has to decide on an arbitrary or discriminatory application of or a failure to act pursuant to contract or board provisions.

The availability of contract grievance machinery and easy access to union attorneys and union staff administrators will, at the outset, increase the volume of challenges to nonrenewal or promotional decisions. Initially, at least, the bird-dogging instincts of a new union trying to establish itself will also encourage such challenges.

In the absence of collective bargaining grievance machinery, the principle external remedy has been the lawsuit. From an individual faculty member's point of view, there are inhibiting factors which discourage the use of this remedy: attorney's fees, court delays, and, most important, the judicial restraint or reluctance to overturn institutional discretionary decisions in favor of faculty. Recourse to grievance is quick and relatively inexpensive from the individual's point of view, and he has the added support of the union.

The effect of all these procedures may be intimidating to institutions with a tendency to discourage nonrenewals in border-line cases because of the potential hassle involved. At some institutions, it might initially result in "instant tenure."

However, grievance machinery offers the potential over the long pull to resolve abuses of the evaluative process and can resolve needless conflict and promote stabilized relationships. Deans, university officials, and departments will eventually familiarize themselves with the grievance machinery, its limitations, and its potential. Thus, disagreements can be avoided at the early informal-grievance stages and can highlight weaknesses in the evaluative process which can be corrected. This correction could result in a disciplined and workable evaluation procedure and a thorough justification of appointment and evaluation decisions. As earlier noted, most grievance systems have informal stages designed to weed out cases which can be informally resolved and to avoid needless controversy at the more formal latter stages.

Without bargaining, I speculate that too many institutions have no workable academic grievance procedure at all. Some institutions have ad hoc arrangements where the president appoints a committee as problems arise. Others have senate committees which are not functional from a practical point of view. Ill-conceived or ineffective academic grievance systems can cause more problems than they solve. Thus, what could be disposed of informally is indiscriminately thrust before a faculty grievance committee and needlessly mushrooms into a cause celebre. Or, the grievance is so broadly defined that issues come before the committee which have no business being there. Or, a grievance is brought against the institution concerning a squabble between faculty involving no challenged institutional policy whatsoever. Sloppy selection methods may result in including members in the academic grievance committee who are totally unskilled, lack practical judgment, or are just plain stupid. Records are not kept of precedent cases; sometimes committee members serve reluctantly and, therefore, do not take their responsibility seriously enough. In other cases, retained faculty attorneys are sometimes permitted in and the whole process turns into a three-ring circus complete with clowns and high-wire specialists. Too frequently, the president and his key representatives simply look upon the academic grievance systems as a sand box for faculty play. He sees it as a means, politically speaking, for "reading the situation" when the recommendation is finally handed to him.

All or a combination of these factors can cause a breakdown of trust in a grievance system. In such situations, collective bargaining grievance machinery can offer an alternative. Although collective bargaining grievance can have the same problems as academic grievance committees, it is less likely because of the nature of the collective bargaining process. It encourages ordered and disciplined procedure, objectivity in the hearing body, credibility in the system, certainty and finality, skilled administrators, maintenance of records of decisions, and continuity in fundamental interpretations of policies.

In sum, matters pertaining to tenure and promotion will become increasingly subject to contract grievance machinery. It will encourage, initially, challenges to nonrenewal and promotional matters. These challenges will entail formal hearings, written decisions, interpretations of promotional criteria, and precedent-setting interpretations of key contract or board policy provisions relating to tenure. The machinery has, however, the long-term potential of reducing disputes and promoting stability.

If tenure systems and related matters are negotiated in a collective bargaining agreement, it will change the fundamental legal relationship between faculty and the institution. In public institutions, tenure rights of faculty in the main derive from policies promulgated by the institution under color of official rules. At many institutions, favorable changes in tenure policies have resulted from pressure by the faculty for improvement or for enhancing the institution's competitive position for recruitment purposes. Such policies were developed over the past twenty-five to thirty years during a climate favorable to faculty and during a time when political and financial contraints upon the institution were not significant. Many elements of the tenure provisions were frequently predicated upon AAUP policy. In public institutions, tenure rules or policies promulgated by action of the governing board of the institution have the force and effect of statute (not a contract), but may be changed or eliminated by similar action of the board. Collectively speaking, the faculty have no legally vested right to prevent a change in the policies. But where there is an authorized bilateral agreement negotiated between the faculty and the public institution, the legal relationship is one of contract and may not be unilaterally changed by the governing board during the contract term. This policy is wholly apart from the complex legal question raised in the event a legislature should enact a law altering an existing contract between a faculty and a state university. It seems unlikely, if not unreasonable, that the public decision-makers would, for example, alter tenure provisions in the face of a state statute authorizing collective negotiations and the resulting contract. The reluctance to change contractually negotiated tenure provisions by law would be particularly true where money was previously appropriated to fund the contract or where it was expressly approved.

The fundamental legal relationships with respect to tenure matters between a faculty member and a private institution have always been contractual in nature and derived from the letter or form of appointment and existing institutional policies. Unionism will likely result in establishing tenure relationships through the collective agreement rather than through an individually negotiated agreement. The entire idea in the preceding sentence is also true of the public institutions. To some extent, a collective agreement disenfranchises the individual faculty member from negotiating his own individually comprehensive contract. On the other hand, it is doubtful that it has ever been the widespread practice to negotiate individually, apart from salary, a comprehensive agreement relating to tenure matters. Most agreements or letters of appointment characteristically recite the salary, rank, and length of appointment with specific reference to institutional policies regarding tenure in the faculty handbook or trustee policies. Thus, in private institutions, so-called individual contracts in the majority of cases are tied to prevailing institutional policies anyway, and the individual has no negotiating leverage over these. Depending on the policies and form of appointment, the institution may well have the right to unilaterally change its tenure policies without causing a breach of contract.

Many of the negotiated agreements have provisions which say that an individual faculty agreement may not be inconsistent with the collective bargaining agreement. This does not necessarily preclude individual contracts or even special salary arrangements so long as they are not less than the minimal contractual norm. But in the main, the collective contract will tend to supplant the individual contract and will shift tenure matters from written board policies to the collective agreement. This will also reduce unilateral board action and flexibility to change tenure policies during the term of the collective bargaining agreement.

If collective bargaining trends so far suggest a businesslike and detailed litany of tenure rights spelled out in the collective bargaining contracts instead of in policies, handbooks, written interpretations, or everyday practice, it is reasonable to assume that collective bargaining will tend to homogenize practices relating to tenure and to reduce discrepancies in practice between departments, schools, and faculties. Unilateral flexibility by the institution to change signals with respect to appointment and tenure because of economic or other considerations will be reduced in both public and private institutions where existing policies and the status quo become baked into collective bargaining agreements. For example, institutional attempts to limit all new appointments to one year with a practice of one year rollovers may well be resisted at the bargaining table where the majority of faculty are young and have no tenure. Likewise, a series of nonrenewals to take advantage of favorable market conditions may result in pressure to establish rank ratios, impose rigorous review procedures on nonrenewals, and demands for a policy of "promotion from within." Retrenchment of "fat programs" will result in pressure for contract retrenchment criteria with, perhaps, built-in seniority concepts tied to tenure status.

This is not to say that collective bargaining will necessarily mean institutional inertia. Quite the contrary, bilateralism implicit in the bargaining process if properly handled can work as a constructive force. The process lends itself to mutual problem-solving, results in disciplined presentation of detailed personnel data necessary to informed tenure decisions, and cultivates an institutional perspective on the problem of tenure.

In the absence of bilateral checks, fiscal crunches can result in haphazard and ad hoc decisions relating to personnel and cause a breakdown in faculty trust. Confronted with this bilateralism in day-to-day operations, institutions will have to be better prepared to rationalize and justify decisions and policies relating to tenure. This is especially true with respect to retrenchment and evaluation.

The law that every action has an equal and opposite reaction may well apply to unionism in some institutions. I believe that at certain institutions, sustained and militant pursuit of unionism by faculty will produce an aggressive management initiative on the part of university officials. This initiative will be abetted by both economic and other pressures outside the university as previously described in the section of this paper dealing with the causes of unionism. For, in practical effect, the thrust of faculty unionism is to circumscribe by a legally enforceable contract the legal authority of the board of trustees and the executive responsibility, wherever it lies. Unionism implies a frontal attack upon the legal control and ultimate institutional responsibility vested in the lay board of trustees.

Depending upon the tone and approach of a particular faculty and the particular type of institution, existing governance schemes, certain notions of collegiality, and faculty prerogatives as we have known them (frequently undefined in a specific sense) will not survive the advent of militant faculty unionism. This raises the chicken and egg argument. Had there been "collegiality" and faculty prerogatives in the first place, there would not have been militant faculty unionism; for it is this very exercise of the so-called management prerogative that causes unionism.

Confronted by self-conscious faculty unions seeking to secure "rights" and prerogatives signed, sealed, and delivered in a written contract, one response is likely to be an escalated "management" reaction and a major redefinition of institutional prerogatives, responsibility, and authority.

At other institutions, however, I believe this problem will be less critical (Rutgers, for example). Much depends upon the faculty tradition and the prebargaining relationships at the particular institution. In some cases, faculty representatives and institutional officials will be reluctant because of strong institutional traditions, if not their trained incapacities to do otherwise, to shrug off collegial roles and relationships characteristic of yesterday for the tough-minded unionism prevalent in some city schoolteacher experiences.

Generalizing, I believe that the potential for a constructive relationship lies in recognizing the problem and exercising restraint on both sides. The accommodation between the bargaining process and the collegial tradition, implicit in the academic enterprise of the past, will be worked out in redefining, over a period of time, the division of labor between the faculty and university. What issues and conflicts can best be resolved through hard negotiation and what issues by more traditional collegial approaches? The answer to this question will be determined by the type of institution, tradition, geographical location, and an understanding of the bargaining process. Where some balance is struck, fundamental changes in tenure are likely to be gradual and on all fours with the then prevailing practices and thinking in higher education.

Assuming a growing "management" awareness takes hold, it is not clear what will be the precise impact upon tenure. The impact could be manifested in contract checks on faculty appointment, promotion, rank ratios designed to protect ultimate board authority. It could be manifested in institutional counterproposals for experimentation in various tenured appointments, such as five-year term appointments or review committees to study the merits of tenure in the context of the particular institution. Managerial initiatives may increase pressure for institutional involvement in the initial appointment process, calling for greater scrutiny and justification or detailed institutional criteria. Institutions may try to place centralized authority over funds over which departments would otherwise exercise control. Managerial initiatives might lead to new types of incentive programs based on productivity concepts or induce large-scale experimentation in teaching methodology. It could well resurrect, in a real way, the merit concept as a tool of encouraging new incentives. It might lead to full-scale programs where the continuing-appointment concept will be virtually nonexistent and involve only a sporadic employment relationship (along the lines of an independent contractor). Clearly, much of this would not be the result of collective bargaining per se or even a new-found management psychology. Forces are building in this direction wholly apart from collective bargaining. Nevertheless, the bargaining process is an unusually flexible process and may well substantially accelerate constructive change because it provides an unusual opportunity for institutional initiative. Assuming a strong and well organized employee bargaining agent, the process affords an unusual opportunity to motivate or gain the collective cooperation of the professional work force based upon hard information. The potential for full and candid communication is enhanced by the process.

Such approaches and the implicit underlying philosophy have no place in certain types of institutions. But, in others, the realities at work upon the institution make it imperative. Understand, too, that a management initiative is not the sole province of administrative officials. Quite the contrary, it can result from a responsible effort by the faculty to improve the institution in spite of "management." The bargaining process has potential for directing collective energy and goodwill for responsible and constructive purposes. It is simply too early to assess whether or not this will be the case.

Some of the unit determinations have resulted in placing nonteaching professional support staff (NTP) in the same bargaining unit with the academic faculty (CUNY and SUNY). This *may* have the effect, as it has in SUNY, of encouraging the NTP groups, such as certain library staff members, student personnel officers, instructional resource personnel, and other administrative staff to seek personnel employment practices similar to faculty. There will unquestionably be pressure from the NTP employees for some sort of job security and perhaps tenure itself. This security will include a defined evaluation process and procedure, certain consultative rights with respect to job functions, and term contract arrangements. For example, in the SUNY negotiations, the NTPs were successful in negotiating three significant elements: acceptance of the principle of term appointments for NTPs; a joint labor-management study committee to make recommendations with respect to developing an

evaluation system; and a joint labor-management study committee
to develop a career promotion plan for NTPs. These joint committees are slated, under the terms of the bargaining agreement, to
make a report and nonbinding recommendations concerning these
matters. Either party may request reopened negotiations concerning
these issues if recommendations are rejected by either party.

Accordingly, I speculate one of the by-products of faculty
unionism will be to encourage NTP employees to organize and pursue job security akin to a faculty tenure system. The SUNY experience seems to indicate that demands by NTP for tenure—like
policies for nonteaching professional staff is encouraged where NTPs
are in the same bargaining unit with faculty. It may also occur even
where they are in a separate unit and employ whipsawing techniques. But I perceive that NTPs will proceed from greater strength
in such demands where they are in the same bargaining unit with
faculty and therefore represented by the same bargaining agent.

The tone of unionism's impact upon tenure will be greatly
affected by the current problems and thinking of tenure. In cata-
loging the impact of collective bargaining upon tenure, it is important to keep in mind that there is nothing immutable about the bargaining process. In part, it will not be a cause, but rather a process
that will absorb existing problems. Constructive results of collective
bargaining will clearly depend upon the imagination, ingenuity,
restraint, and the goodwill of the leadership involved. It will also
depend upon a clear understanding of the bargaining process, its
limitations, and its potential. In the last analysis, these factors will
be decisive in avoiding needless damage to the university tradition
and in keeping current problems in perspective.

If, on the other hand, men pursue narrow interests and
irresponsible positions and thereby generate conflict it is, of course,
bad. In my judgment, there is nothing inherent in the collective
bargaining process which necessarily produces the latter. Debilitat-
ing conflict versus constructive conflict is more often the result of
head-in-the-sand institutional officials who have not assumed their
responsibility for understanding the bargaining process and who
fail to appreciate its potential as a stabilizing influence for achieving institutional objectives. Needless conflict can also be the result
of mediocre men thrown by accident into employee leadership

capacities, and who, as men of principle, have neither the intelligence nor sophistication to realize where their principles are leading them.

Systems of conflict resolution which force both sides to rationalize their positions in terms of institutional objectives can be productive in spite of the so-called confrontation styles frequently associated with unionism. In the last analysis, the people and the problems remain the same. If a given representational system can in a conflict situation produce constructive decisions which the parties will accept, if not agree with, it can be a productive process.

Chapter 10

Tenure

Under Attack

Robert M. O'Neal

A tenured music teacher in New Jersey recently underwent a sex-change operation during spring vacation. The school board at once announced its concern and took the issue under advisement. Some weeks later, the board ruled that the teacher (newly female) "could keep her job but would have to give up his fourteen years of tenure." In the controversy that followed, both teacher and school board seemed to feel that tenure, rather than the opportunity to teach, was the crucial issue.[1]

The role of tenure may be more symbolic than real. Behind the symbol, the deeper concern of those who mounted the recent attack on tenure is nothing less than the prerogatives of professors in American colleges and universities. The academic profession, not the tenure system, is the real object of the attack. Yet the status of tenure is not a wholly irrelevant target. Its protections seem to

[1] *San Francisco Chronicle,* Aug. 13, 1971, p. 9.

make professors relatively immune to public pressure and criticism. There is a pervasive feeling that faculties would become more vulnerable—reduced to size, some would say—if only they could be stripped of these special safeguards. (The extent to which tenure *does* confer a special immunity upon university professors is itself a debatable issue; in any event, most persons outside the university probably believe the status is special.)

The attack upon tenure has taken several forms. Occasionally the attack is direct—legislation designed to abolish tenure, for example, and recurrent demands that the tenure system be re-examined. Far more significant, if less clearly perceived, are a host of indirect attacks, which have begun to chip away the prerogatives and the power of the senior faculty. These latter pressures have come from a variety of sources—some internal to the academy, others external; some conservative, others liberal. Few have tenure as their focus; yet many of these indirect attacks have the inevitable effect of making tenure a less valuable and less certain guarantor of academic freedoms for those who hold it.

The senior faculty have recently lost relative power and prestige in two distinct ways. On the one hand, there have been serious incursions by external forces: hostile legislatures; angry governing boards; insensitive judicial and law enforcement agencies; and the like. Such incursions have seriously impaired the autonomy of the entire academic community, even though the senior faculty have suffered disproportionately since they have traditionally held the major share of academic power. Meanwhile, their status has also been threatened by internal reallocations of power and responsibility. When students gain voting rights in the faculty senate, when nontenured teachers participate more fully in departmental affairs, when senior professors are made more accountable for decisions that affect the other constituencies, the inevitable consequence is a relative lessening of the authority of the tenured faculty. The general university community may well gain from such reallocations and re-alignments, since the process of academic decision-making becomes more democratic and more visible. For the tenured faculty, however, the net result may be very much the same, whether the source of impairment is an internal transfer or an external incursion.

It is not the purpose of this essay to appraise the validity of the attack and defense of tenure; other contributors to the present volume have done so. Nor is this the place to review alternatives and substitutes, also canvassed in other chapters. The focus here will be upon the attack itself—its nature, its dimensions and manifestations, its underlying assumptions, and an appraisal of its targets and objects. Hopefully, the defense of an embattled profession may be aided by clear understanding of the assault.

The direct attack upon tenure has come principally from state legislatures, although the incidence of bills designed to "abolish tenure" has been exaggerated. The California legislature did adopt in 1970 a joint resolution requesting the university regents to mandate a probationary period for all academic employees, so that no one could be hired from outside the system to an initially tenured position.[2] But the cutting edge of this action was blunted by several factors. The regents (apparently invoking their constitutional autonomy) paid no attention to the request. Moreover, to require a probationary period of at least a year is very far from abolishing tenure; indeed, though this was hardly the intent of the framers, the joint resolution might even have enhanced the tenure system by improving the review and promotion process. (Some faculties, like that of the University of Oklahoma, have voluntarily imposed such a constraint on their own hiring policies.) Finally, the California resolution cited relevant policies of the American Association of University Professors (AAUP) and urged the regents to set a seven-year limit on the probationary period (when present university policy, whether the legislature knows it or not, permits an eight-year term).[3] The resolution was, then, an attack of sorts on the tenure system. At least it was presumably intended to be an attack. But it could hardly be considered a fatal blow to the prerogatives of California's faculties.

Bills have now been introduced in the legislatures of between six and eleven states to abolish tenure, usually by substituting contract terms of four or five years.[4] Such proposals have evoked head-

[2] California Assembly Concurrent Resolution, No. 102, 1970 Regular Session.

[3] *Handbook for Faculty Members of the University of California* (Berkeley: Regents of the Univ. of Calif., 1970), 28.

[4] See *Chronicle of Higher Education*, March 22, 1971, p. 1;

lines about the jeopardy of the tenure system, and they have quite understandably frightened many academic people. But no such measure appears to have passed any state legislature. Had there been a serious chance of any of these bills becoming law, the faculties would have mobilized in opposition, probably with the rare support of regents and trustees alarmed by the implicit threat to their own autonomy in personnel matters. But mobilization has not proved necessary and probably will not become necessary until and unless there is a new wave of campus disorder, reconstitution of classes, and the like.

If the professoriate should have expected harsh treatment from state lawmakers, few would have anticipated the unkind words it has received from its friends. A succession of high-level study commissions, drawn mainly from within the academic community, have taken faculties to task in the course of appraising campus problems. In each instance tenure has been singled out for special concern—not so much because tenure is the cause of faculty dereliction (at least no causal connection has been proved, as Eble argues in Chapter Six) but because tenure is both a symbol and a safeguard. The American Council on Education Committee on Campus Tensions suggested a thorough reexamination of the tenure system, which it felt has "sometimes been a shield for indifference and neglect of scholarly duties."[5] The Scranton Commission concurred five months later, adding that tenure "can also protect practices that detract from the institution's primary functions, that are unjust to students, and that grant faculty members freedom from accountability that would be unacceptable for any other profession."[6] In the spring of 1971, a special task force report to the Secretary of Health, Education, and Welfare called for "a revision of standard tenure policies leading toward short-term contracts for

---

Time May 10, 1971, p. 62; *Wall Street Journal,* April 16, 1971, pp. 1, 23.

[5] *Campus Tensions: Analysis and Recommendations—Report of the Special Committee on Campus Tensions* (Washington, D.C.: American Council on Education, 1970), 42.

[6] *Campus Unrest: The Report of the President's Commission on Campus Unrest* (Washington, D.C.: U.S. Government Printing Office, 1970), 201.

at least some categories of faculty positions."[7] Individual members of the academic community, too, have been severely critical. Perhaps most outspoken is Boston University President Silber (see Chapter Three), who fears that "granting a sinecure is clearly a device of the devil to let sloth into the world."[8] Alone among the major recent reports, that of the Assembly on University Goals and Governance (of the American Academy of Arts and Sciences) recognized that, "despite the abuses common to permanent positions, professorial tenure needs to be retained as a guarantor of academic freedom against political and other pressures."[9]

Despite occasional parries at the institution of tenure, it is problematical whether tenure per se is under serious attack. Indeed, a deeper analysis of the current plight of the academic profession suggests the target is not the tenure system, notwithstanding its role as scapegoat or symbol. Those proposals that dealt most explicitly with tenure have received least support from legislators and others, and the reluctance to repeal or dilute traditional academic safeguards cannot be attributed primarily to fear of AAUP reprisal. Moreover, the attacks that have received substantial support have seldom bothered to differentiate between tenured and nontenured teachers, suggesting this distinction holds limited significance for the critics. In fact, the really controversial faculty members who draw the sharpest legislative and regental ire do not have tenure and are unlikely to get it under present conditions. (One notable exception is Herbert Marcuse, but he was already beyond retirement age, as well as tenured, when the California Regents discovered him. After the board unwittingly delegated to the San Diego chancellor full authority for over-age appointments, the issue became moot.) Finally, there has been no broad attack on the underlying principle of employment security; that principle is widely accepted through civil service in the public sector and collective bargaining in much

[7] *Report on Higher Education* (Washington, D.C.: U.S. Government Printing Office, 1971), 100 (advance draft).

[8] Quoted in *Chronicle of Higher Education,* March 22, 1971, p. 4.

[9] Assembly on University Goals and Governance, *A First Report* (Cambridge, Massachusetts: American Academy of Arts and Sciences, 1971), 18.

of the private sector. Thus the fault found with academic tenure apparently reflects its *academic location* much more than its *protective function*.

If tenure per se has seldom been under direct attack, the same cannot be said of other professorial perquisites. And since tenure is one of the prime incidents of academic status, any attack upon the status of the senior professoriate is an indirect threat to tenure. Indeed, most such attacks disproportionately harm the holders of tenure, since they also hold a disproportionate share of academic authority and responsibility.

As suggested earlier, challenges to the hegemony of the senior faculty are of two distinct types. There are, on the one hand, serious incursions by hostile forces outside the academy—repressive legislation, governing board directives, grand jury reports, and the like. The entire academic community suffers from such attacks, though the wounds to the senior faculty are especially grave. At the same time, the senior faculty has also lost power simply by sharing it with the other constituencies and by becoming increasingly accountable to them. While the implications for the tenured professoriate may be similar, the sources and nature of these two convergent forces manifestly differ. Keeping this distinction clearly in mind, it seems appropriate to discuss them together in this essay. For purposes of analysis, the various indirect threats to tenure may be grouped functionally; that is, in terms of the professorial prerogative which they impair. This approach will facilitate a more thorough appraisal of the current health of the tenure system than is possible through undifferentiated analysis.

There has been much anti-faculty legislation of late. Several states have enacted laws prescribing harsh penalties for faculty members who commit certain offenses; some statutes preclude reemployment or even reentry to the campus for a certain period following conviction. Apparently the harshest measure to date is Ohio House Bill 1219, passed in the wake of the Kent-Cambodia crisis in 1970. In its original form, as enacted by the lower house, the bill required automatic suspension of any faculty member following his arrest for any of a variety of offenses, including several new crimes created by the bill itself. Dismissal was to be mandatory upon conviction. The Ohio Senate refused to adopt the bill until some concessions were made to due process. Under the substitute measure which eventually passed both houses, the arrest of a faculty member for any of the enumerated offenses triggers a rather complex process which begins with a hearing before a referee (an attorney in the county, selected by the Board of Regents) to determine whether the faculty member should be suspended while awaiting trial. An adverse judgment by the referee effects a suspension—without pay. If a criminal conviction eventually results, dismissal from the university is automatic without any further proceedings. If acquitted, the defendant must be reinstated but apparently without back pay or other amends. Conviction carries certain collateral consequences: A faculty or staff member dismissed from one state-supported institution may not be hired by another such institution for at least one year. Even after that time, his employability is contingent upon express approval of the governing board.[10]

Since the provisions of this law apply without regard to a faculty member's status, its implications for tenure are twofold: First, the procedure completely bypasses all internal tribunals and leaves an arrested professor's fate in the hands of an outside referee and a criminal judge or jury; and second, dismissal may be decreed with no inquiry into the offender's fitness to teach or his compliance with *academic* norms. (There are limits, however. The first faculty case under H.B. 1219 involved a tenured black professor at Ohio State who got into a fight with a Columbus policeman at a local high school. A hearing was scheduled following his arrest, but the referee correctly held the law did not apply to off-campus activity which did not involve another member of the university community.)[11]

Although legislatures seldom interfere quite this directly with basic faculty freedoms and employment security, governing boards occasionally do. After the Kent-Cambodia crisis, the University of Missouri's Board of Curators suspended without pay for ten days the tenured chairman of the sociology department because he refused to tell the board which of his colleagues had cancelled or restructured

---

[10] Page's Ohio Revised Code, § 3345.22 (Supp. 1971).
[11] *In the Matter of Charles O. Ross,* Decision of Referee Thomas E. Palmer, June 11, 1971.

classes.[12] The University of California Regents, soon after delegating to campus chancellors the responsibility for non-tenure appointments, reclaimed that power just long enough to terminate the employment of Angela Davis following disclosure of her Communist Party affiliation.[13] These are perhaps the most notorious but not the only such instances.

Academic autonomy also has been recently jeopardized by criminal courts and grand juries. The academic community has viewed with proper alarm the indiscriminate resort to criminal charges as a deterrent to campus disorder: the grand jury indictment and subsequent prosecution of Hobart and William Smith Colleges; the Ohio grand jury report excoriating the Kent State faculty and indicting one of its members; the contempt citation of the Stony Brook (State University of New York) faculty members for refusing to reveal student confidences to a grand jury in the aftermath of a drug raid; and the arrest and prosecution of forty-five faculty members at SUNY-Buffalo for a peaceful Sunday morning sit-in in the president's office. These and other recent applications of the criminal law have undeniably threatened academic freedom. They bear upon tenure in the most obvious way: While a tenured professor cannot be summarily dismissed because of an arrest or criminal conviction, tenure no better enables him than his junior codefendant to conduct his courses from a county jail.

While academic autonomy is being impaired by such incursions, the authority of the senior faculty is being challenged by two forces of a different sort. One source of change, of course, is the rapid expansion of collective bargaining in higher education. While unionization does not make tenure irrelevant (and may under some conditions strengthen tenure), it does tend to redistribute power and broaden the base of academic decision-making. In the preceding chapter McHugh develops at some length the complex relationship between collective bargaining and tenure; it would be inappropriate to pursue the theme further here.

At the same time, the way in which senior professors exer-

[12] *Washington Post,* Oct. 30, 1970, p. A24.
[13] *New York Times,* June 20, 1970, p. 47.

cise their responsibility for the careers of junior colleagues has been made more visible and accountable. Several courts have held that a probationary teacher is entitled at least to an explanation of a decision not to renew his appointment and sometimes to a hearing at which he may challenge the basis of an adverse judgment. Nor are these concerns exclusive with the courts. The AAUP's Committee A on Academic Freedom and Tenure recently recommended improved procedures for nonreappointments. This statement, adopted by the Association's council and endorsed at the annual meeting in 1971,[14] underscores a developing AAUP concern for the status of nontenured faculty members by suggesting that the senior members of a department should be prepared to explain the basis on which they decide to terminate the services of a junior colleague.

Strengthening the rights of probationary teachers is clearly not an attack on tenure in the conventional sense. Yet these developments do affect the status of tenured faculty in two respects. First, they serve to diminish somewhat the historic difference between those who have tenure and those who do not by giving some rights to the latter. At the same time, the effect is not—as some have mistakenly suggested—to create "instant tenure" for everyone. Continuation of probationary appointments may be denied for a broad range of reasons that would not remotely constitute "cause" in a dismissal proceeding. Yet in subtle ways the status of the tenured faculty is diluted by sharing with junior colleagues certain protections and safeguards that were once theirs exclusively.

Meanwhile, the greater visibility which such safeguards give to the promotion and tenure process imposes upon the senior professoriate an unaccustomed measure of accountability. When a decision not to promote or retain an assistant professor must be explained upon request, the method by which that judgment is made is itself affected. Tenured faculty do not, to be sure, forfeit the power to make decisions about the status and future of junior colleagues. But they do come under a measure of scrutiny that restricts their latitude, if only by denying them the right to be arbitrary, or petty, or vindictive in individual cases. To the extent nontenured professors

[14] *AAUP Bulletin,* 1971, *57,* 206–210.

gain in these respects, the system of higher education also probably benefits. But to a degree the senior faculty, whose authority in this area was until recently beyond challenge, are the losers.

Tenure has suffered indirectly as a result of threats to a second and related set of faculty interests. The authority to determine academic policy and shape the curriculum is a vital tenet of professorial autonomy, and threats on this authority have come from a variety of sources. The California Regents, for example, withdrew power long delegated to the Academic Senate's committee on courses for the sole purpose of denying credit given by the faculty to students enrolled in the symposium of which Eldridge Cleaver was to have been a major participant. (Most of the students eventually got credit through some other route.) Cleaver, of course, left the country. Suit was brought by the Senate Academic Freedom Committee, challenging the propriety of the regental action.[15] When the Missouri Board of Curators suspended the sociology department chairman, they also rescinded an agreement between the chancellor at Columbia and a faculty-student group under which course credit could be obtained on the basis of work completed before the Kent-Cambodia crisis.[16] In New York, a comparable threat to curricular autonomy came from the legislature. The Office of Legislative Research (at the behest of a group of lawmakers) asked presidents of more than thirty state university campuses for detailed information about various courses in the social sciences. The focus of the inquiry was courses dealing with "revolution," "the Establishment," and sociology and urban studies, with particular attention to the instructor's orientation.[17]

Courts have also threatened the academic authority of the faculty in several recent cases. Most notable was the suit brought after Kent-Cambodia by a group of students at Queens College, claiming they had been denied instruction to which they were entitled because of the restructured conclusion of the academic year. The basis of the suit was a May 10 resolution of the board of higher

[15] *Searle, et al. v. Regents of the University of California,* 1 Civil. No. 28,240; *Tabucchi et al. v. Regents of the University of California,* 1 Civil No. 29,234 (Calif. Ct. of Appeal).

[16] *Washington Post,* Oct. 30, 1970, p. A24.

[17] *New York Times,* Jan. 30, 1971, p. 47.

education requiring that all units of the city university "remain open to continue to offer instruction to the students. . . ." The resolution also provided that "colleges may adjust their programs of courses, attendance, examinations and grading as in their judgment may seem necessary and appropriate." The court held in the plaintiffs' favor and ordered the Queens faculty to provide special compensatory instruction in specified subjects, since it was impractical to reopen the whole college in the summer just for a few students. While the board had left considerable flexibility to each campus and its faculty, the judge found no latitude for individual adjustment to the end-of-the-year crisis.[18]

Meanwhile, threats to the curricular hegemony of the senior faculty may come from a very different quarter. A case in point is the strike in the spring of 1970 by the Teaching Assistants Association at the University of Wisconsin (Madison). Ostensibly the conflict was between TAs and the administration over tangible benefits, terms of employment and the like (and even, at one point, a TA demand for something resembling "tenure"). But the real battle was between junior and senior faculty and related centrally to the shaping of the curriculum in the large introductory courses. Just as an agreement was about to be adopted that would have shared considerable responsibility with the teaching assistants, intense opposition developed within the senior faculty, which had remained esentially on the sidelines up to that point. Ultimately the senior professors insisted that the contract qualify any commitment to TA participation in curricular planning with this proviso: "Such mechanisms shall not infringe upon the ultimate responsibility of the faculty for curriculum and course content." The TAs won many victories on tangible issues but lost on the one intangible issue that many felt had precipitated the strike. The senior faculty was apparently willing to yield on most of the tangible issues but prevailed on the vital question of who shaped the curriculum.[19]

A similar issue arose a year later at the University of Cali-

[18] *DeVito v. McMurray*, 311 N.Y. Supp. 2d 617 (Sup. Ct. 1970).

[19] See Arlen Christensen, "Collective Bargaining in a University: The University of Wisconsin and the Teaching Assistants Association," *Wisconsin Law Review*, 1971, 210.

fornia. Student leaders had been pushing for some time for a stake in departmental decisions. The senior faculty had adamantly opposed these efforts, just as they had long resisted attempts to admit students to membership in the extremely powerful academic senate. Suddenly the students gained an unexpected but valuable ally—a group of conservative regents, who supported a proposal to broaden and democratize the base of departmental decision-making. For a long time it appeared that a coalition of strange and seldom allied bedfellows might succeed in diluting the power of the professoriate where neither adversary alone had succeeded in the past. (In some respects the whole Free Speech Movement of 1964–1965 was an attack by junior against senior faculty, very much like the Wisconsin TA strike. But studies of Berkeley five and six years after the FSM have shown remarkably little redistribution of academic power.) At the last moment, President Hitch supported the faculty position and the regental proposal died.[20] But the threat to senior faculty hegemony at the departmental level had been real and substantial. Had the change been made as proposed, it would have drastically increased the visibility and accountability both of decisions about tenure and promotion and decisions on other matters by the tenured faculty—prerogatives jealously guarded in the past against both regental and student scrutiny.

The impact of collective bargaining in the City University of New York has created a comparable threat to faculty autonomy at the departmental level. Shortly after the Legislative Conference obtained for its members (the senior CUNY faculty) a contract with the highest salary schedule in history, the law committee of the Board of Higher Education recommended that department chairmen—traditionally elected by their colleagues for a three-year term—should be appointed. The change was justified by the special needs of collective bargaining: Under the new contract the chairman serves as the first formal step in a complex grievance machinery and performs other duties arguably incompatible with elected status.[21] The proposal drew an angry response from the union and other

[20] *Los Angeles Times*, Feb. 19, 1971, pt. 1, p. 3; *id.* May 21, pt. 1, p. 3.
[21] *New York Times*, Dec. 11, 1969, p. 31.

faculty groups. It also evoked the editorial concern of the *New York Times,* which felt the appointment of chairmen would be "a blow to faculty morale" and would "force an increased reliance by the rest of the faculty on shop stewards in a further departure from academic traditions."[22] Here, as with the other changes and proposals reviewed in this section, the gravest threat may well lie in the challenge to the traditional dominance and independence of the senior, tenured faculty. If any constituency stood to lose power by altering the manner in which department chairmen were selected, it would be this group. The governing board and administration would gain power; the students and the junior faculty would neither gain nor lose; but the senior faculty would forfeit a very valuable perquisite of participation in university governance.

One of the potentially gravest threats to campus autonomy is federal agency review of the composition (by race and sex) of university faculties. Minority groups and women account for only a low percentage of senior faculty; female and minority shares of lower academic ranks and in lower paid academic fields are somewhat higher. The surprise, in fact, is that these inequities have gone nearly unnoticed and unrequited by the academic community for so many decades. The condition has made the professoriate extremely vulnerable to outside ameliorative pressure.

Recently such pressure has come from the Department of Health, Education, and Welfare. Armed initially with the nondiscrimination mandate of Title VI of the Civil Rights Act of 1964—applicable to all recipients of federal funds and thus covering most colleges and universities—HEW compliance officers in the late sixties began to ask embarrassing questions about the underrepresentation of minority groups. Following the promulgation of specific guidelines, the agency has insisted on development of "goals and timetables" for the increased participation of women and minorities in campus employment. In several instances—notably at Columbia and the University of Michigan—HEW has demanded rather extensive data from personnel files as a further check on institutional compliance. Substantial sums in federal contracts and grants were

[22] *New York Times,* Dec. 16, 1969, p. 46.

withheld from Columbia pending submission of a satisfactory plan to remedy the underrepresentation.

It is clear how campus autonomy as a whole may suffer from such inquiries and demands. The effect upon faculty autonomy is less apparent. A governmental mandate to consider women and blacks in filling academic positions does, however, restrict the historically unfettered discretion of many departments and colleges in choosing junior colleagues. Moreover, the prospect that termination of a nontenured teacher may bring a charge of discrimination and may be reviewed by federal agents carries an even graver threat. Finally, the prospect of governmental access to academic personnel files may restrict the future contents of those files and, in a way, circumscribes the evaluation by senior professors of their junior colleagues.

It is too early to tell whether affirmative action programs will jeopardize professorial autonomy or threaten the tenure system. Like court review of nonreappointments, HEW compliance proceedings may serve chiefly to keep the senior faculty honest and to enhance opportunities for groups long denied full equality in the academic profession. In less sensitive hands, however, affirmative action mandates could have harmful effects on the confidentiality of personnel files, on the exercise of experienced professional judgment about qualification for academic positions, and on academic freedom itself.

In various important ways, tenure serves to divide one group of faculty from another—the journeymen from the apprentices. Indicia of the distinction are many and sometimes subtle. In part, the achievement of tenure means higher salaries—if not at once, then after a few years. Tenure usually also means a higher proportion of graduate courses, more time (and money) to conduct research on subjects of one's own choosing, opportunities for paid sabbatical leaves, expanded access to rewarding activities and associations outside the university, and so on. To the extent these perquisites are jeopardized, tenure status is itself threatened. This is precisely what has begun to happen, however,—partly as a result of the austerity that has suddenly beset higher education but for other reasons as well.

Most visible of these threats have been the "workload conditions" attached to the university budget by several state legislatures. The process began in Michigan, which has a special history of conditions on appropriations for higher education. The 1970 budget, encumbered by myriad complex conditions affecting many aspects of the state's college and university system, declared the intention of the legislature "that each full-time faculty member who is paid wholly from the line item instruction budget will teach a minimum of not less than fifteen classroom contact hours at technical colleges, developing colleges and universities, regional colleges and universities, and complex universities; and ten classroom contact hours at graduate institutions."[23] While the stipulations seem not to have been fully enforced, at least at the larger institutions in Michigan, the implication was clear. Law professors at Ann Arbor, for example, who regularly meet five or six classes each week, and may not (under policies of the Association of American Law Schools) be compelled to teach more than eight, were now expected to be in the classroom for a minimum of ten hours. Because of these and other conflicts, the University regents took the extraordinary step (extraordinary, that is, except in Michigan, where it has been done several times before) of bringing suit against the state to invalidate the conditions. The central claim was that the legislature had violated the state constitution (whence derives the authority of the regents) by attempting to circumscribe university policy and operation in this fashion.[24] (One caveat is important, if obvious, in any discussion of *faculty* autonomy: The regents argued not that University of Michigan professors should necessarily be free of any workload mandate but only that any power to impose it resided with the governing board and not the legislature.)

A year later New York followed suit. In a separate act declaring the intent of the legislature, both houses cited a "recognized educational observation that greater amounts of the educator's time [are] being expended upon research and nonclassroom scholarly endeavors"—a commitment which apparently diluted the value

[23] Enrolled Senate Bill No. 1179, § 12, 75th Michigan Legislature, Regular Session of 1970.

[24] *Regents of the University of Michigan v. State of Michigan,* Civil Action No. 7659-C (Ingham County Circuit Court).

of "the generous sums of public monies appropriated and expended
. . . for higher educational purposes." In order to ensure "a fair
return in the form of commensurate productivity on the part of the
respective faculties" of New York's colleges and universities, the
resolution prescribed fifteen classroom contract hours weekly for the
community colleges, twelve hours for undergraduate instruction,
and nine hours for graduate instruction at all other SUNY and
CUNY campuses. Though the health sciences were exempted, the
work-load conditions were expressly extended to the faculties of
private institutions receiving state funds. Compliance was strongly
encouraged by a warning that further appropriations of state funds
would be "proportionate to the extent to which administrators . . .
implement this expression of the public policy of the state."[25]

The New York legislation followed a tortuous course which
finally brought about its demise. Recalled by the legislature on its
own motion following intense criticism from educators, the resolution was reenacted later in the summer, only to be "disapproved"
by Governor Rockefeller. (It was not a law, so a refusal to approve
was the only course legally open to him.) In a brief explanatory
message, the governor acknowledged that the bill "reflects a growing
concern among students, parents, educators, and public officials
about the amount of time some college and university faculty members spend on nonstudent related matters." But the concern could
not be so crudely implemented: "the determination of a reasonable
teaching load depends on a number of complex factors, including
the number of students in a class, the type of course involved, and
the nature of the faculty member's other responsibilities. Moreover,
the degree of a faculty member's commitment to the student is not
embodied solely in the hours devoted directly to classroom teaching
functions."[26]

While the New York episode reached this relatively happy
denouement, similar workload provisions were pending in several
other states, including Ohio and Illinois. Florida enacted a set of
conditions more onerous than those of Michigan or New York but

[25] S.6299, New York Legislature, 1971–72 Regular Sessions.
[26] Message of Governor Nelson A. Rockefeller Concerning
S.6299, July 6, 1971.

containing a wider range of exceptions for graduate and professional faculties. The Florida law also attempted to establish equivalency formulas for teachers assigned to spend part of their time on research and other noninstructional activities.[27]

The impact of the workload conditions on tenure status is readily apparent. If the legislature can determine how many hours a senior professor will teach, then his autonomy is seriously impaired. If, moreover, the legislature makes that determination without regard for length of service, type or size of course, tradition, or any of the myriad factors which led Governor Rockefeller to disapprove the New York resolution, then the threat to tenure status is substantially greater. One of the most valued perquisites of the senior professor has been endangered by the work-load-condition approach.

Meanwhile, other privileges have also been threatened by external action. New York's legislature, in the spring of 1970, struck a second blow at faculty status, this one almost inadvertent. Without warning, the legislature simply cancelled all sabbatical leaves for the following academic year, except where a preexisting contractual right to a leave was enforceable prior to enactment of the law.[28] (The director of the budget was given a very limited power of dispensation in circumstances where a leave would "inure to the benefit of the state.") The impact of this legislation upon tenure was even more direct than the work-load formulas. While nontenured teachers may sometimes accumulate sufficient credit to merit a salaried leave, sabbaticals are mainly a reward for longevity of employment associated with tenure. Where the institution requires, as many do, six years of full-time service prior to taking such a leave and an additional year following the leave, nontenured faculty simply do not receive sabbaticals. Elimination of paid leaves, therefore, imposes a disproportionate hardship upon the tenured professoriate.

Most of the attacks and threats recounted here affect faculties as a whole. In certain cases (for example, the cancellation of

[27] *Higher Education and National Affairs*, 1971, XX, *26*, 1971.
[28] S.6300, New York Legislature, 1971–72 Regular Sessions.

sabbaticals in New York) the tenured faculty actually suffer disproportionately. There may be slight evidence of large-scale effort to eliminate tenure as such. But to the extent that such measures reach the tenured and untenured professor even *equally,* the status of tenure suffers a special blow. For tenure was meant to afford its holders an exemption from political pressures, fiscal fortunes, and assaults upon the academy. If the net effect of being tenured is that one is *no worse off* than his junior colleague—as is the consequence of many of the current restrictions, conditions, and disabilities—the status earned through seniority and academic distinction is to that extent impaired. Equal treatment of both groups, in the eyes of the academic community, means one thing; equal treatment in the eyes of legislators, tax-payers, some governing board members, and students, means quite another.

It is difficult for persons on the periphery of the academic community to appreciate both the significance and the fragility of tenure. In turn, it is hard for the professoriate to understand the insensitivity of outsiders toward academic freedom and autonomy. To the academician, it is perfectly obvious why the working conditions of a professor must be determined more delicately than the working conditions of a municipal bus driver or state auditor. To the auditor or the bus driver, it is very far from clear why there should be any such distinction. Indeed, those outside the academy sometimes suppose the professor should be more accountable than other public employees, not less. Any discussion of the current status of the academic profession must take account of these popular feelings and their significance for tenure.

The fact is, as we have seen, that most external critics of the faculty either do not know or do not care enough about tenure to attack it head on. Others may fear that courts, faculty organizations, unions, and other groups would come to the defense of the tenure principle and would receive substantial public support— where lesser perquisites may be chipped away virtually without challenge. Thus, to the extent tenure has been under attack, its role has been more symbolic than functional. But there can be little doubt that the academic profession has become a target of considerable hostility.

Why has the professor fallen from grace, and what does his

reversal of fortune have to do with tenure? The very independence which tenure to a degree confers and protects may be a major source of tension between faculties and other constituencies. It is this independence that permits professors to teach what they wish, to spend their time as they will, to consult for government agencies (or not), to criticize others with little fear of reprisal, to dress and live in ways that are abhorrent to the average citizen and that would not be tolerated among IBM employees or even public school teachers. Part of the tension derives from misunderstanding and misinformation: The average citizen-taxpayer simply does not know how independent a professor is and therefore assumes the worst—especially when the worst seems to be confirmed by a few outrageous examples of dereliction. Nor does the lay critic have any clear notion of what a professor does for a living; the widespread belief that faculty members who are assigned to *teach* six hours a week really *work* only six hours no doubt explains the popularity of workload conditions appended to university budgets. Just below the surface is a belief that if tenure could be removed, professors would be accountable just like everyone else, could be made to conform in dress and life style, compelled to teach a full forty-hour week, and so on. In this sense, tenure is surely not irrelevant to the popular concern.

Second, public hostility focuses not only on the right to be different but on the exercise of that right. There is in fact greater diversity of political expression and activity, life style, diligence, and commitment in the professoriate than is possible anywhere else save in the tiny group composed of full-time creative and performing artists. Moreover, Angela Davis, Eugene Genovese, Staughton Lynd, John Froines, and other visible "radicals" are always clearly identified in the press as university teachers. When the Illinois legislature launched a major investigation into campus disorder during the summer of 1970, the committee chairman held a press conference to announce the inquiry. "We want no Angela Davises in Illinois," he declared, explaining that the committee would "try to find ways to remove tenure from faculty members, where necessary, to keep them from agitating further violence."[29] Similarly, the hostility of

[29] *Chicago Tribune,* Aug. 21, 1970, p. 3.

the Portage County, Ohio, grand jury toward the Kent State faculty reflected more than anything else an abhorrence of life style and political views. The jurors cited, with a mixture of shame and regret, the presence at Kent of professors who "teach nothing but the negative side of our institutions and government and refuse to acknowledge that any positive good has resulted during the growth of our nation."[30]

As a corollary of the life-style and political gulf, there is a conviction that professors have contributed to or caused the alienation of the young. Higher education is always a subversive force; but at a time when 60 per cent or more of our students come from non-college families, the potentially divisive force is magnified. Many citizen-taxpayers no doubt reflect the view described in a recent pseudonymous article in *Change* magazine: "The professor gets even with the lathe-operator (who has a trade); the businessman (who can organize the production and distribution of goods); the Madison Avenue account executive (who uses some professors' learning for commercial purposes); and even the minister (whose scholarship is presumably passé and too unsecular) by teaching their children to despise their parents' culture."[31] The charge is as ironic as it is pervasive. Faculties may indeed have contributed to the alienation of disaffected young people but surely not by design. And few groups have less capacity to draw those students, once alienated, back into the mainstream than the rank and file of professors.

Then, too, there is a feeling that many professors are shirkers. Suspicions bred by rumors about three- and four-hour work weeks are reinforced by occasional extreme cases. When a tenured department chairman at Los Angeles State College was shown to be teaching no courses on his own campus for over a year, but was in fact being paid extra for conducting a class at a nearby private university at the very same hour the catalog said he was teaching at State, confirmation of faculty dereliction was provided beyond even the critics' resourceful imagination.[32] (The professor was dismissed

---

[30] *New York Times,* Oct. 17, 1970, p. 22.

[31] A. Lambeth, "The Academic Class Machine," *Change Magazine,* 1971, III, *4,* 43.

[32] *San Francisco Chronicle,* Nov. 25, 1970, p. 6; *Los Angeles Times,* Nov. 25, 1970, pt. 1, pp. 3, 13.

—the first tenured teacher in the system to be discharged in recent times—and was later sued by the state for back salary and other alleged wastage of state funds.) Perhaps the public believes, as university officials try to assure them, that such cases are extremely rare. But the fact that they occur at all draws very special attention to the academic profession.

Finally, the changing economic position of the faculty may reinforce other concerns. When professors were desperately poor, as most were until the mid-1950s, their indiscretions could be tolerated more easily. Today, when faculty salaries fail to keep pace with rising living costs, few professors are wealthy (save by independent means) and many are not yet even comfortable. But there is a widespread belief that faculties are reasonably well paid, perhaps because of publicity given to the few salaries like those of the Schweitzer and Einstein professors in New York and the medical school faculties at the University of California. The number of professors who are actually paid less than high school teachers and laborers seldom receives any public note.

The relationship between economics and the status of higher education has not been studied. It may well be, however, that taxpayers have become increasingly angry about an apparently inverse correlation between the *costs* of the system and its *performance*. The correlation is in trouble not only because of campus turmoil and disorder, but more recently because higher education (and the degree evidencing its completion) seem both essential and superfluous at the same time. One must go to college if he is to succeed, so higher education remains the nearly universal aspiration. Yet the kind of experience that college classes provide seems not to prepare graduates for the work that awaits them upon graduation. Thus radical student claims that much of higher education is "irrelevant" have begun to be echoed by corporate personnel officers and others whose views on most questions could not be more remote from those of the radicals. Thus the faculty and its teaching tend to be blamed by both sides for a maladaptation between campus life and real life.

Clearly all is not well within the academic community. There is a malaise, a loss of morale among the faculties of all types of institutions of higher learning. There is a great deal of bad teaching.

Some of it is extremely bad, and students are legitimately aggrieved on a range of curricular and instructional concerns. Most thoughtful observers would agree that the tenure system did not bring about this situation and probably does relatively little to perpetuate it— or that in the absence of tenure other pressures and conditions would produce similar results. The remedy is not to destroy a cornerstone of academic freedom and faculty security in the attempt to improve instruction and professional responsibility. These problems should be addressed directly by trying to enhance the classroom performance of those who will respond and, if necessary in extreme cases, to dismiss those who will not respond, whether or not they have tenure. The current attacks will serve none of these ends and may, in the process, prove dangerously counterproductive.

Chapter *11*

Academic Freedom, Tenure, and Countervailing Forces

Bardwell L. Smith

Tenure, since it was advocated by the newly-formed American Association of University Professors (AAUP) in its 1915 Declaration of Principles, has never been regarded as a sufficient deterrent to the abuse of academic freedom, only as a necessary step toward the protection of such freedom. What is evident now is the relative ineffectiveness of tenure against what currently hampers the academy's determination of its own goals, programs, and methods of evaluation. As long as academic freedom is construed in the classical sense, involving the Lehrfreiheit of the professor as teacher, scholar, and citizen, tenure and due process combine to assist, though not guarantee, its protection for tenured and nontenured alike. While abolishing tenure would render even relative academic freedom more vulnerable, the key point is that tenure alone cannot protect the academy against increasing losses of self-determination. The thrust of this essay is to suggest how self-determination has in fact diminished, in what ways academic freedom is at stake, and along what battle lines the controversy will be drawn.

In order to perceive what new threats to academic freedom have emerged since 1945, one must describe the earlier scene, note the factors that brought about changes, and assess the meaning of academic freedom in its complex institutional and cultural setting. The first section deals with the academic world of 1915, the developments leading to the formation of the AAUP, and the growing acceptance of academic freedom as necessary for both teaching and research and of tenure and due process as its principal safeguards. Section two examines the picture from World War II on, noting the massive federal involvement in higher education, the spiraling enrollments of the past three decades, the serious challenges to traditional patterns of authority, and the rapid politicizing of elements within and outside higher education. All of these developments compound the existing confusion over the purposes of colleges and universities. The final section reviews various current tensions within higher education, each of which presses for a more thoughtful understanding of academic freedom and requires that academic tenure be viewed within a broader framework.

Academia: 1915–1945

In an essay written for the fiftieth anniversary of the AAUP Metzger analyzes the American academic scene of the late nineteenth and early twentieth centuries leading to the founding of that Association. It was a period which "despite its archaic features bears significant resemblances to our own."[1] The thirty years before World War I, similar to the period after World War II, brought a large-scale expansion in American higher education. Metzger examines three concerns which resulted from this expansion: self-improvement, stemming from the fear that expansion would lessen the quality of staff, research, and instruction; self-government, proceeding from an awareness that more students and faculty would

[1] W. P. Metzger, "Origins of the Association: An Anniversary Address," AAUP, *Bulletin*, 1965, 5, 229.

create enlarged administrations whose powers would stifle newly-born aspirations for "guild autonomy"; and self-defense, in response to the continuing need for procedural safeguards against arbitrary treatment, guarantees against violations of academic freedom, and a salary scale that might attract persons of the highest ability.

While these concerns were hardly new, the dimensions of the problems and the upward mobility of the academic profession, resulting partially from increased university involvement in research, contributed to predictable clashes between the professoriate, administrations, and governing boards. Furthermore, the public was generally ignorant of any connection between academic freedom and the common good, regarding the former as unwarranted privilege for a special class. Accompanying the expansion of higher education during the late nineteenth century was a rapidly growing professional self-consciousness. While little consensus existed within the professoriate, the dominant movement was toward a degree of guild autonomy. Although familiar to England and the continent, this autonomy had never been part of the American context.[2] The uniqueness of American higher education, with charters granted by the state to lay governing boards, provided limits as well as opportunities not found in Europe. Modelled originally after Oxford and Cambridge, American colleges, however, resembled the German Gymnasium or French lycée until the mid-nineteenth century, when the German university began to present an alternate model—a university designed for disinterested research and learning, intellectually independent of both state and ecclesiastical control.

The German separation of authority between the guild of scholars and the state was neither acceptable nor possible in the United States, however.[3] It was not possible because of the legal

[2] R. Hofstadter and W. P. Metzger, *The Development of Academic Freedom in the United States* (New York: Columbia University Press, 1955), p. xii. Compare also F. Machlup, "European Universities as Partisans," in *Neutrality or Partisanship: A Dilemma of Academic Institutions,* Bulletin 34 (New York: Carnegie Foundation for the Advancement of Teaching, 1971), pp. 7–30.

[3] Compare L. L. Rockwell, "Academic Freedom—German Origin and American Development," AAUP *Bulletin,* 1950, *36,* 225–236; W. P. Metzger, "The German Contribution to the American

charters and it was unacceptable for a variety of reasons, most stemming from the longstanding interplay between American higher education and the culture at large. The American public was also against granting students the freedom implied by Lehrfreiheit. Nor was the American professor willing to relinquish his freedom as a citizen to criticize the state, as his counterpart in Germany had in exchange for autonomy within the academy. Neither has the American intellectual often settled for pure research, independent of applied possibilities, being a pragmatist by disposition if not by ideology. American colleges from the outset had prepared men for the professions and, through the Morrill Act (1862) and the land-grant movement, had woven applied sciences into the fabric of higher education.[4]

It was only toward the end of the nineteenth century that social criticism provoked serious conflicts of interest between the "liberals" among the professoriate and the "conservatives" among the academy's benefactors. The two decades prior to World War I reveal continuing ideological clashes over the nature of society's ills and the corresponding reforms. A key point in the 1915 AAUP declaration was society's need for dispassionate analysis of social, political, and economic institutions—a need which the AAUP felt the university was designed to fulfill. The "menace to academic freedom" was no longer ecclesiastical; it suddenly was perceived to issue from business and legislative interests. The 1915 report was outspoken about the potential tyranny of public opinion, arguing that of all institutions a university should be an "inviolable refuge from such tyranny."[5]

As crucial as ideological independence and a dispassionate role in encouraging society's willingness for self-criticism is the correlative obligation of academia to analyze its own enterprise and avoid the suppression of divergent opinion. From the start, the AAUP concerned itself not only with guarding academic liberties

Theory of Academic Freedom," AAUP *Bulletin*, 1955, *41*, 214–230; W. P. Metzger, "The German Influence," in Hofstadter and Metzger, pp. 367–412.

[4] Hofstadter and Metzger, p. 418.

[5] Committee on Academic Freedom and Academic Tenure, "Report," AAUP *Bulletin*, 1915, *1*, 32.

but with the maintenance of professional standards. Its success in arguing for the procedural safeguards recommended in the 1915 report contributed to a more constructive relationship between faculty, administrators, and trustees. The changed tone was reflected in Seligman's influential AAUP presidential address in 1922, during which he advocated a new phase in the relationship between administrators and faculty—one of "cooperation rather than suspicion."[6] Seligman stressed the tension between the rights of the academic profession and the acceptance of responsibilities if these rights are to be honored by others. While viewed as standard today, these rights were not axiomatic fifty years ago nor can they be taken for granted now: reasonable compensation; security of tenure; liberty of thought and expression; and adequate leisure. Seligman's main thrust in balancing rights with responsibilities remains suggestive and, in light of the decade just past, appears almost prophetic.

A more extensive treatment of the years 1915–1945 would explore in detail the threats to academic freedom spawned during various periods of stress. Briefly, the perceived danger of "foreign elements" during and after World War I and the fiscal instability of higher education during the depression years[7] were the two most prominent causes of insecurity. During this same period, however, one also finds a widening acceptance of academic freedom as essential to higher education, of academic tenure as an effective deterrent to attacks upon this freedom, of due process as crucial to the academy as to society at large, and of the professoriate's role in decision-making within the institution. Full acceptance of the last concept had to await the next stage, although cooperative efforts within higher education anticipated the concept of shared partnership which was articulated finally in the 1960s.

The periods before World War I and after 1945 were characterized by power struggles, accelerated growth and diversification, accentuation of research, and confusion about goals and purpose. During the period between the war and 1945 earlier gains were consolidated without adequate preparation for what ensued. The

[6] E. R. A. Seligman, "Our Association—Its Aims and Accomplishments," AAUP *Bulletin*, 1922, *8*, 90–110.

[7] W. M. Kotschnig, "Depression, Recovery and Higher Education: A Review and Pre-view," AAUP *Bulletin*, 1938, *24*, 19–28.

era of paternalistic administrators was all but gone, and the hired-hand status of faculty was no longer acceptable, yet almost no attention was given to what structures of authority might be adequate for the future. Theoretically, teaching and research were maintained in balance, but the reward system belied this claim; the curriculum was diverse but fragmented; the gains of specialization were offset by a diminished sense of coherence. The elective system had come home to roost; general education was soon to react, though in vain.

The twenties and thirties were an interlude between two periods of struggle characterized by immense energy, accomplishment, and inevitable confusion. If the battles of seventy and eighty years ago stimulated faculty desire for increased self-determination, the irony of the past twenty years has been the erosion of control at the very pinnacle of the academy's prestige. C. Wright Mills, writing in 1944, helps to put this phenomenon into a broader context, providing a clue to what has transpired since World War II. He identifies the dilemma of illusions turned into despair:

We continue to know more and more about modern society, but we find the centers of political initiative less and less accessible. This generates a personal malady that is particularly acute in the intellectual who has labored under the illusion that his thinking makes a difference. In the world of today the more his knowledge of affairs grows, the less effective the impact of his thinking seems to become. Since he grows more frustrated as his knowledge increases, it seems that knowledge leads to powerlessness. He feels helpless in the fundamental sense that he cannot control what he is able to foresee. This is not only true of the consequences of his own attempt to act; it is true of the acts of powerful men whom he observes.[8]

Present Threats to Academic Freedom

The most blatant assault on academic freedom since World War II took place during the McCarthy era. Since then, threats have had more devastating potential but have been launched more

[8] C. W. Mills, "The Powerless People: The Social Role of the Intellectual," AAUP *Bulletin*, 1945, *31*, 232.

subtly and gradually. The past two decades have made it clear that academic freedom can be undermined by friend and foe alike. But, beyond all the charges and countercharges emerging from a profound cultural malaise, lies the fact that the world for which the classical theory of academic freedom sufficed no longer existed. Metzger characterizes the original 1915 AAUP statement, refined through the years but not fundamentally altered, as having outlived its day. "Nothing was said about threats to the autonomy of the university that were not, at one and the same time, threats to the livelihood of its members; indeed, it was not even clearly acknowledged that a corporate academic interest, as distinct from an individual academic's interest, existed and had also to be preserved."[9] Metzger's 1969 judgment complements Mill's 1944 analysis of a profound sense of powerlessness: "Organized irresponsibility is a leading feature of modern industrial societies everywhere. On every hand, the individual is confronted with seemingly remote organizations and he feels dwarfed and helpless."[10]

Examining the components of this phenomenon in higher education since World War II, at least three interrelated developments stand out which, taken together or separately, affect any reconception of academic freedom: the scope, complexity, pervasiveness, and influence of the university since 1945; the degree to which the university, through unprecedented funding, sponsored research, and interlocking activity, has been grafted onto the corporate world of business, industry, and government; and the continuously shifting power alignments in all institutional contexts which stem not only from challenges to old forms of authority but from a basic confusion over the meaning of authority itself.

In short, one no longer finds the academy isolated from societal pressures and interventions. Accompanying this change is a degree of ambiguity in society's image of the academy. As academic man responded to the allurements of status, power, and monetary gain, a certain disenchantment set in, compounding further the confused role for teaching and scholarship in a technocratic

[9] W. P. Metzger, "Academic Freedom in Delocalized Academic Institutions," in W. P. Metzger and others, *Dimensions of Academic Freedom* (Urbana, Illinois: University of Illinois Press, 1969), p. 3.
[10] Mills, p. 234.

society. The present task is to define new modes of responsibility consistent with the need for sufficient self-determination. Before examining this task, however, the three developments noted above, each of which has affected the academy's ability to define its own purposes and call its own shots, need explication.

Complexities of Magnitude. The recent concepts of "open admissions," "universities without walls," and "non-traditional education" are only logical extensions of a process that began in the postwar years. Beginning with the GI Bill of Rights and expanded through community colleges, educational TV, and continuing (or never-ending) education, man's right to be ignorant has been forever abrogated. The inevitable accompaniment has been more and larger institutions. Spurred by Sputnik, national pride in education became involved in ways that made it relatively simple to secure massive appropriations, particularly for the natural sciences. In all fields specialization was rewarded. The graduate level spun off institutes, centers, and bureaus whose accountability to the university as a whole often remained undefined. Entrepreneurial leadership capitalized upon the existence of a largesse that was proffered at the expense of intellectual coherence within the academic community.[11]

The very size of expanding institutions guaranteed fragmentation, resulting in a sensed loss of community and even deeper impressions of impersonalization. The infrastructures required to organize, monitor, and service the multiversities created not only distance between categories of people but ultimately breakdowns in communication, competition for funds and special privilege, and resentment by faculty and students alike that the quality of education was not infrequently being shortchanged. While it would be unfair to discount the important achievements in research, even in education, and while there was sometimes a touch of the romantic in the critics' preferences, the period was clearly one of uneven growth, basic planlessness, considerable waste, and much sloganeering. Innovation for its own sake took command, giving persuasive credence to the suspicion that no one was clear about the purpose,

[11] R. Nisbet, *The Degradation of the Academic Dogma: The University in America, 1945–1970* (New York: Basic Books, 1971), pp. 76–77.

goals, direction, or meaning of a liberal education. The rate of change, exhilarating at the outset, in the end exhausted everyone. The rarest commodity of all was time to reflect in leisure, without which all teaching eventually becomes superficial and scholarship impossible. As Seligman put it in 1922, "the lack of a decent amount of leisure saps the enthusiasm and circumscribes the ambition, until the mettlesome steed becomes the steady but dull dray horse."[12] The image of the dull dray horse seems even more apt today.

Beyond the impact of size, expanded bureaucracy, and a killing rate of change the most telling development since 1945 has been the extent to which all these have contributed to a sense of frustration and impotency. The basic issue is again one of control, of self-determination, of relative independence. "Richer, larger, more complex than ever before, the typical modern institution of higher learning is less self-directive than ever before."[13] (The most obvious example is the financial plight of education when the economy is not in an upswing.) But increased size provides opportunities as well as new problems. The outreach of higher education into different sectors of society becomes unfortunate only when it compromises its vocation or overextends its resources. Specialization is not inappropriate if comparable effort is also made to overcome fragmentation. Research institutes are crucial to a complex culture, yet they should be restrained from siphoning energy, personnel, or funds from other equally important tasks of a university. Graduate education is a necessary feature of higher learning, but it becomes self-defeating when favored at the expense of the undergraduate years. Systems of higher education are necessary, in order to coordinate isolated contexts and to stimulate new trends, but only if they foster both authentic diversity and considerable local control. The task of maintaining, indeed encouraging, these and other tensions is of crucial import, however difficult.

Costs of Sponsored Research. In a 1967 address, retiring AAUP General Secretary William Fidler examined a number of "clouds on the academic horizon." One of these was whether

[12] Seligman, p. 18.
[13] Metzger, "Academic Freedom in Delocalized Academic Institutions," p. 15.

government-sponsored contracts did not constrain the freedom of the scholarly community, since the increasing costs of research inevitably affected the academy's power of self-determination.[14] From Eisenhower's famous nunc dimittis in 1960, in which he warned of the military-industrial complex, there was continuing awareness of how heavily various universities had been implicated in sponsored research and how much of this research had been for space, defense, and war purposes. This had originated during World War II, a time that furnished the most dramatic contract of all— the Manhattan Project—which indelibly identified the academy with the state. The issue is not whether technological expertise is needed or will be employed, but in what context and for what ends. The crisis for the university has become that of multiple accountability, a dilemma we shall examine later.

The most thoroughgoing critique of the direction of higher education since World War II is Nisbet's *The Degradation of the Academic Dogma*. While Nisbet sketched out portions of this book a decade earlier, many problems were not completely visible until the bubble of affluence had burst. The book appeared at the perfect moment, when it was obvious that the free ride of the sixties was over and that the Faustian dream of limitlessness had been a fantasy from the outset. Nisbet's essay is essentially concerned with the purpose of the academic community, which he sees to have been not only lost but violated, more or less deliberately if not systematically, since 1945. Defining the academic dogma, or its raison d'être, as "the ideal of dispassionate study," he catalogs the ways by which its function and authority underwent a process of fundamental self-contradiction in the ensuing quarter century.

If money is not the root of all evil, Nisbet believes it has a way of luring men from first principles and, in good satanic fashion, of making worse appear the better reason. "The first million dollars to a university for project research was far too much. Today ten billion dollars is not enough. So have we fallen."[15] Entrepreneurial man arose, and with the windfall the autonomy of higher

[14] W. P. Fidler, "From the Retiring General Secretary," AAUP *Bulletin,* 1967, *53,* 114–115. Compare also J. S. Millis, "Unfinished Faculty Business," AAUP *Bulletin,* 1967, *53,* 210–212.
[15] Nisbet, p. 72.

education became an anachronism. Temptation took the form of project research. Gemeinschaft blurred into Gesellschaft in the wink of an eye. While the American academic scene has had from the start a strong tradition of service to the community, Nisbet is correct in asserting that its form had been essentially indirect. "Few things, however, are more spectacular about the contemporary American university than its plunge into direct service to society."[16] In all spheres, on all socio-economic levels the shift involved the academy in ways that strained its budget, exhausted its members, dissipated its common efforts, undermined its teaching function, polarized elements within the institution, compounded factions within society, and politicized the context of learning almost to destruction. Seeking to be all things to all men, higher education guaranteed the consequence would be a contradiction. The roles the university accepted for itself—"of higher capitalist, chief of research establishment, superhumanitarian, benign therapist, adjunct government, and loyal revolutionary opposition"[17]—were those ensuring chaos.

The degradation of dispassionate study was not the result; it was the cause. But, in the process, it has been claimed that the academy's true service was direct involvement in society, that only a community free of vested interests could resolve the problems vested interests had created. The claim was unalloyed hubris. The full cost of sponsored research, though the latter was but a channel, can be measured not in dollars but in loss of identity. It is Nisbet's expectation that from this loss will follow the demise of academic freedom and academic tenure, for there is danger that a society with which the academy has become this interlocked may not continue to tolerate special privileges.

[16] Nisbet, p. 129.
[17] Nisbet, p. 8. Compare W. P. Metzger, "Institutional Neutrality: An Appraisal," in *Neutrality or Partisanship: A Dilemma of Academic Institutions,* pp. 49–54, in which he discusses the decline in institutional independence and the "diversification of institutional functions," both of which made institutional neutrality difficult. Similar to Nisbet, he writes that "the passage of time has produced yet another difference—the difference between a university and a multiversity, between service as a concept and a cult."

Struggle for Authority. If the degree of involvement of higher education in the concerns of society has posed new dangers to academic freedom, the heart of the crisis lies in the struggle for authority that has preoccupied both the culture and the academy during the past decade. Again, it is helpful to note earlier developments that generated new concepts of authority and strengthened the claims for both academic freedom and tenure. There can be no question of the conviction of the founders of the AAUP that the right of self-determination must be balanced by the duty of self-regulation. This was affirmed on both the individual and corporate levels. Within the legal authority granted to the trustees (or regents) of each institution (under the law of the state concerned), the primary task of exercising responsible academic freedom in research and teaching fell to the faculty itself. In counsel ahead of its time, the 1915 AAUP statement was unequivocal over the locus of authority and the seriousness of the problem. It is "unsuitable to the dignity of a great profession that the initial responsibility for the maintenance of its professional standards should not be in the hands of its own members. It follows that university teachers must be prepared to assume this responsibility for themselves. They have hitherto seldom had the opportunity, or perhaps the disposition, to do so."[18] When one considers the discrepancy between this affirmation and the traditional lack of faculty authority, the statement holds great significance. Its self-critical implications carry remarkable irony.

During the next thirty years there was a discouragingly gradual conversion of authority from the patriarchal to the collegial pattern. A study of the position and function of faculties in college and university government in the late thirties revealed a continuing pattern of noninvolvement in many areas basic to their welfare.[19] It was only with the emergence of higher education in

[18] Committee on Academic Freedom and Academic Tenure, 1915, p. 35.

[19] Committee T, "Place and Function of Faculties in College and University Government," AAUP *Bulletin,* 1940, *26,* 171–216. There was in the typical institution, for instance, no definite procedure to consult faculty in the selection of a new president, dean, or depart-

its politically and scientifically influential postwar form, accompanied by the attack on academic freedom during the early fifties, that a rapid coalescing of forces within the academy and the society reopened the question of authority.

Statements by the American Civil Liberties Union in the mid-fifties, as well as decisions by the United States Supreme Court, not only gave crucial support to the concepts of academic freedom and due process but an awareness that all levels of education constituted a seamless robe. Moreover, a conviction was emerging that "the distinction between teacher-freedom and student-freedom [was] artificial and should be discarded."[20] This distinction, inherited from the nineteenth century German model, had lain dormant in the American context for over a century. Once raised in the courts, however, it became an issue of major importance and inevitably extended the question of authority into a consideration of all constituencies with claims upon the academy. Therefore double-edged, presenting threats as well as the prospects of more responsible freedom, it has created an agenda that cannot be avoided.

As long as the struggle for authority was against a familiar

---

ment chairman. Also, there were seldom any definite plans for facilitating exchange of opinion between faculty and trustees.

[20] American Civil Liberties Union, "Academic Freedom and Academic Responsibility: Their Meaning to Students, Teachers, Administrators, and the Community," AAUP *Bulletin*, 1965, *42*, 519. Compare also the ACLU statement entitled "Academic Due Process," AAUP *Bulletin*, 1956, *42*, 661–665; an essay by R. K. Carr entitled "Academic Freedom, the American Association of University Professors, and the United States Supreme Court," AAUP *Bulletin*, 1959, *45*, 5–24; and one by W. P. Murphy, "Educational Freedom in the Courts," AAUP *Bulletin*, 1963, *49*, 309–327, which discusses the need for educating the public regarding tenure, the constitutional protection of academic freedom, the cruciality of due process, and the violations of academic freedom through censorship; P. Monypenny, "Toward a Standard for Student Academic Freedom," *Law and Contemporary Problems*, 1963, *28;* S. Jacobson, "Student and Faculty Due Process," AAUP *Bulletin*, 1966, *52*, 196–204; "Joint Statement on Rights and Freedoms of Students," AAUP *Bulletin*, 1968, *54*, 258–261; and "Draft Statement on Student Participation in College and University Government," AAUP *Bulletin*, 1970, *56*, 33–35.

adversary, whether administration or governing board or political chauvinist, the academic ranks traditionally held firm. When the community itself became politicized, however, there was no limit to the camps that could be formed, and few positions could be apolitical. What had passed as the "extramural utterances" of academic man as citizen now sought the official support of colleagues and institutional backing. As unfamiliar and foreign as this seemed to many Americans in the 1960s, Machlup has shown that the principle of institutional neutrality has gained acceptance only in this century.[21] What had become accepted in principle by one generation was anathema to many in the next. The present confusion regarding the twin values of scholarly pursuit and social concern has caused divisions not only within the professoriate itself but within individual professors.[22]

The struggle for authority is not embodied simply in a battle between faculty and various constituencies. While often taking that form, the basic struggle is for an authority that the academy itself has lost in its confusion over its role in an age unable to afford the absence of either expertise or social conscience. If it is true that these are opposite sides of the same coin, complementary aspects of a responsible technological society, many profound questions arise as to the nature and goal of a liberal education, the standards by which performance is evaluated, the ways in which disciplines may complement each other, the means by which the learning experience can become genuinely corporate yet remain uniquely personal, the nature and process of governance within the academy, and the interrelationship among the educational communities within a society.

The political activity of professors was sometimes the reflection of a confusion that saw no way to maintain the tension between social consciousness and dispassionate study. The fitful quest for new models of governance, however well-intentioned, produced only way-stations between archaic patterns long dysfunctional and future

[21] Machlup, p. 7.
[22] S. M. Lipset and E. C. Ladd, Jr., "The Divided Professoriate," *Change,* 1971, *3*(3), 60. This article is based upon "a national sample of professors at more than 300 institutions, in a study under the general sponsorship of the Carnegie Commission on Higher Education" taken in 1969.

forms still unconceived. The emergency codes of rights and responsibilities were a protective response to the threats of anarchy on the
one hand and authoritarianism on the other. The lemming-like
rush by some into the arms of collective bargaining bought familiar
but questionable models of security in the face of financial exigency,
communal insecurity, and pressures within and upon the academy.
In the process, confusion born out of a sudden collapse of self-
control reinforced a profound sense of powerlessness.

    If higher education is to argue convincingly for academic
freedom, let alone validate the need for tenure, it must address
itself to profoundly new realities and expectations in a society in
which no authority is beyond question, no priority self-evident. The
shattering experiences of the past decade, while ambiguous, have
created an extraordinary necessity for honesty, sensitivity, and discipline. The real struggle for authority, the struggle for real authority,
is in this direction.

Autonomy, Accountability, and Countervailing Forces

    To focus primarily upon the issues of governance and to
debate the merits of shared responsibility versus collective bargaining, is to miss the principal tension out of which new forms of academic freedom must emerge. However pressing the problems of
governance, they are subordinate to the tension between autonomy
and accountability. "The intimate relationships of many universities
with government, industry, and the military raise serious questions
of ethical responsibility and intellectual independence for both
faculty members and institutions. . . . Individuals find themselves
accountable to other members of the academic community and to
the institution itself. Both faculty members and their institutions
are also publicly accountable in manifold ways. These forms of
accountability are multiple and sometimes conflicting."[23]

    In the face of this dilemma between accountability and
autonomy, the temptation may be to retreat from areas of controversy within society. To submit to this temptation would default

    [23] T. R. McConnell, "Faculty Interests in Value Change and
Power Conflicts," AAUP *Bulletin*, 1969, *55*, 342.

responsibility to some sectors of society even less restrained from partisanship. Such default would dissolve the tension towards a form of autonomy that would reduce, not enhance, the potential for critical objectivity. Dispassionate study which ignores all claims of accountability soon evolves into specious autonomy.

It is equally true that stressing certain forms of accountability at the price of autonomy may evolve into brutal power conflicts. The academy's recent failure to resist this temptation should engender self-criticism, however, not unresponsiveness. Again, the dilemma is to reestablish the primacy of dispassionate analysis, in Nisbet's sense, without withdrawing to issues that lack controversy. Metzger writes: "It is the task of the civilized man to uphold not one, but several values; not autonomy 'or' freedom, but autonomy 'and' freedom; not social justice at any price, but social justice and other goods besides."[24]

Metzger's analysis of the 1915 AAUP statement (the so-called Lovejoy formula) underscores AAUP advocacy of institutional neutrality in a power sense without suggesting that "the university had to be neutral in a value sense." The advocacy of restraint was not the counsel to be devoid of values. Only as the academy became enmeshed with the social order through extended services and contracts did the Lovejoy formula require reinterpretation. "The advent of the all-purpose university creates concern about subtle unneutralities that do not apply primarily to research and teaching and are not remedied by official self-restraint." These unneutralities, even more than blatant partisan declarations, render the task of institutional neutrality more difficult. The myriad ties between the academy and society began to compromise the former's ability to dissociate itself from the prevailing values, even when choosing to, thus casting doubt on its claims to objectivity.

The notion of countervailing forces suggests a complexity that has emerged since World War II, especially since the late fifties. The expanding scale of higher education created the need for associations, consortia, and systems that disturbed old balances

---

[24] Metzger, "Institutional Neutrality: An Appraisal," p. 55. The remainder of this essay is a judicious discussion of the task of institutional neutrality in the present period.

of power and fostered new ones. Until recently, however, the predominant countervailing forces were internal. Clearly, a primary impetus for the collective bargaining movement was the power vacuum that existed as a whole constellation of forces developed in relatively short order. "In the absence of common goals and a shared sense of purpose, authority is difficult to legitimize. In such a situation old methods are apt to seem either impotent or illicit. When new methods are sought, collective bargaining stands available as an option for faculties which have never been enfranchised, or which see traditional prerogatives being lost to students, to managers, and to politicians."[25] The crisis of authority that inheres in the battle between forces within higher education and between the respective bargaining agents (AFT, NEA, and AAUP) will influence profoundly the shape of academic freedom and the destiny of academic tenure.

Even more important, the crisis of authority within the academy mirrors the crisis of the culture at large. The sensed loss of autonomy is shared by modern man everywhere, and the contest between egalitarian and meritocratic principles raises age-old issues about access to power within educational circles and in the society. Again, the academy's principal calling may be to make more vivid "the necessity for intellectualizing problems without dehumanizing them or blunting their urgency."[26]

Summarizing the threats to academic freedom, I conclude by noting five areas that require sustained attention: combining overall planning within higher education with the enhancement of diversity; strengthening governing boards in order to preserve academic freedom and provide sympathetic outside criticism; developing varied patterns of institutional accountability and governance; reconciling exploration of new areas with comparable attention to

[25] W. B. Boyd, "Collective Bargaining in Academe: Causes and Consequences," *Liberal Education*, 1971, *57*, 311. Compare also G. W. Bonham, "The New Class," *Change*, 1971–1972, *3*(7), 13–14. The most extensive bibliography on this subject is J. W. Gillis, "Academic Collective Bargaining," *Liberal Education*, 1970, *56*, 594–604; and "The Continuing Development of Academic Collective Bargaining," *Liberal Education*, 1971, *57*, 529–540.

[26] McConnell, p. 345.

coherence; and attending to renewed emphasis on teaching and accountability which evoke levels of self-examination previously uncalled for by either society or higher education. Each of these points is central to the viability of academic freedom and needs expanding here.

First, it is clear that without long-term national planning higher education will continue to be victimized by fashion and powerful interests at the expense of continuity, reasoned analysis, and the needs of society at large. The variability of the academic marketplace alone, whose wild fluctuations breed insecurity and unreliability, argues for rational planning on the federal level which respects regional, state, and local interests and contributions. The efforts of the Carnegie Commission in its proposal for a National Foundation for the Development of Higher Education, though now languishing for lack of federal and educational support, are a promising beginning. The principal dilemma is to balance national planning with local autonomy. Indeed, paradoxically, only through systematic planning on such a scale can genuinely strong heterogeneity be encouraged.

The call for either egalitarianism or meritocracy creates an invalid dichotomy. Few societies can justify one at the expense of the other. The need is for models that accommodate the diverse requirements of the times. Attempts made in certain states are again promising, but ultimately the problems must be confronted on a national level. Countervailing measures within the funding and regulating processes are required to insure not only that these monies are responsibly used but that sufficient freedom is granted to institutions (public and private) to determine educational policies independent of mercurial and repressive public pressures.

Second is the need to redefine and strengthen the role governing boards play in the support and critique of higher education. A series of AAUP Committee A reports between 1949 and 1952, at the height of the McCarthy period, stressed the "peculiar and necessary" service a lay governing board may render in the battle for academic freedom that is never wholly won.[27] Even more

[27] Committee A, "Academic Freedom and Tenure," AAUP

double-edged than tensions between faculty and administration are those between an institution and its board of regents or trustees. Representing the public's basic interest in maintaining academic freedom and intellectual quality, a board's mandate is not to control but to foster a climate of independent thinking. The peculiarity of the American system, having endured more than three centuries, may afford distinct advantages in the future. An alert and responsible board should assist in maintaining tension between autonomy and accountability, between various forms of freedom and the several claims upon the academy's time and resources. As the tissue connecting elements within higher education extends, influence of an important sort could fall to associations of governing boards at state and federal levels. In this sense, lay boards can mediate between partisan interests and at the same time remind the academy of its unique role within, as well as separate from, society.

Third, among the easiest mistakes, as institutions evolve from traditional to collegial forms of governance, is the assumption that an ideal type does exist, which all forms should approximate. Instead, an institution's size, history, style, current and past composition, pressures within and upon it, geographic location, and financial condition will determine the appropriate shapes and processes of governance. Accountability remains the essential issue. It is as much an art of responding to legitimate needs as it is political or legal insurance of responsibility. There are as many ways of building accountability into systems of governance as there are forms of human ingenuity. The danger of standardized procedures is as great as procedures which are not acceptable to all. The necessity of combining standardization with local options is clear to anyone who seeks to foster quality as well as fair play. Although attention is rightfully focused upon due process and careful modes of evaluation, it would be fatal for academic freedom and the assessment process to slip into a one man/one vote approach to decision-making. It should become increasingly incumbent upon administrators, whose accountability must be measured by their commitment to due process and their responsiveness to the entire institution, to insure that appropriate parties be consulted in ways pertinent to the decision. While peer evaluation remains central, the hierarchy of decision-making can be responsible only as long as it takes into account all relevant constituencies.

Beyond, but related to, tenure decisions is the clamor of previously silent factions: students; teaching assistants; nontenured faculty; professional librarians; administrative and student personnel staff; alumni; and so on, now articulate interests and issues that threaten, complicate, and enrich the process of governance. The obvious need is to weld significant unity out of diversity; the hidden danger is that both quality and leadership may be sacrificed in the process. New structures will be called for, but in the end the process must allow for both accountable authority and forms of governance that emerge naturally from varied contexts. The academic scene is presently a testing ground for this process, and it may create a number of models useful to society at large.

Fourth, basic to the converging interests of higher education and society is the continuing requirement for new forms of investigation and patterns of coherence. Specialization without attempts at discovering relationships leads to intellectual fragmentation and confusion. Behind any cry for "relevance" are potential relationships between areas of knowledge; the cry is as much for coherence as for utilitarian ends. The dichotomy between research and teaching need not be absolute. Both can be sophisticated efforts at coherence; each can be oblivious of the proper balance between exploring new areas and weaving discoveries into existing or new frameworks. Whitehead's model of a continuing dialectic between exploration and synthesis holds for both teaching and research. It illumines also the current debate between knowledge-centered and man-centered, or developmental, approaches to learning, suggesting that neither is dispensable.

The fundamental issue here is balance. While research can compromise finite conceptions of the university, teaching can attempt too much in certain respects and too little in others. By exposing students to new data and previously neglected areas, today's teaching provides a richness which is spectacular though bewildering. But its general education programs are an incoherent reaction to specialization and are no less confusing to faculty than to students, a fact of which the latter are not unaware. The implications for academic freedom may seem obscure until one recalls how accessions to social, fiscal, curricular, and bureaucratic pressures constrain the academy. The very tempo of life, accelerated by entrepreneurial energies, eventually debilitates the academic capacity for reflective analysis. We can neglect neither new areas of exploration nor the continuing need for coherence. Attempts to serve either extreme to the exclusion of the other inevitably result in exhausted frustration.

Fifth, the most noteworthy development stemming from discussions over academic tenure may be the renewal of serious attention to teaching. While these issues are separable, and while there has always been stress upon effective teaching in theoretical discussions of tenure, concern for the evaluation and improvement of teaching has only now become widespread and sincere. The armor's first chink appeared during the sixties, as students began to articulate complaints. The financial bind finally galvanized action, as larger numbers of tough decisions had to be made. It became obvious that existing procedures had been casual, to say the least. No area more quickly identified the countervailing forces than teaching evaluation; yet no area more profoundly reveals the common benefits which result from serious commitment to its improvement.

Accountability to students is only one facet of a serious commitment to teaching. The task of dispassionate analysis is a continuing one, involving colleagues in relationship to each other as much as to students. Persons teach in as many ways as they learn and the stakes for improved teaching are as high for the intellectual community as a whole as for its younger members. If one asset of tenure's existence is the necessity of making difficult decisions, no criterion can be higher on the scale than the ability to stimulate others to reasoned and self-critical analysis. Whether the tenure system continues or not, the improvement of teaching will remain a constant assignment. One likely outcome of present discussions will be continued emphasis on teaching improvement even after the granting of tenure. While initially threatening, such a development would ameliorate the tension between autonomy and accountability.

Sixth, the most difficult and ambiguous tension between autonomy and accountability, however, involves the academy's role of fostering critical responsibility in the social order. The issue goes beyond neutrality versus partisanship. Although I believe that both the academy and society suffer when academic institutions take partisan stands on social issues not directly affecting their own welfare, I believe the refusal to face power realities and to debate existent or proposed priorities is equally destructive. Indeed, to insist "that the university preserves a value-free intellectual environment leads to a displacement of the active, creative marketplace of ideas away from the university."[28] The dimensions of freedom implied here are founded principally in the responsibility of colleges and universities to discuss openly and participate freely in fostering "a lively, critical, constructive 'engagement' in the activities of an evolving society."[29] The dilemma is to preserve intellectual independence on the one hand and to stimulate social experimentation on the other. To resolve the tension by ignoring the requirements of either reasoned analysis or social concern diminishes the academy's capacity for self-determination and simultaneously proffers a superficial response to demands for accountability thrust upon it by its own members and society. While its contribution is potentially immense, the academy must exercise restraint in its undertakings and afford honest appraisals of its own judgment. While its vocation is to be critical of all values, priorities, and structures, higher education needs to see itself in constructive tension with the society of which it is inevitably a part.

Despite the importance of current discussions about tenure, it is as crucial now as in 1915 to retain the focus not upon it but upon the centrality of both academic freedom and academic responsibility and to design measures effective for the furtherance of each. The essentiality of due process is indisputable, as its frequent violation attests. The relative effectiveness of tenure itself, whatever its drawbacks, is not necessarily under dispute, though important mod-

[28] S. E. Luria and Z. Luria, "The Role of the University: Ivory Tower, Service Station, or Frontier Post," *Daedalus*, 1970, *99*, 80.

[29] Luria and Luria, p. 83.

ifications will begin to emerge. Beyond the necessity of maintaining a climate of independence within higher education is the task of regaining a degree of independence from new forms of outside pressures. The academy must do this, however, without losing sight of accountability to its own membership and to the common good. It would indeed be a surprise if countervailing forces presently existing within and outside higher education should permit the academy to neglect either the difficulty or the necessity of this dual task.

Chapter 12

The Distribution of
Academic Tenure in
American Higher
Education

Martin Trow

I̲n recent years academic tenure has been increasingly the subject of discussion and the object of criticism. Its chief justification, as other essays in this volume point out, lies in its relation to academic freedom. It is criticized as a protection of incompetence and a major

This chapter is based in part on data gathered by the National Surveys of Higher Education, sponsored by the Carnegie Commission on Higher Education and supported in part as a cooperative research project by funds from the United States Office of Education. The interpretations put forward in this publication do not necessarily reflect the position of the U.S. Office of Education, and no official endorsement by the Office of Education should be inferred.

barrier to academic innovation. The current and probably chronic financial crisis of our colleges and universities also carries implicit arguments against the granting of tenure to men whose salaries remain a permanent charge on the institution and defeat efforts of trustees and administrators to make rational allocations of resources, perhaps in directions other than the continued support of men for whose services there may be little need or justification. Whatever the weight of these or other arguments, it may be useful to examine some elementary statistics about the extent and distribution of tenure in American higher education. Who has it? In what fields? At what ages? And how does this vary in different kinds and qualities of institutions? This essay avoids the policy arguments and confines itself to a differentiated description of the extent and distribution of tenure in American higher education.

The data from which these figures are drawn were gathered in 1969 through a large national survey of academic men and women in over 300 institutions. The achieved sample consists of over 60,000 teachers in the full range of American colleges and universities. The respondents were asked early in the questionnaire, "What kind of appointment do you have here?" The distribution of responses was in Table 1.[1]

About 1 per cent of those questioned did not reply to this question. They are excluded from the foregoing distribution and from subsequent analysis.

We see in Table 1 that just half of the faculty in colleges and

---

[1] Tables in this chapter are based on a subsample of 27,191 cases, containing all respondents to the survey at four-year and junior colleges and a systematic 1:4 sample of all those in universities, where the original numbers were very large. Respondents have been weighted to compensate for biases caused both by differential sampling ratios within strata of institutions and by differential institutional rates of response. These weights are used in all tables, and percentages and totals are therefore population estimates for the universe of American college and university teachers (excluding teaching assistants) in 1969. (See M. Trow and others, *Technical Report: National Surveys of Higher Education,* Carnegie Commission on Higher Education, Berkeley, California, 1971, for a description of the sample, the weighting procedures, and the measure of institutional "quality" introduced in Table 3.)

Table 1. TYPE OF ACADEMIC APPOINTMENT, ALL FACULTY

Regular with Tenure	50%
Regular without Tenure	46
Acting	2
Visiting	3
	101%
	(442,076)

Table 2. TYPE OF APPOINTMENT BY PUBLIC/PRIVATE CONTROL

	Public	*Private*
Regular with Tenure	53%	45%
Regular without Tenure	43	49
Acting	2	2
Visiting	2	4
	100%	100%
	(271,911)	(170,155)

universities hold tenured appointments in their present institutions. Table 2 shows the distribution of these kinds of appointments in public and private institutions. The distributions are very similar; a little over half of the men in public institutions and a little less than half of those in private institutions hold tenure rank.

Differences by the quality and kind of institution are also very slight (Table 3). In every category within a few points of 50 per cent of teachers hold a tenured position. Moreover, there is little difference between public and private colleges and universities in all categories of "quality" (Table 4).

Table 5 gives the distribution of tenured and nontenured appointments within a different classification of colleges and universities used in a number of studies and reports issued by the Carnegie Commission. Theological seminaries, engineering schools, and other specialized institutions show conspicuously low proportions of tenured faculty—perhaps because of their relatively high proportions of part-time faculty.

Table 3. Type of Appointment by Quality of Institution

Quality

	Universities			Colleges			Junior Colleges
	High	Medium	Low	High	Medium	Low	
Regular with Tenure	49%	56%	49%	52%	48%	44%	54%
Regular without Tenure	43	40	47	42	48	52	43
Acting	3	2	1	2	3	2	2
Visiting	5	3	2	4	2	3	1
	100%	101%	99%	100%	101%	101%	100%
	(55,521)	(80,043)	(69,973)	(25,171)	(48,257)	(98,368)	(64,743)

Table 4. Proportion Having Tenure by Quality and Control

Quality

	Universities			Colleges			Junior Colleges
	High	Medium	Low	High	Medium	Low	
Public	52%	58%	51%	54%	51%	46%	56%
Private	47	50	47	50	44	41	44

Table 5. TYPE OF APPOINTMENT BY TYPE OF INSTITUTION

TYPE OF INSTITUTION

	Leading Research Universities	Other Research Universities	Other Doctoral Granting Universities (10 + Ph.D.s)
Regular with Tenure	52%	51%	52%
Regular without Tenure	43	45	44
Acting	2	2	2
Visiting	3	3	2
	100%	101%	100%
	(111,669)	(39,468)	(21,434)

TYPE OF INSTITUTION

	Other Doctoral Granting Universities (less than 10 Ph.D.s)	Broadly Comprehensive Colleges	Other Comprehensive Colleges
Regular with Tenure	44%	45%	55%
Regular without Tenure	53	50	41
Acting	1	3	2
Visiting	2	2	1
	100%	100%	99%
	(21,420)	(74,574)	(29,214)

Table 5. Type of Appointment by Type of Institution (cont.)

TYPE OF INSTITUTION

	Highly Selective Lib. Arts Colleges	*Other Liberal Arts Colleges*	*Theological Seminaries*
Regular with Tenure	49%	39%	18%
Regular without Tenure	44	56	82
Acting	2	2	0
Visiting	5	3	0
	100%	100%	100%
	(18,258)	(45,672)	(651)

TYPE OF INSTITUTION

	Schools of Engineering and Technology	*Schools of Business and Management*	*Schools of Art, Music, or Design*
Regular with Tenure	43%	50%	18%
Regular without Tenure	53	50	82
Acting	0	0	0
Visiting	5	0	0
	101%	100%	100%
	(2,109)	(519)	(255)

Table 5. TYPE OF APPOINTMENT BY TYPE OF INSTITUTION (cont.)

TYPE OF INSTITUTION

	Other Specialized Institutions	All 2-year Colleges and Institutes
Regular with Tenure	29%	54%
Regular without Tenure	61	43
Acting	4	2
Visiting	6	1
	100%	100%
	(7,395)	(65,319)

In Table 6 we see the distribution of tenure by rank. Nearly 90 per cent of the full professors in all our colleges and universities hold tenured rank; nearly three-fourths of the associate professors, but less than one-fourth of assistant professors, and about 1 in 5 instructors hold tenured positions. In the small number of institutions which do not designate ranks (most of them junior and community colleges), two-thirds have tenure.

Table 7 shows us the distribution of tenured positions by institutional quality and individual rank. Variations in the proportions of professors holding tenure are small in all categories except the weakest four-year colleges, where the proportion is slightly less than 80 per cent, and in the junior colleges, 81 per cent. The proportion of tenured assistant professors in the first quality universities is notably lower than in the other institutions: fewer than 10 per cent as compared to 21 per cent in the "weaker" universities and nearly a one-third in the medium and low-quality colleges. It may be that the leading institutions are wary about granting tenure but try to hold promising faculty with pay and title while the decision is being made.

Table 8 shows the variation in tenure by age. Overall, we see that a comfortable majority of the men forty-one and over teaching in American colleges and universities hold a tenured position. Among those between thirty-six and forty the proportion is almost half—48 per cent. The big break occurs at about that age. Of the men between thirty-one and thirty-five, only one-fourth hold tenured rank.

Table 6. Type of Appointment by Rank

	Professor	Associate Professor	Assistant Professor	Instructor	Lecturer	No Designated Rank	Other
Regular with Tenure	89%	73%	24%	20%	8%	67%	31%
Regular without Tenure	9	26	73	73	59	28	54
Acting	0	0	1	4	13	3	6
Visiting	2	1	2	3	21	3	9
	100%	100%	100%	100%	101%	101%	100%
	(100,832)	(94,043)	(122,279)	(84,150)	(12,739)	(17,216)	(10,097)

Table 7. Proportion Having Tenure by Rank and Quality

Quality

Rank	Universities			Colleges			Junior Colleges
	High	Medium	Low	High	Medium	Low	
Professor	94%	94%	89%	93%	88%	79%	81%
Associate Professor	69	82	74	78	71	64	75
Assistant Professor	8	17	21	18	29	32	40
Instructor	5	11	8	8	14	13	41
Lecturer	11	8	2	6	7	5	8
No Ranks Designated	7	26	0	13	38	45	71
Other	9	21	27	14	18	34	58

Table 8. Type of Appointment by Age

AGE

Appointment	61 and older	56–60	51–55	46–50	41–45	36–40	31–35	26–30	Under 26
Regular with Tenure	78%	79%	76%	69%	61%	48%	25%	9%	9%
Regular without Tenure	17	19	22	27	35	48	70	83	81
Acting	1	1	1	2	2	2	2	4	7
Visiting	3	2	2	2	2	3	3	4	3
	99%	101%	101%	100%	100%	101%	100%	100%	100%
	(32,801)	(28,330)	(40,560)	(56,242)	(65,670)	(71,530)	(73,074)	(57,511)	(8,947)

Table 9. Proportion Having Tenure by Age and Quality

Age	Universities			Colleges			Junior Colleges
	High	Medium	Low	High	Medium	Low	
61 and older	85%	89%	80%	87%	80%	69%	68%
56–60	82	88	81	83	89	69	67
51–55	75	82	76	85	78	71	71
46–50	68	77	75	75	69	60	67
41–45	66	70	59	73	58	50	63
36–40	44	52	48	50	48	40	57
31–35	20	23	20	20	24	22	45
26–30	4	8	5	7	6	9	21
Under 26	4	14	8	2	6	11	14

Quality

Table 9 shows age variation in the different quality universities and colleges. While variations might be noted, the general impression is of the surprisingly small variation in the proportions having tenure in different age categories within these quite different colleges and universities.

In Table 10 we see the distribution by broad fields of teach-

Table 10. TYPE OF APPOINTMENT BY FIELD

	Business	Biological Sciences	Education	Engi- neering	Fine Arts
Regular with Tenure	45%	60%	52%	57%	50%
Regular without Tenure	51	38	45	40	46
Acting	2	1	2	1	2
Visiting	2	2	2	2	2
	100%	101%	101%	100%	100%
	(25,605)	(29,936)	(50,516)	(27,230)	(34,021)

	Medicine and Law	Humani- ties	Physical Sciences	Psychology and Social Sciences	New and Semi- Profes- sions
Regular with Tenure	46%	45%	52%	48%	50%
Regular without Tenure	47	50	43	47	45
Acting	1	2	2	2	2
Visiting	6	3	3	3	3
	100%	100%	100%	100%	100%
	(17,646)	(86,976)	(58,962)	(52,659)	(48,990)

ing without regard to age and rank. Faculty in the biological sciences show the highest proportion holding tenure (60 per cent), as compared, for example, with less than 50 per cent of those in psychology, and the social sciences, humanities, or business. But a more interesting and informative table shows the variation by age in the proportions holding tenure in these subject areas (Table 11).

In Table 11 we see that, while majorities in all the fields eventually gain tenure, the proportions for the oldest age-group range from 91 per cent in the biological sciences to 77 per cent in the humanities and 64 per cent in medicine and law. Moreover, if we chart these figures we find different career patterns for different fields. For example, 59 per cent of the biologists between thirty-six and forty hold tenure; the proportions of tenured faculty in education and the humanities in that age bracket are only 45 per cent or 42 per cent. The picture is even clearer when we look at the same table but confine our attention to the teachers in the three categories of universities (Table 11A), where, for example, in the thirty-six to forty age bracket nearly two-thirds (63 per cent) of physical scientists have tenure, as compared with a little over one-third in education and only 38 per cent in the humanities.

These tables, however, obscure sharp differences between teachers in medicine and law since they are grouped together. The difference between law and medicine becomes very clear when we look at variations in tenure by the highest degree earned (Table 12). Nearly 60 per cent of all men who earned the Ph.D. and are teaching in colleges and universities have tenure as compared with 42 per cent of those who hold only a master's degree. The proportions holding differing kinds of professional degrees show interesting differences; of those holding an M.D. degree, only 43 per cent have tenure as compared to those with a first degree in law, of whom 55 per cent have tenure. This reflects the very sharp differences in medical and law school practices in giving tenure and their practices in employing adjunct and part-time faculty. That contrast is sharpest when one looks at the leading universities where these practices are most deeply entrenched (Table 12A). In those institutions only 38 per cent of those holding M.D. degrees have tenure as compared with 73 per cent of those with law degrees.

In Table 13, we confine our attention to those with a Ph.D. and examine how the length of time they have had their Ph.D. affects their chance of holding tenure. We see there that beyond ten years there is a plateau—men who have held the degree for ten years show about the same proportions (between 84 and 90 per cent) holding tenure regardless of how long they have held their

Table 11. Proportion Holding Tenure by Age and Field, All Institutions

Age	Business	Biological Sciences	Education	Engineering	Fine Arts	Medicine and Law	Humanities	Physical Sciences	Social Sciences	New and Semi-Professions
61 and older	73%	91%	75%	83%	87%	64%	77%	81%	81%	73%
56–60	87	87	76	83	74	67	77	83	80	80
51–55	72	88	79	73	80	64	72	84	78	72
46–50	61	82	64	80	67	60	65	81	77	65
41–45	50	70	54	70	65	56	59	72	61	54
36–40	42	59	45	53	46	37	42	61	52	42
31–35	27	22	28	32	22	10	23	31	23	20
26–30	17	8	11	10	11	4	6	8	6	10
Under 26	5	0	13	28	8	0	4	9	6	25

Table 11A. Proportion Holding Tenure by Age and Field in Universities

Age	Business	Biological Sciences	Education	Engineering	Fine Arts	Medicine and Law	Humanities	Physical Sciences	Social Sciences	New and Semi-Professions
61 and older	78%	94%	86%	81%	89%	63%	87%	91%	95%	79%
56–60	91	86	84	91	83	68	86	92	85	81
51–55	64	90	79	86	83	64	77	90	86	68
46–50	80	90	67	88	66	60	74	86	77	66
41–45	54	71	50	75	65	55	62	82	68	57
36–40	44	58	35	58	45	37	38	63	61	45
31–35	22	20	19	35	16	11	16	27	24	18
26–30	10	7	7	9	5	4	2	7	3	9
Under 26	0	0	0	25	0	0	6	10	0	18

Table 12. TYPE OF APPOINTMENT BY HIGHEST DEGREE HELD

	Ph.D.	1st Professional Medical Degree	1st Professional Law Degree	Ed.D.	Other Doctorate
Regular with Tenure	59%	43%	55%	65%	56%
Regular without Tenure	38	49	39	33	40
Acting	1	2	4	0	1
Visiting	3	7	3	1	4
	101%	101%	101%	99%	101%
	(172,829)	(17,695)	(5,492)	(16,675)	(7,300)

	Doctor Arts without Disser.	Other 1st Professional	Master's	B.A.	Less than B.A.	None
Regular with Tenure	44%	46%	42%	26%	32%	46%
Regular without Tenure	50	49	53	63	65	45
Acting	3	3	3	7	2	4
Visiting	3	3	2	3	2	5
	100%	101%	100%	99%	101%	100%
	(7,059)	(30,023)	(135,563)	(21,646)	(2,165)	(1,353)

degree. Among men who have had their Ph.D.s between six and ten years, nearly two-thirds already hold tenure and among those who had earned their degrees only three to five years before the survey, a bit under a third were already tenured.

Table 13A shows this variation in different fields of study. It is interesting that in the fine arts, contrary to expectations, fully two-fifths of the men who had gained their Ph.D.s as recently as three to five years before the survey already held tenure. By contrast, only 22 per cent in physical sciences and math who had earned

Table 12A. TYPE OF APPOINTMENT IN LEADING UNIVERSITIES
BY FIRST PROFESSIONAL MEDICAL AND LAW DEGREES

Type	First Professional Medical Degree	First Professional Law Degree
Regular with Tenure	38%	73%
Regular without Tenure	53	21
Acting	2	1
Visiting	8	5
	101%	100%
	(8,094)	(1,418)

their degrees that recently held tenure. The latter were undoubtedly much younger men who had less time as teachers in their present institutions, having earned their degrees while still in graduate school or shortly thereafter, rather than (as is more common in fine arts) after years of teaching.

This question of the relation of tenure to length of time affiliated with an institution is examined in Table 14. Here a plateau starts somewhat sooner: by the time men have served seven to nine years, over 80 per cent have earned tenure. And if they stay long enough, almost all earn tenure. Indeed, within four to six years in an institution over half of all college and university teachers hold tenure. Of course, this table makes no distinction between men whose original appointment was at a high rank or with tenure. Nevertheless, it seems clear that tenure is awarded to most men within five years of their appointment in a university and to over 80 per cent within ten years. We may ask which faculty remain untenured after ten, fifteen, twenty or even thirty years of service in an institution. It may be that they hold administrative posts or are part-time teachers, but this is a question that deserves further exploration.

A slightly different picture appears when we look at Table 14A. We see that the majority at leading universities do not achieve tenure until they have served at least seven years in the institution. This undoubtedly reflects both the long-standing practice of these

Table 13. TYPE OF APPOINTMENT BY HOW LONG HAS HAD PH.D.—PH.D. HOLDERS ONLY

Type	Over 20 Years	16–20 Years	11–15 Years	6–10 Years	3–5 Years	2 Years or Less
Regular with Tenure	87%	90%	84%	67%	32%	14%
Regular without Tenure	9	8	14	31	64	81
Acting	0	0	0	0	1	1
Visiting	3	2	2	2	3	3
	99%	100%	100%	100%	100%	99%
	(24,578)	(20,490)	(26,314)	(36,742)	(33,702)	(30,384)

Table 13A. Proportion Having Tenure by Field
by How Long Has Had Ph.D.—Ph.D. Holders Only

	Business	Biological Sciences	Education	Engi- neering	Fine Arts
Over 20 years	86%	96%	90%	82%	94%
16–20 years	89	92	89	90	87
11–15 years	82	84	89	90	90
6–10 years	76	55	68	71	71
3–5 years	45	26	38	40	40
2 years or less	12	10	20	17	13

	Medicine and Law	Humani- ties	Physical Sciences	Social Sciences	New and Semi- Professions
Over 20 years	61%	82%	89%	88%	93%
16–20 years	66	90	93	88	88
11–15 years	48	86	84	82	78
6–10 years	53	72	60	72	66
3–5 years	26	36	22	30	36
2 years or less	0	18	8	11	28

institutions and the influence of AAUP guidelines. By contrast, in weaker universities we see that within four to six years of service, half the faculty hold tenure, as compared with 38 per cent in the leading universities and 75 per cent in the junior colleges. The contrast is similar at the leading colleges, where, again, over half the faculty have tenure within the first four to six years of service. In the leading universities, tenure is granted more slowly but as surely as elsewhere if faculty can remain with the university long enough.

In Table 15 we introduce a new consideration: whether tenure is related to research activity, and whether this varies in different kinds of institutions. Table 15 shows us first the relation of

Table 14. Type of Appointment by Years in Same Institution

Type	One Year or Less	2-3 Years	4-6 Years	7-9 Years	10-14 Years	15-19 Years	20-29 Years	30 + Years
Regular with Tenure	9%	19%	54%	82%	86%	90%	94%	90%
Regular without Tenure	79	76	43	16	13	9	6	8
Acting	5	3	1	1	0	0	0	0
Visiting	8	2	1	1	1	1	1	2
	101%	100%	99%	100%	100%	100%	101%	100%
	(71,386)	(111,724)	(84,522)	(42,492)	(47,320)	(27,602)	(33,076)	(9,724)

Table 14A. Proportion Having Tenure by Years in Same Institution by Quality

	Universities			Colleges			Junior Colleges
	High	Medium	Low	High	Medium	Low	
One Year or less	12%	11%	8%	8%	5%	8%	8%
2–3 Years	20	22	17	15	16	14	27
4–6 Years	38	54	54	53	51	50	75
7–9 Years	75	80	86	87	86	81	85
10–14 Years	77	90	88	89	94	82	86
15–19 Years	90	89	95	94	94	87	88
20–29 Years	91	95	96	96	97	92	87
30 + Years	87	96	91	95	92	81	87

Table 15. Type of Appointment by Number of Articles Published

Number of Articles

Type	None	1–2	3–4	5–10	11–20	More than 20
Regular with Tenure	38%	44%	55%	57%	69%	82%
Regular without Tenure	57	52	40	39	28	15
Acting	3	2	1	1	1	0
Visiting	2	3	3	3	3	3
	100%	101%	99%	100%	101%	100%
	(178,954)	(84,268)	(42,919)	(46,218)	(30,105)	(43,649)

tenure to research or scholarly publication over the entire academic career and for the entire sample. Academics who have published a great deal are much more likely to hold tenure than those who have not. Table 16 indicates that the relationship obtains in all kinds of institutions, though most strongly in the leading universities. (The reason for discrepancies among heavy publishers in junior colleges is unclear; they are a highly atypical group in those institutions.)

But lifetime publication is related to age, and age often brings tenure independent of publication. It may be more illuminating, therefore, to look at the bearing of current research activity on tenure. Our typology is based on the number of publications within the previous two years and whether the respondent was currently engaged in research for publication. (Research activity, unlike lifetime publication, is almost wholly unrelated to age.[2]) Table 17 shows the relation of current research activity to tenure for the entire sample. Men who are currently very actively engaged in research (as measured by their publications in the past two years and whether they are currently engaged in research for publication) are more likely to have tenure than are those not doing research, but the relationship is smaller than we might have anticipated. Overall, 65 per cent of those very actively engaged in research hold tenure, as compared to slightly less than 50 per cent of those who are wholly inactive. Interestingly, those who are active but have no recent publications are less likely to be tenured than those who are totally inactive. This may be accounted for by the concentration of young men among the former (active but not *yet* publishing) and of older men at the end of their active careers among the latter. Certainly the table shows no support for the notion that the doctrine of publish or perish governs the system of higher education as a whole.

However, the story is rather different when we look at the same pattern in different kinds of institutions. As we see in Table 18, of those doing no research at all in the leading universities less

[2] See Oliver Fulton and Martin Trow, *Research Activity in American Higher Education,* University of Edinburgh, Centre for Research in the Educational Sciences, April 1972, pp. 59–60 and Tables 20 A and B.

Table 16. Proportion Having Tenure by Number of Articles Published by Quality

Number of Articles	Universities			Colleges			Junior Colleges
	High	Medium	Low	High	Medium	Low	
None	19%	28%	28%	33%	38%	37%	52%
1–2	25	40	40	51	49	46	56
3–4	35	50	59	60	59	59	73
5–10	44	60	59	58	66	56	63
11–20	60	73	78	75	69	55	34
More than 20	83	85	81	84	74	55	62

Table 17. TYPE OF APPOINTMENT BY
TYPOLOGY OF RESEARCH ACTIVITY

Typology of Research Activity

Type of Appointment	Inactive, not Currently Publishing	Active, no Recent Publications	Few Recent Publications	Many Recent Publications
Regular with Tenure	48%	39%	53%	65%
Regular without Tenure	47	56	43	31
Acting	3	3	1	1
Visiting	2	2	3	3
	100%	100%	100%	100%
	(138,171)	(82,059)	(155,972)	(44,552)

than one-third hold tenure, compared with those who are involved with research and publishing, of whom two-thirds have tenure. The relationship is weaker in other kinds of universities and colleges, absent in the weakest four-year colleges, and reversed in the junior colleges.

We see differences among kinds of institutions more clearly in Table 19, which shows the joint effect of current (or continuing) research activity and age on tenure in three different kinds of institutions. In the leading universities less than a quarter (22 per cent) of those in the thirty-five to thirty-nine age bracket who are inactive are already tenured, as compared with 62 per cent of those in the same age bracket who are actively publishing. And in the next age bracket, forty to forty-four, the proportions are 35 per cent and 79 per cent. The rewards for publication in tenure, rank, and pay are very great in high quality universities, still clear between thirty and fifty-five in low quality universities, much smaller in the weakest universities and colleges, and absent in junior colleges.

While we have seen notable differences in the distribution of tenure among different fields of study and differences too in the relation of research activity to tenure in different institutions, the major finding of this survey is that the frequency and distribution

Table 18. PROPORTION HAVING TENURE BY TYPOLOGY OF RESEARCH ACTIVITY BY QUALITY

Typology of Research Activity	Universities			Colleges			Junior Colleges
	High	Medium	Low	High	Medium	Low	
Inactive, not currently publishing	32%	48%	44%	47%	48%	44%	55%
Active, no recent publications	27	38	35	44	41	39	49
Few recent publications	48	58	55	56	52	45	55
Many recent publications	66	69	66	68	54	43	40

Table 19. PROPORTION HAVING TENURE BY RESEARCH
ACTIVITY, AGE, AND QUALITY OF INSTITUTION

Typology of Research Activity

High Quality Universities	Inactive, not currently publishing	Active, no recent publications	Few recent publications	Many recent publications
Age				
61 and older	78%	77%	91%	91%
56–60	52	72	81	92
51–55	51	57	80	89
46–50	42	54	72	84
41–45	35	40	65	78
36–40	22	18	44	62
31–35	10	7	20	32
26–30	5	3	3	9
Under 26	4	10	2	**
Low Quality Universities Age				
61 and older	79%	80%	85%	78%
56–60	84	80	86	85
51–55	64	66	80	90
46–50	61	66	79	82
41–45	47	46	66	72
36-40	28	34	47	62
31–35	12	10	22	33
26–30	5	5	5	9
Under 26	4	8	3	**
Medium Quality Colleges Age				
61 and older	79%	76%	81%	**
56–60	93	82	88	**
51–55	80	68	79	**
46–50	68	75	68	**
41–45	56	54	62	**
36–40	46	49	50	**
31–35	23	17	29	**
26–30	4	4	13	**
Under 26	6	12	**	**

NOTE: This table is based on the complete sample of over 60,000
cases. The double starred cells include too few cases for reporting.

of tenure is very much the same throughout our system of higher education. And this is true despite the very great differences among American colleges and universities and the men and women who teach in them.

But similarities in the distribution of tenure should not be mistaken for similarities in its functions in various institutions. Whatever forces of competition or emulation have given rise to such remarkably similar patterns of employment across such a heterogeneous range of institutions, academic tenure has quite different consequences in research universities than it has, for example, in small local colleges. And that raises the question whether there can be any national policy on academic tenure that does not do violence to the quite different roles tenure plays in the different institutions which together make up American higher education.

Index

251